Artistic Instructional Guide to Casting Molds with Urethane

I0483418

Ch 1 Pouring Molds

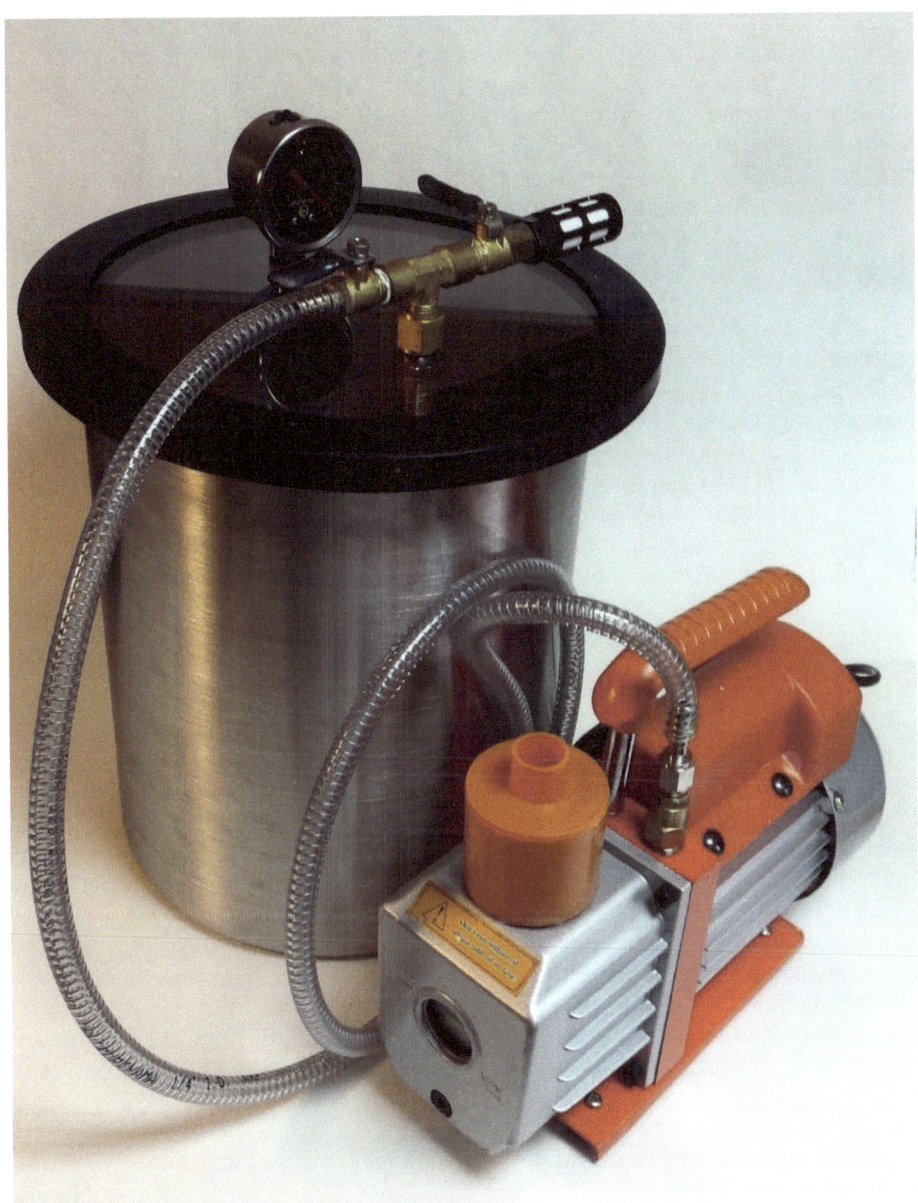

This art form of creation with molding technique is used in the film industry; stop animation & special effects and in archaeology preservation and display.

I used reverse engineering to re-create discontinued vintage dolls, turning the idea into a one-of-a-kind art form that is worth the effort and fun to do. I construct the figures from industrial urethane with silicone molds. You are sure to find similar instruction in this area on the internet but I will illustratrate how to add hair, costume, features and accessories to complete the piece. You may also use this guide to assist in restoration of vintage original figures.

There are many kinds of materials in which to mold objects and even more to sculpt using molding process to re-create an object. I chose industrial urethane, for it's durability, flexability and the infinate possibilities of adding pigments, glitter and effects.

One thing to consider when buying molding materials is to plan to use them immediately. Old chemicals can darken and eventually becomes unusable when they are stored too long. It is a good idea to store previously opened containers inside an air-tight totes to prevent residual gas exposure.

A good vacuum chamber is an absolute necessity in creating sculpture with silicone and urethane in order to draw out bubbles that are suspended within the viscous materials created in the mixing process. These bubbles will rise and create flaws in the upper extemities of your figure if they are not extracted.

I can't stress enough about the necessity of good ventalation. These chemicals in their seperate forms, when they are first combined and while curing & "gassing off," are known to cause cancer.

The gasses don't only affect the lungs. It may affect the liver, kidneys and brain so all precaution should be undertaken to prevent materials from getting on your skin and into your eyes besides being inhaled. Wear a long sleeved shirt to protect your arms. You might need to use a painter's face mask too. You can't be too careful.

It is easy to accidently drop a full container or the cup of materials as you are pouring liquids, combining or scraping the sides or while holding a mold open while finessing a small quantity of materials into tiny spaces. The cup might crack down the side and you must make a quick decision whether to save the materials or start over. This is a messy process no matter how careful you might be.

A brightly lit work space is important for the precision that is necessary. Temperature control prevents premature oxidization of the chemicals and it helps materials cure properly.

Learn to hold your breath when looking closely at details to avoid breathing gasses while you work the urethane into small extremities of your figures.

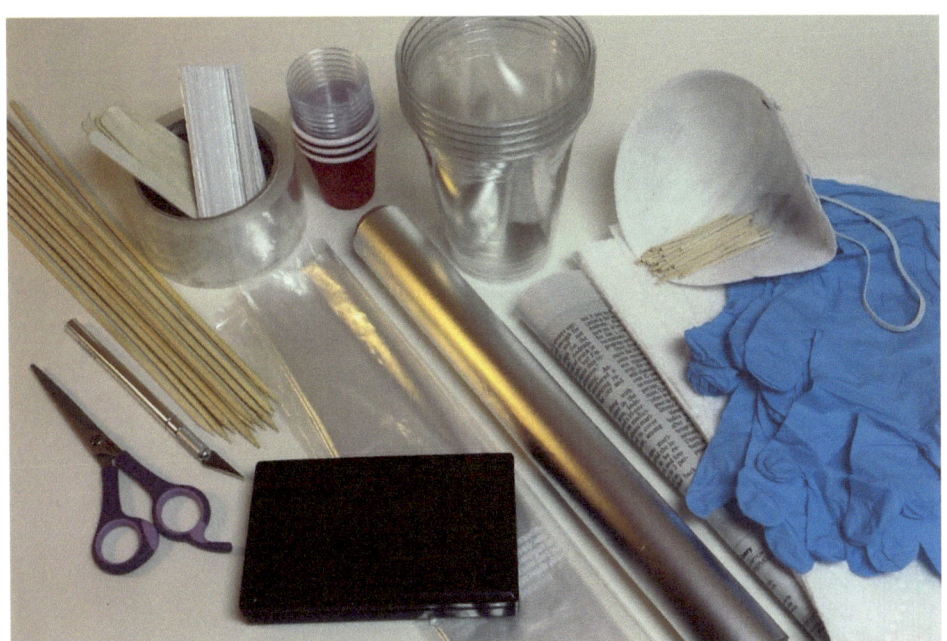

Materials list:

Vacuum Chamber and pump compressor, Good ventalation system, Newspapers for masking work area, Plastic cups, various sizes, Paper towels, Foil, Bamboo skewers, Tooth picks, Nitrile disposable gloves, Face mask, Pigments chemically compatable with molding materials, Scales to 1/10 gram, Dry gas blanket, Plastic bags for chemical disposal , Bypass pruning shears, Craft sticks, Packing tape, Twist ties, Xacto knife, Effects powders and glitters, Scissors , Cornstarch baby powder, More paper towels and a first aid kit, Self sealing totes to store chemicals, Various sized plastic containers.

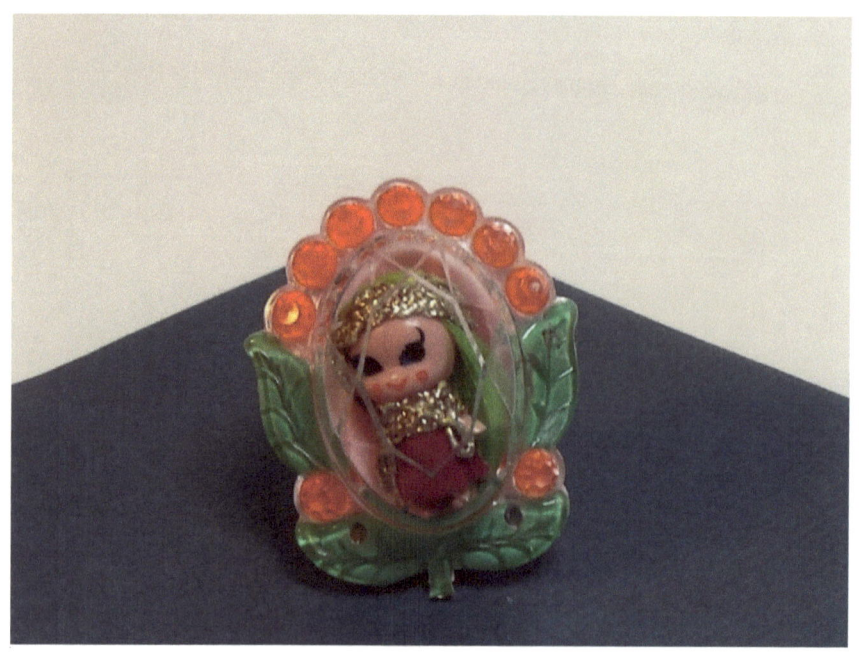

I used a commercially made vintage doll as my model to reverse engineer.

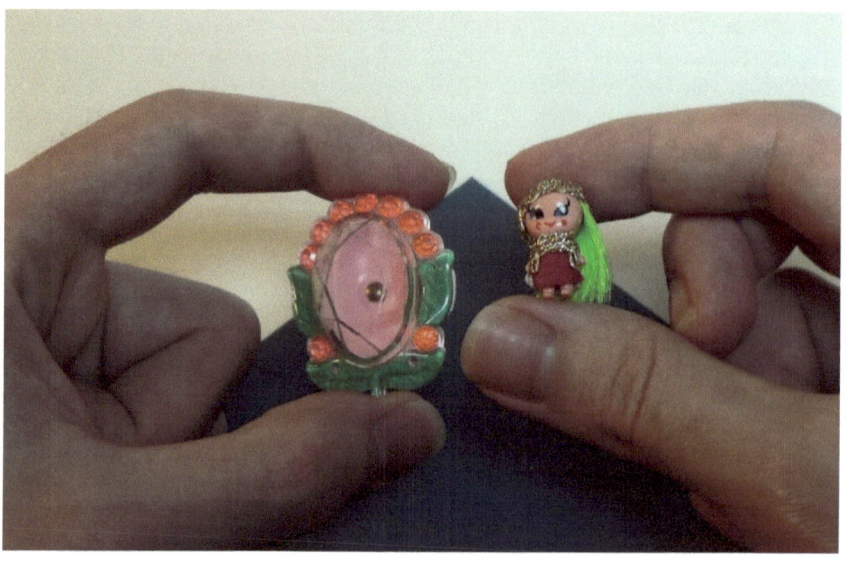

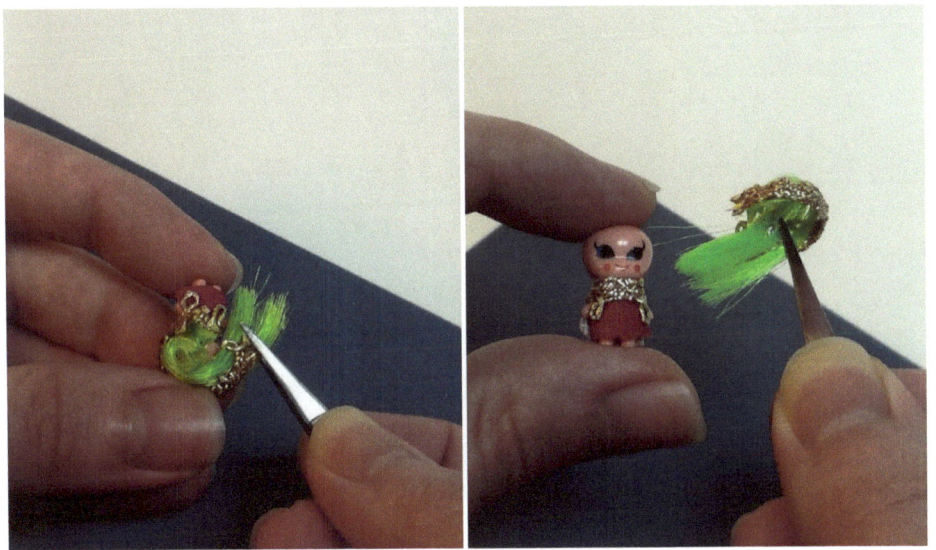

In preparation, I first removed the vintage doll's hair very carefully. I then removed the original costume with tweasers. I cleaned and dried the figure to remove anything that might cause a problem with the silicone chemicals it will come into direct contact with.

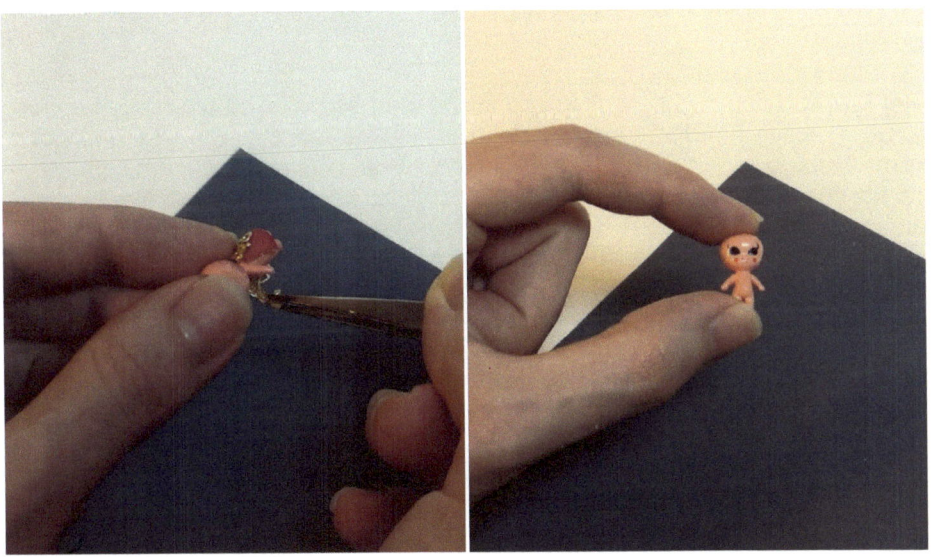

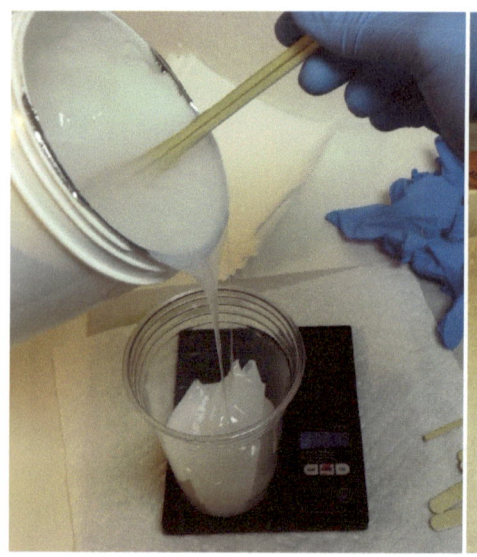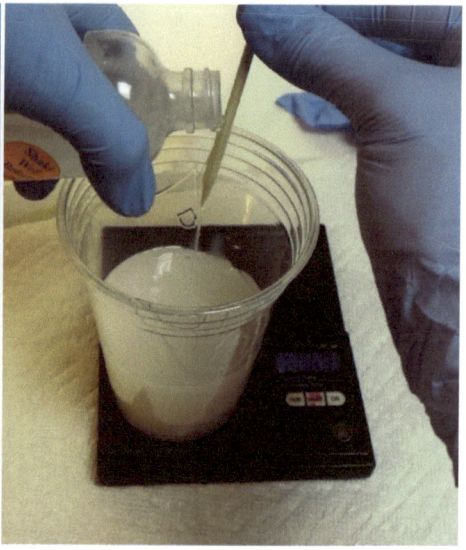

Prepare silicone according to manufacturers instruction.

Being precise is important in this step. The two part silicone I use is 100 part A to 10 part B. Part A has the consistancy of cool honey and care should be taken while stirring this product not to allow it to spill over the container. I use 2 or 3 thick bamboo skewers together to mix this well before pouring the chemical into the measuring cup. Part B is thin like warm baby oil-like consistancy and should be shaken for up to ten minutes before attempting to pour. It has particluates that settle and need to be in a perfect suspension or the silicone will not set up correctly.

After Part B is thoroughly shaken and suspended evenly, you are ready to pour part A. Place the mixing cup upon digital scales and set the scales to tenths of a gram. Tare down the scales to zero out the weight displayed. Pour a quantity into the cup. I generally eyeball Part A and like to have a round number to work with to quickly add the correct fraction to the equasion before the digital scales sometimes automatically turns off. This happens to me as a battery saving feature I can't seem to turn off, so time is of the essence in that regard.

The chemicals begin to react to both the atmosphere surrounding the product and as the second product begins to come in contact with the first as it is being measured. Take this into consideration.

If Part A weighs 60 grams, then I need to add exactly 6 grams of part B and not a drop more. While pouring part B, note the quantity of drops required for a single tenth of a gram. There is not a single number to this equasion because the product could be cold and thicker at the moment, thus rendering larger drops or warmer and having a thinner consistancy so more drops are required per tenth of a gram. The total weight in this example should be 66 grams.

8

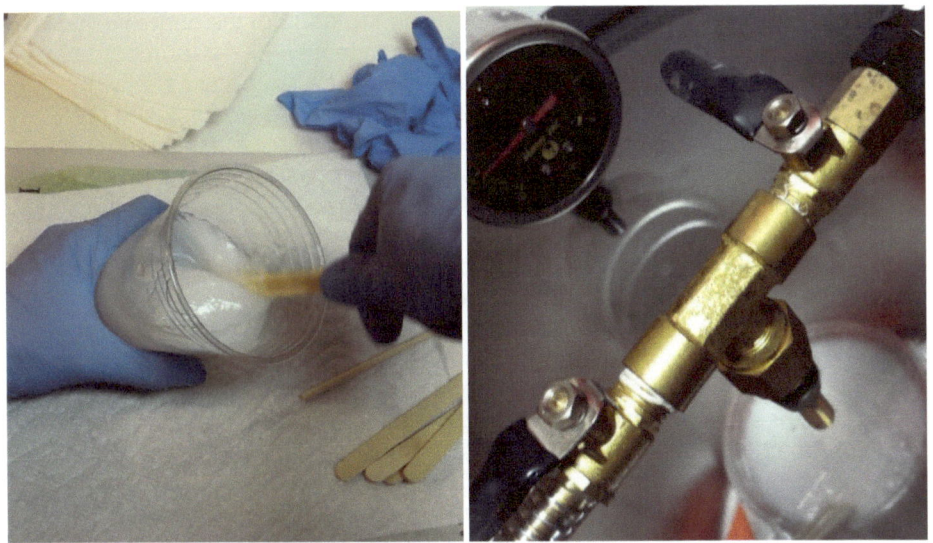

Stir the the two parts, mixing well, for about three minutes. Next, place the cup, craft stick and all into the vacuum chamber to pull trapped air bubbleos from the chemicals. Use -32psi until the silicone "boils" up, producing foam where the trapped bubbles are escaping the mixture. When the raising foam drops, most of the bubbles should be extracted. Stop the vacuum process and reverse the pressure. Remove cup from the chamber and pour into a shallow contaner and let stand, undisturbed to cure for 48 hours in a well ventilated room.

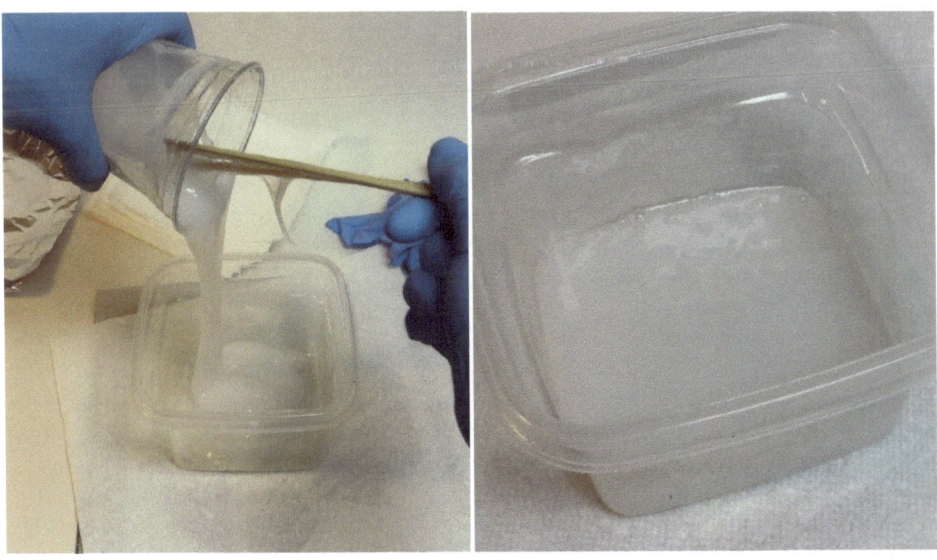

Between pouring each chemical, you must wipe the edge of the container down thoroughly to prevent cross contanimation and place clean foil over mouth of large containers and "hand crimp" into place, giving it a temporary seal while measuring and mixing.   When you are completely finished working with the chemicals, and while it is undergoing the vacuum process, take this time to wipe down and re-seal containers with clean foil and gas blanket before scrweing on the cap(s) for storage. Keeping your work space clean is important.

 If you accidentally over pour part B, you can quickly add a tiny bit more of part A and re do the math and then add the correct quantity of part B again. If part A weighed 60 grams and you accidentally poured 7.5 grams of part B, you must add at least 15 more grams of part A. Chances are because of the thick viscosity of the this part of the product, you might add too much which is fine but just don't add too little because that won't work. So if Part A over pours as aformentioned, you do the math as follows; The second blob of part A turns out to be 18 additional grams instead of 15, totaling 85.5g total parts weight instead of the 82.5 grams that was required, you must add .3 grams of part B to correct the ratio. You can do this by dipping a tooth pick into the small jar of part B and adding drops at a time. The materials drop weight varies as mentioned before so use your previous noted quantity by earlier observation.

If at this stage, you accidentally over pour part B a second time, too much time has passed to add more to fix the problem and the rate of inaccuracy increases. Throw out the product, cup, picks, newspapers and gloves and start over. There are many reasons to start over and this is one of them and where patience is required.

After the correct quantity of both parts are measured, it must be stirred until combined thoroughly about 2-3 minutes depending on humidity and temperature with a craft stick scraping the sides, bottom and corners often. The container for part B should be resealed with foil and sprayed with a dry gas blanket to prevent oxidization that degrades the product.

The mouth and sides of the container must be wiped off thoroughly with paper towel to prevent any residual product contaminating the exteriors. Un-mixed materials are toxic. The silicone components don't last long and should be used and not stored. Unopened, stored materials do not last either. Extreem temperatures cause degradation of this product. Un-mixed product gasses off (cancer causing gasses) at a longer rate and care needs to be taken to avoid spills and contamination.

After mixing parts A & B thoroughly, place into the vacuum chamber, seal and apply vacuum pressure to -32 PSI or until the product foams and collapses within the mixing cup. This collapse ensures that micro bubbles have escaped. This is why the mixing cup should have up to 4 times the volume of the product that is poured to prevent spilling within the vacuum chamber. Release pressure slowly to prevent another spill due to air rushing into the chamber.

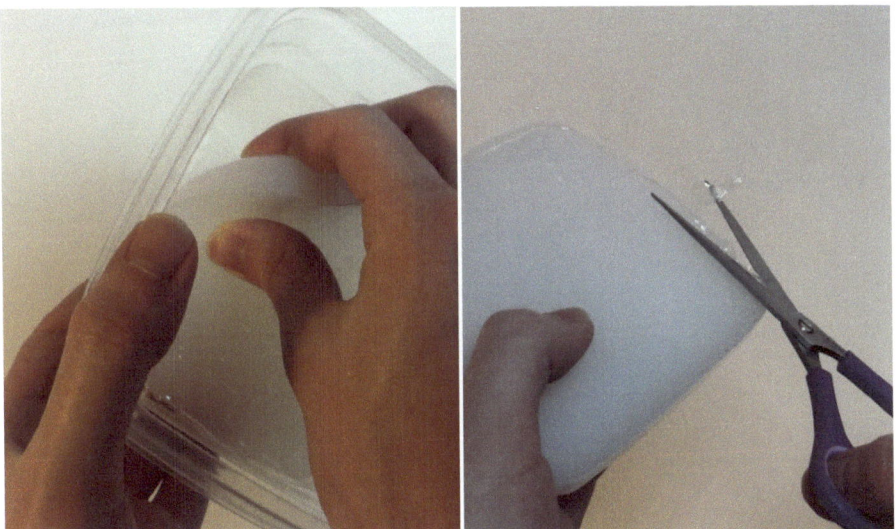

After the silicone is cured according to manufacturers instructions, remove it from the mold. The edges are trimmed with scissors to remove flashing. Avoid overhandling the smallest pieces of flashing from fresh silicone molds, the small strands tend to not cure at the same rate as the solid form. Use this ½ inch sheet of silicone to create spacers for the molding process and tools by cutting it into workable pieces with an xacto knife.

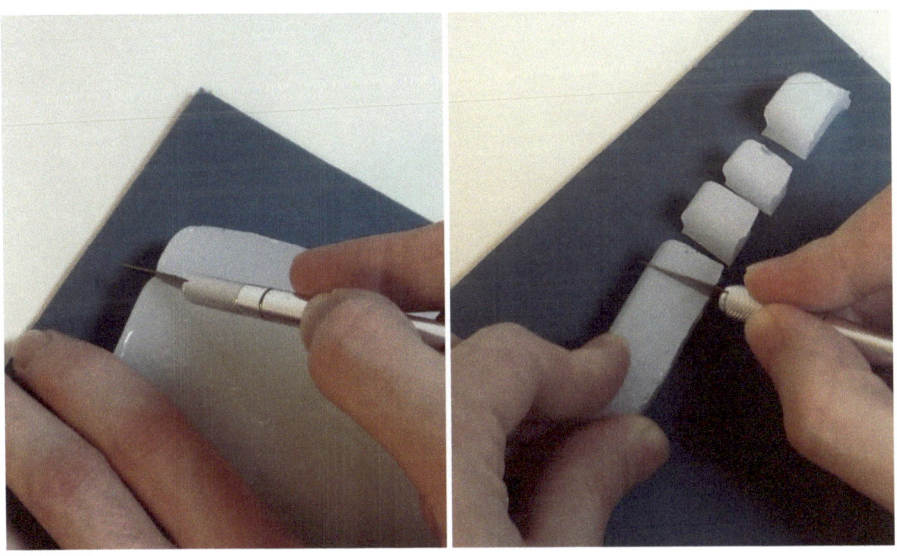

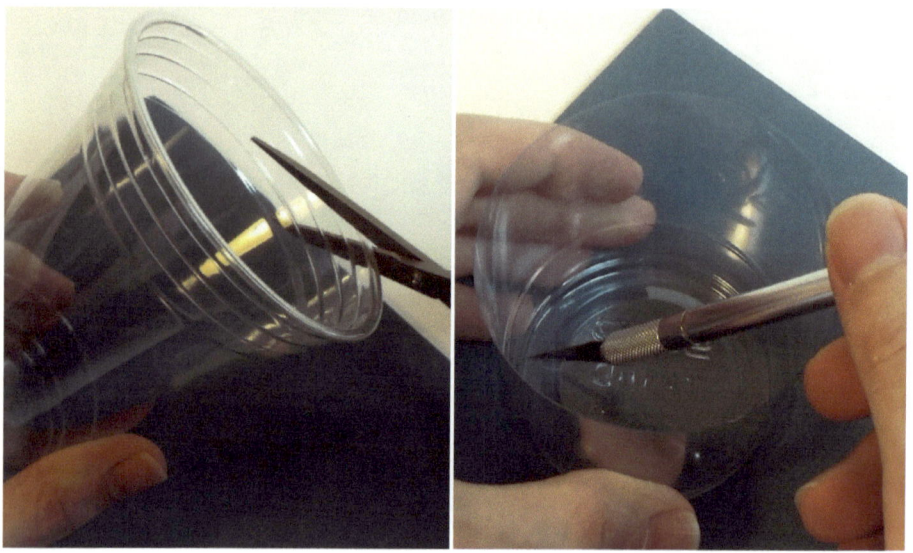

Trim a plastic disposable cup down to a more useful size. Lightly score an indicator arrow to show the front and sides of your mold. Arrange the silicone cubes inside molding cup to hold the figure in a stable position while suspending it within the silicone. New silicone will adhere perfectly to these silicone cubes becoming a cradle to hold the figure and another part of the eventual mold.

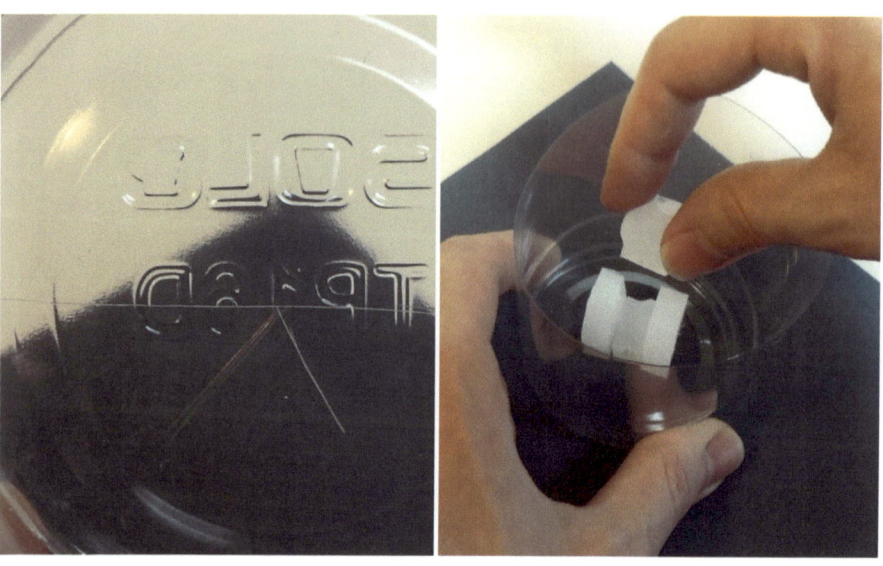

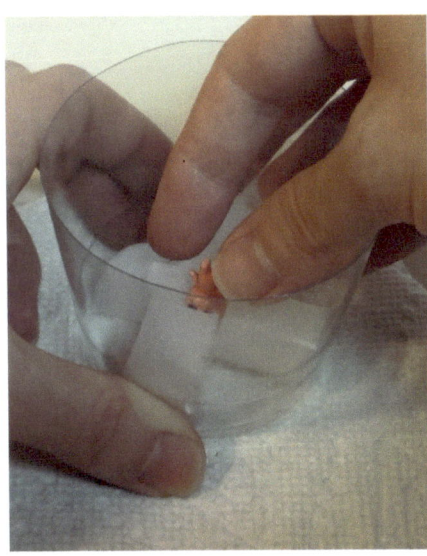 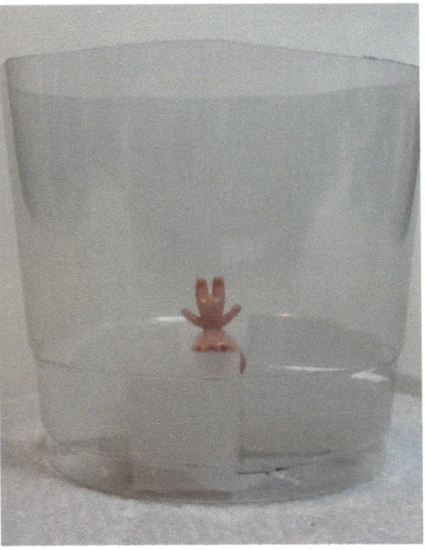

I placed the figure, upside down and facing the noted the direction scored in the bottom of the cup. After removing the silicone from the vacuum chamber, give it a fold to check for the presence of micro bubbles. Pour silicone slowly into the mold, near but not the onto the object as it may knock it over. Allow the rising line of the silicone fold slowly around the figure's arms and legs or object creases. You may use a paint brush to apply the silicone straight onto the object, then replace it into the cradle assembled from silicone. You might need to use a pick to hold the figure into place because of the slow wave action while pouring. After it is completely covered by silicone, let it cure 48 hours undisturbed.

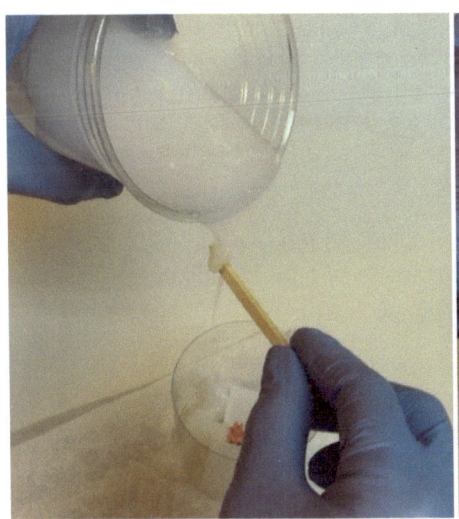 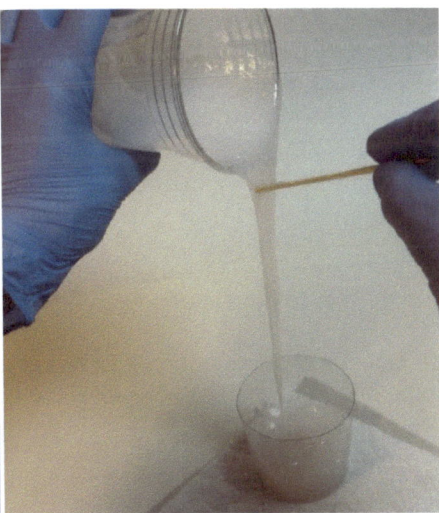

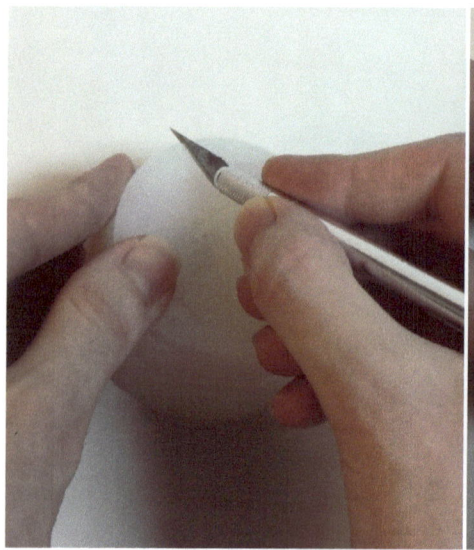 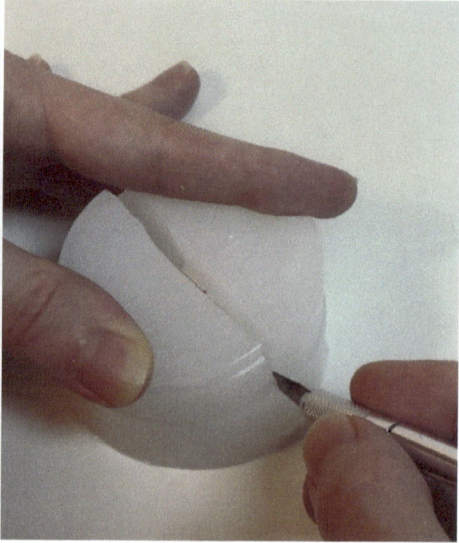

You have from between 15 to 20 minutes before the viscosity changes too much to work with. It is important that when this figure is enveloped within the silicone that it is placed upside down at this point because the bottom of the mold within the cup will become the top of the mold. Bubbles rise so keep that in mind when making the decision of figure positioning. The feet and hands of the figure I chose point downward so it would be logical that I would want them to point downward in the molding process because air bubbles will escape away from these points and not toward these extremities.

After the material is poured into the mold cup with the original, prototype or master, the instructions on the silicone advise not to remove from the mold until after 24 hours but I like to allow 48 in case the chemicals are a tiny fraction off or if the air temperature is not optimal. A few degrees of varying temperature in the curing process alters curing time. This allows it to further "gas off" any residual fumes or oils that are created in the molding process and is ready for safe handling and removal.

After 48 hours, cut the plastic cup away carefully, not to slice into the silicone material. Carefully determine where the cut line is and the direction the figure is facing in order to have clean flashing lines.

Store any cured silicone in plastic to prevent oxidization. This material will become brown, similar to how an apple turns brown after exposure to the atmosphere.

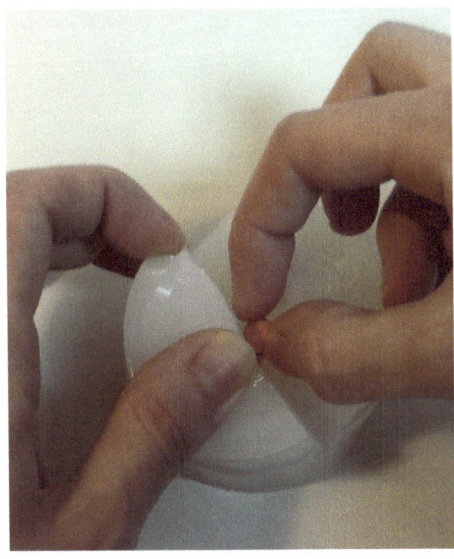
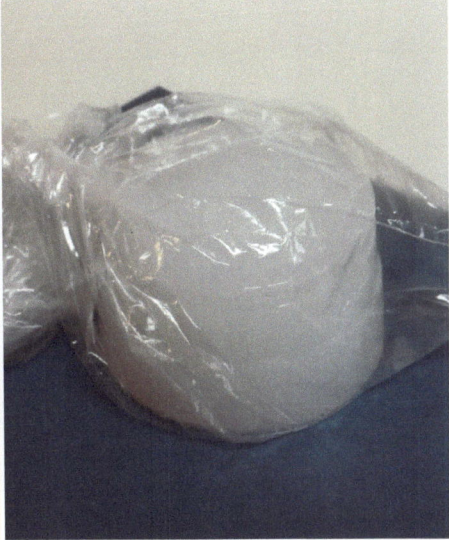

When using an xacto knife, be very careful and use a new blade. It makes all the difference in creating a clean, even cut. Wipe all oils off new blades to prevent chemical reaction with a paper towel until completly dry.
Do not cut yourself. Slipping while holding a fresh sharp xacto knife is to be avoided at all cost because you can cut yourself badly and need ER treatment. This is why I recommend having a first aid kit handy. If you have ever cut yourself while carving a jack-o-lantern for Halloween, imagine worse and don't do that.

Trim any flashing from the silicone edges, these "strings" and thin flashing edges don't cure well and can be removed easily with scissors. They may have an oily residue where the solid mass is not completely cured through. Handle these with paper towel and dispose of immediately.

Locate the top center of the figure previously etched line in the cup and slice down the sides of the top of thefigure's head. Working between the negative space, slowly with the blade pointed away from the figure so as not to accidentally cut into and damage the original object.

Apply even pressure, peeling back the silicone as it is slowly sliced open. These dolls require a cut line that starts from the top of the head to the fingertips or the waist then slowly wiggle the figure to release it from the lowest parts of your mold. Inspect the interior of the mold for tears and perform any additional cuts at this time to prepare for the next step.

Carefullly and properly dispose of all garbage that come into contact with chemicals by securely bagging and dispose of immediately outside.

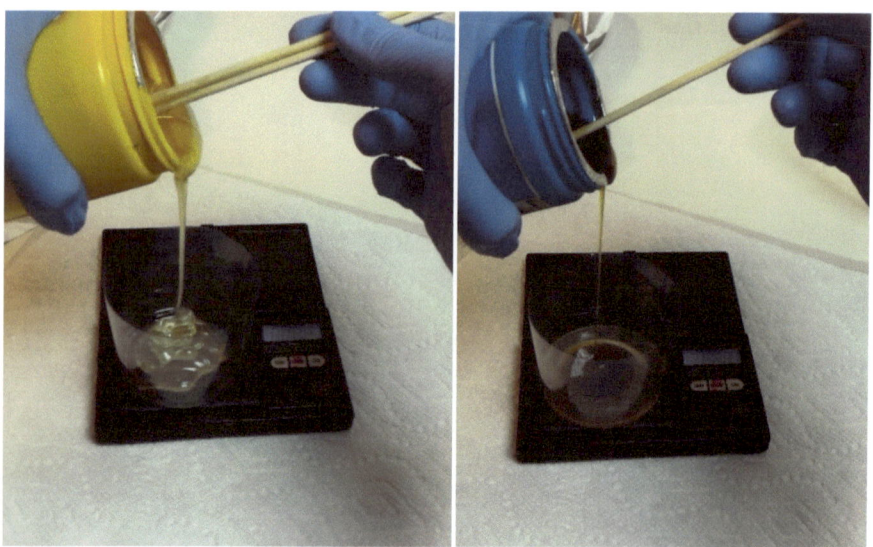

This urethane product is of industrial strength rubber compound is flexible both physically and in its many uses. The ratio is 2 parts to 1 part so I weigh the master figure to determine its weight then add enough weight to account for flashing and residual material. Mix chemicals well according to manufacturers instruction.

It is better to err on the side of mixing too much than too little at this stage. I am going to use the aproximate target total weight of 10 grams. I keep in mind that the consistancy of part A is similar to cold corn syrup and part B viscosity is similar to warm pancake syrup. My target for part A is about 6 grams. The actual weight of part A poured according to the scales is 6.2g so 3.1g of part B must be added to total of 9.3 grams.

If you over pour, you can correct the weight by performing a little quick math and then adding parts with a toothpick one drop at at time for more controlled and acurate measurements. But you must do this quickly and while being mindful not to breathe the toxic fumes.

Another way to correct an over pour of part B is to dip a corner of a paper towel into the cup until the correct weight in that chemical was apsorbed by the paper towel leaving the exact measurement needed in the cup.

The reason precision is necessary when measuring small quantities, it is easier to make an error that might ruin an entire batch of urethane. If it does happen, start over.

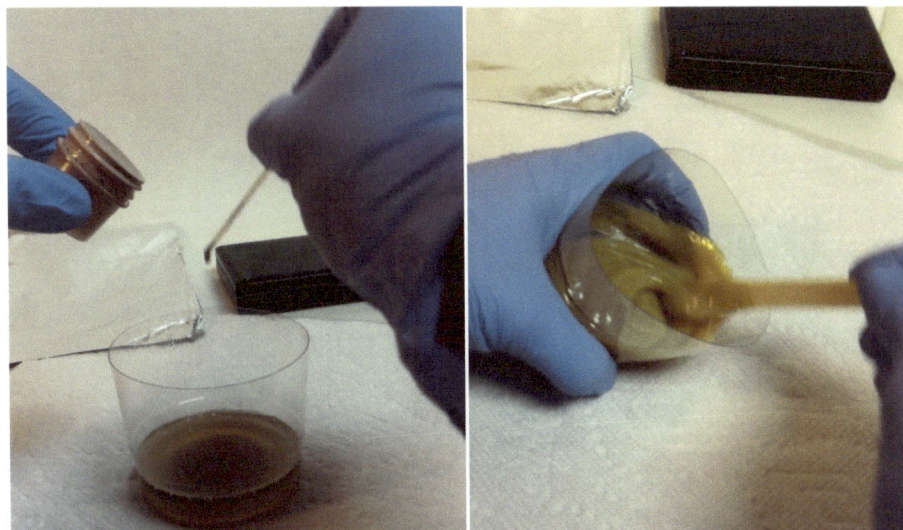

 Add small quantities of pigments at a time with a toothpick because you can always add more if the resulting color is not rich enough. Scrape the bottom, corners and sides of the cup often. Hold your breath if you are looking closely because you don't want to accidentally breathe in the fumes.

 After the parts are throroughly mixed, you may stir in effects powders. Place cup with craft stick and all into the vacuum chamber and apply -32psi for about 3-5 minutes or until the foam on the surface collapses. Remove, stir and begin to scoop small quantities of urethane and place carefully inside the silicone mold.

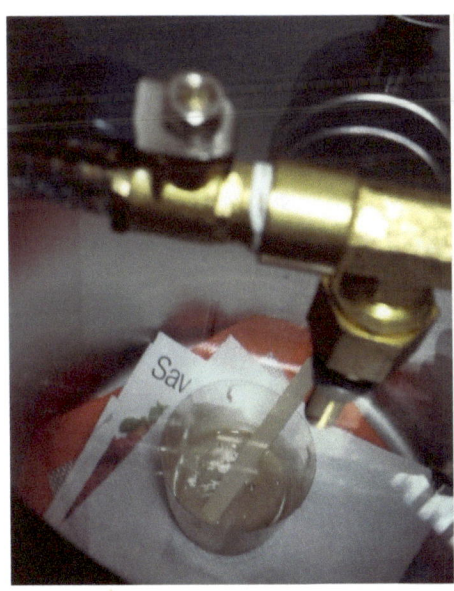
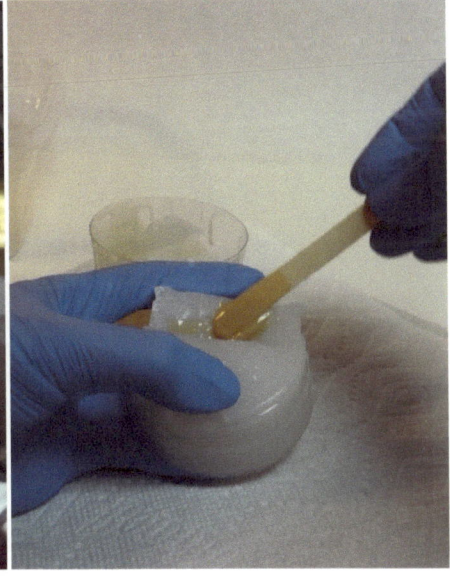

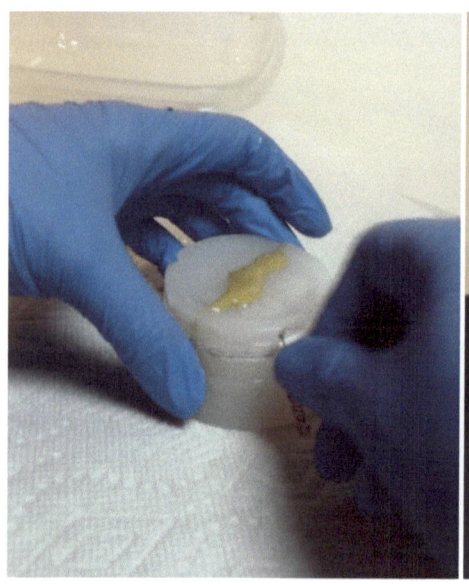
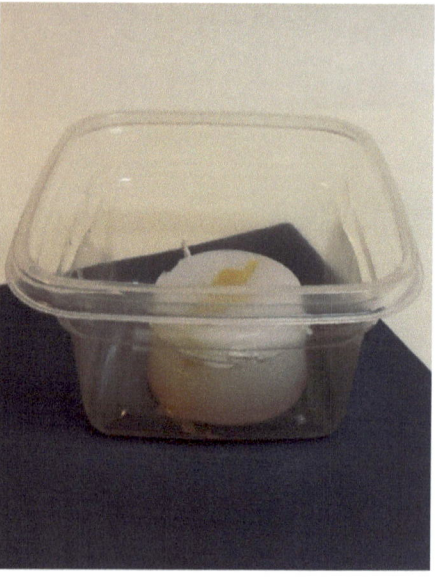

Work from the lowest parts of your figure to the upper parts, teasing residule air bubbles out as you add more urethane. When a sufficient quantity was added with enough to spare, secure with a twist tie and let it cure in a temperature controlled enviornment that is well ventillated.

After the manufacturer's recommended cure time, use a tooth pick to determine the consistancy before attempting to handle it to remove it from the mold. Pull apart mold, and gently pull, squeeze and manipulate silicone until the doll or figure is free. Inspect the figure for flaws, bubbles and missing limbs.

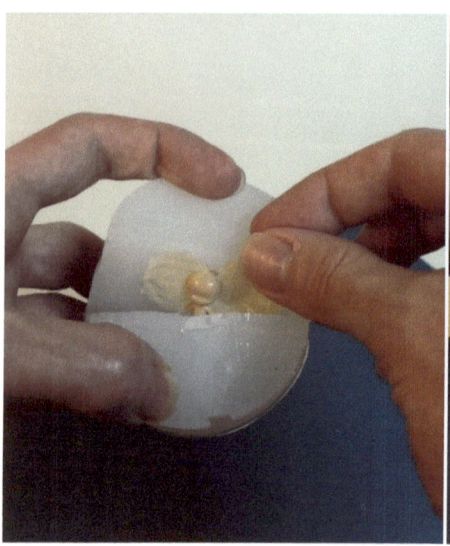
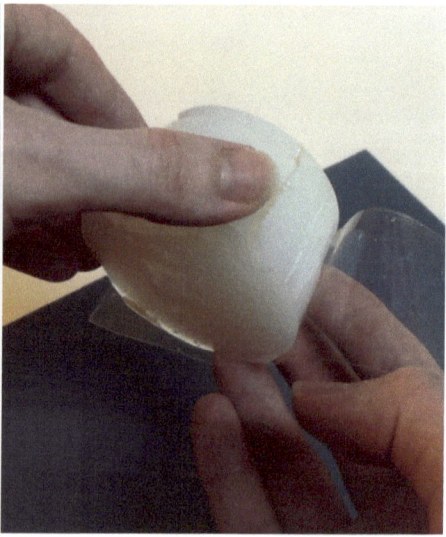

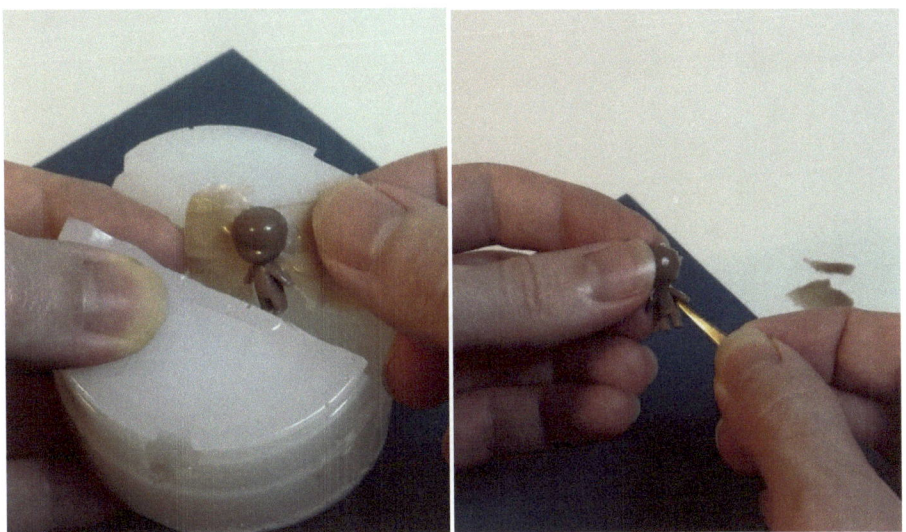

Remove the flashing carefully with tweezers. I allow the figures to cure an additional day before dressing them.

If the doll is without flaws, proving the mold is good enough to re-use, congratulations! You may re-pour urethane into the mold and create another figure!

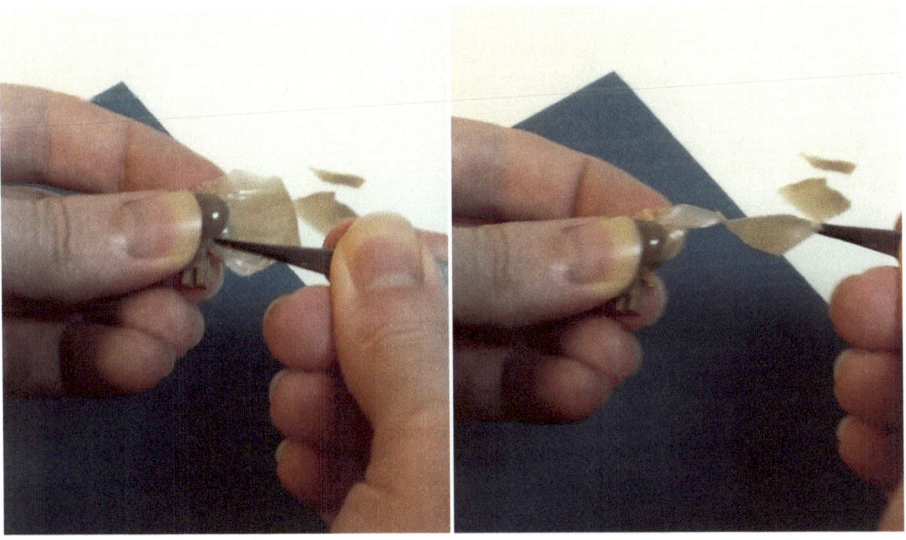

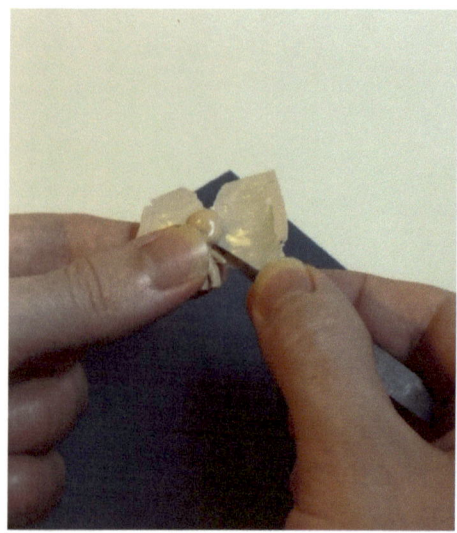 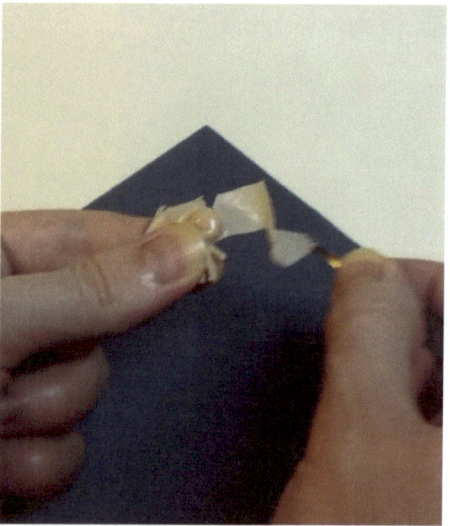

If the doll is not complete, you will have to repour until you obtain a complete figure to ensure the mold is good enough for re-use.

As you re-pour urethane, take care that you don't tear the silicone. Pouring molds is a destructive process and creating new molds is a requirement and part of creation.

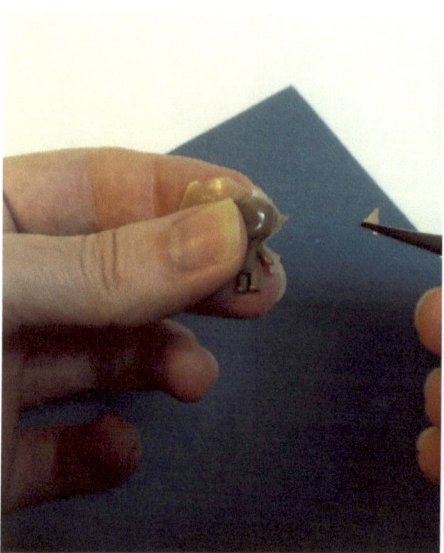 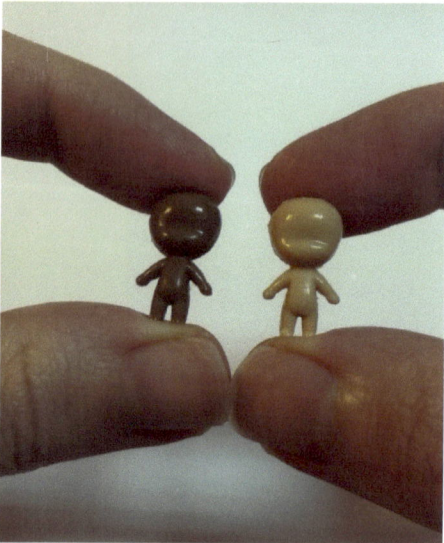

Ch2 Costume Design

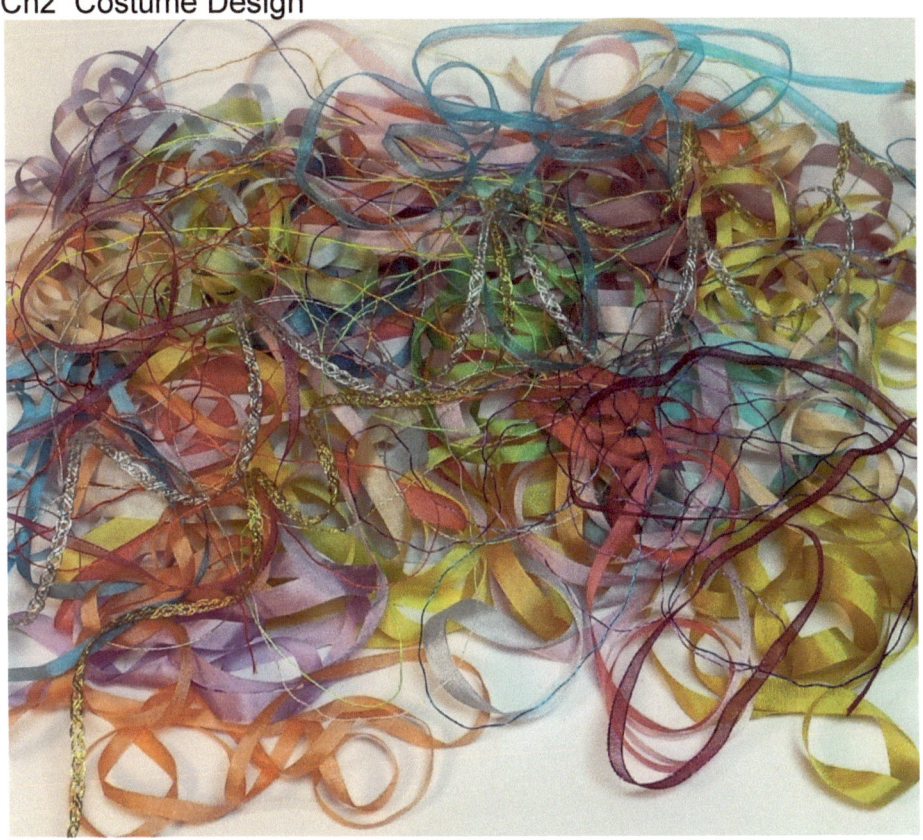

When making the decision to dress this size of figure or doll, which is under an inch, you are faced with limitations and with any limitation, there are unique opportunities. Rather than concentrate on what you can't do because of size constraints, I will show you what I was able to create and how.

If you have a color wheel, it might help with designing costumes or in re-creating characters. These materials are only suggested, the options are truly endless.

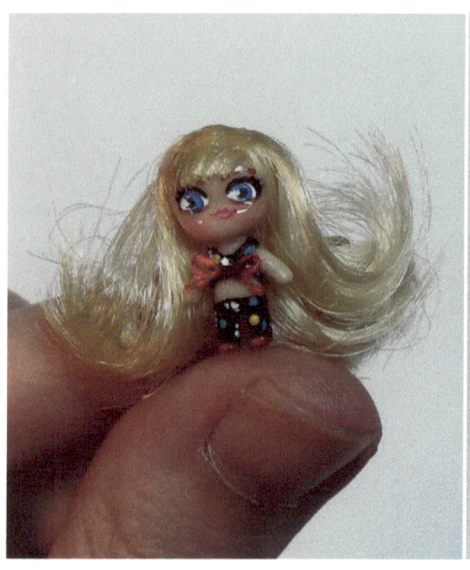 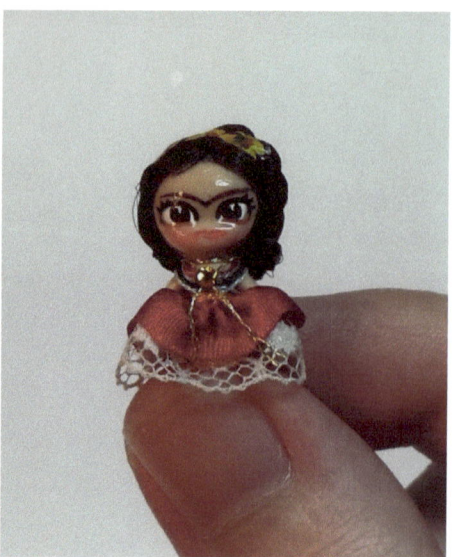

Tools;

Sharp sewing shears
Various size needles
Super glue
Toothpicks
Paper towel
Wax paper
Silicone tools that you create
Bamboo skewers
Packing tape
A well lit and very clean work space
Various sized zip-lock bags
Ruler
Magnifying glass
Artists brushes
A friend to hold your figure while you are working on details
Keeping your hands clean to prevent fabric stains
Just as much patience as when pouring molds, but not as much breath holding

Suggested Materials;

Embrordary floss
Ribbons in varying widths and colors
Acrylic paint
Glitters and effects powders

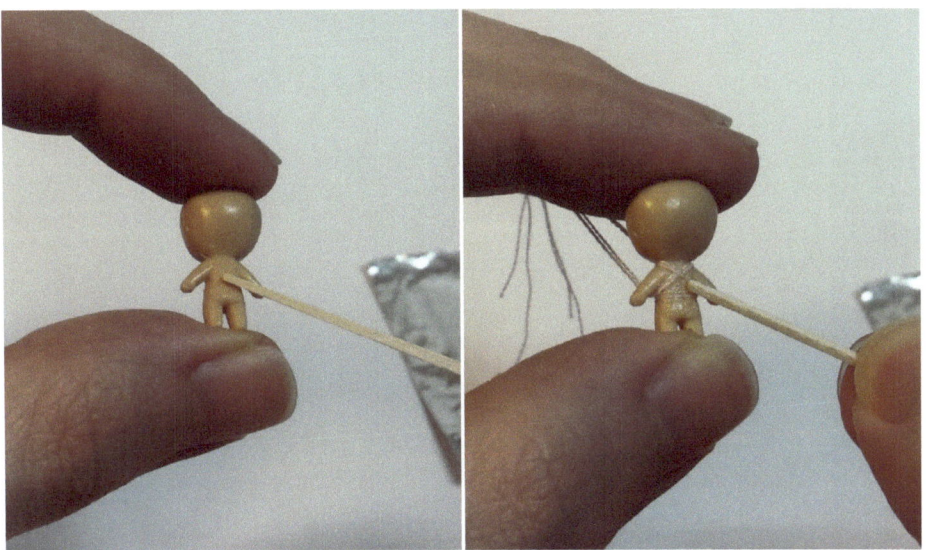

While designing, I like to see various combinations before settling on a final choice. Silk embrordary ribbon, vintage lace, plaids, jaquards and brocades in about ¼" widths or narrower all work well.

In these examples, the model is prepped with super glue and wrapped with deconstructed floss to create a bikini.

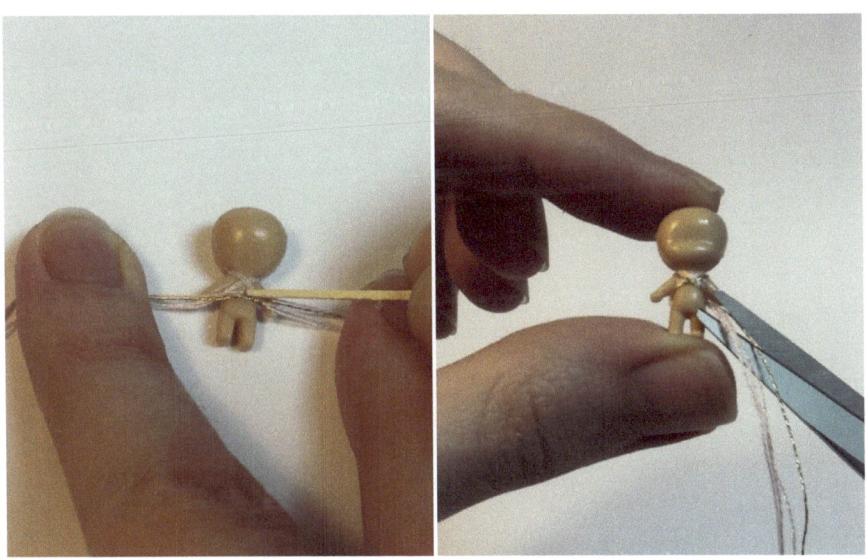

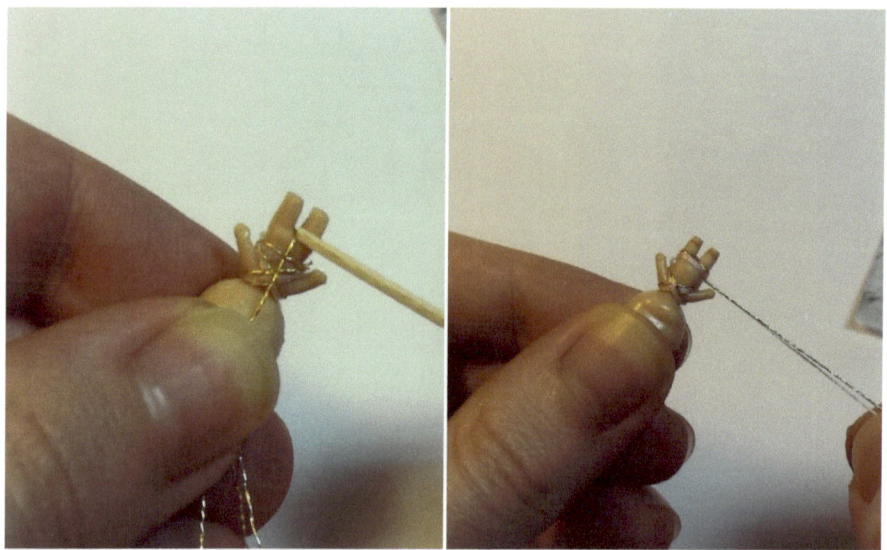

I start by choosing the largest materials and work my down to the smallest. I often layer costumes with varying hues and pair complimentary shades and highlights to finish the piece.

I apply the smaller elements first and often the top portion of the costume.

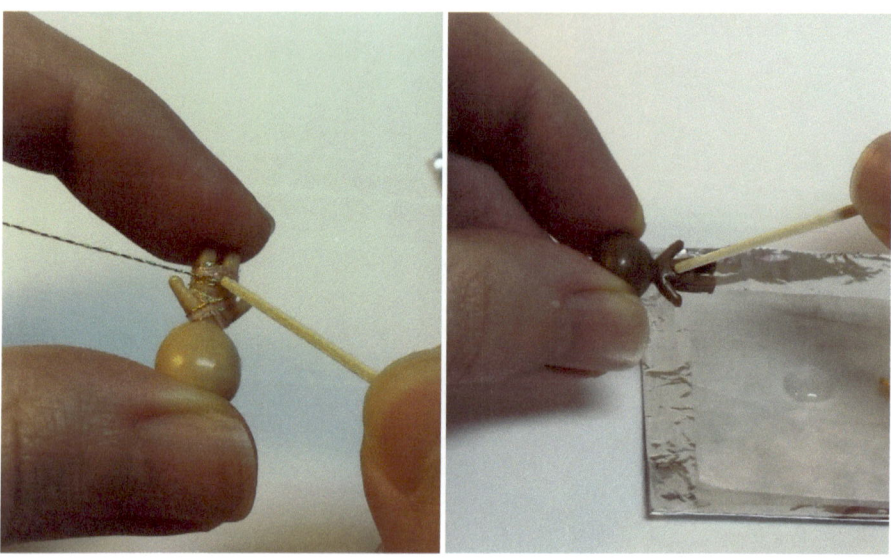

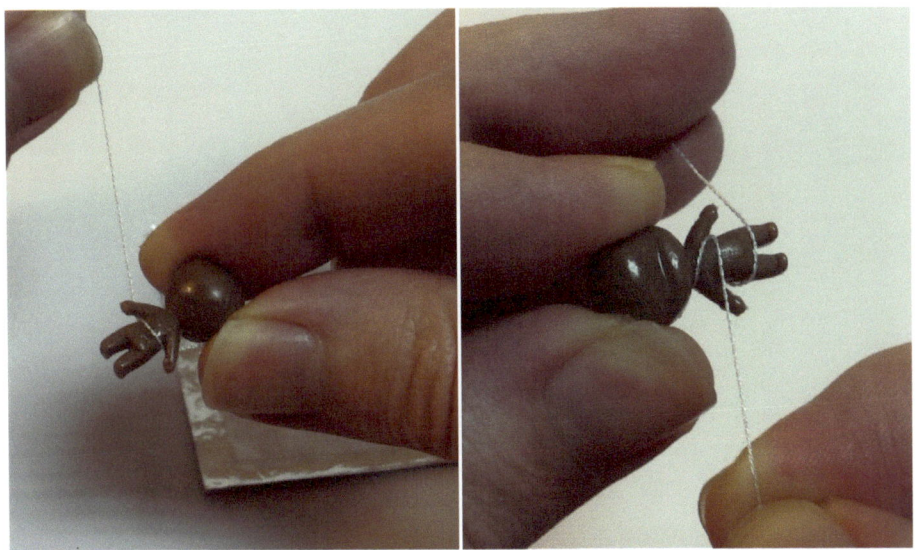

Silver floss is applied first to outline an asymetrical bikini top.

Shiny aqua floss is added to become the primary color of this design.

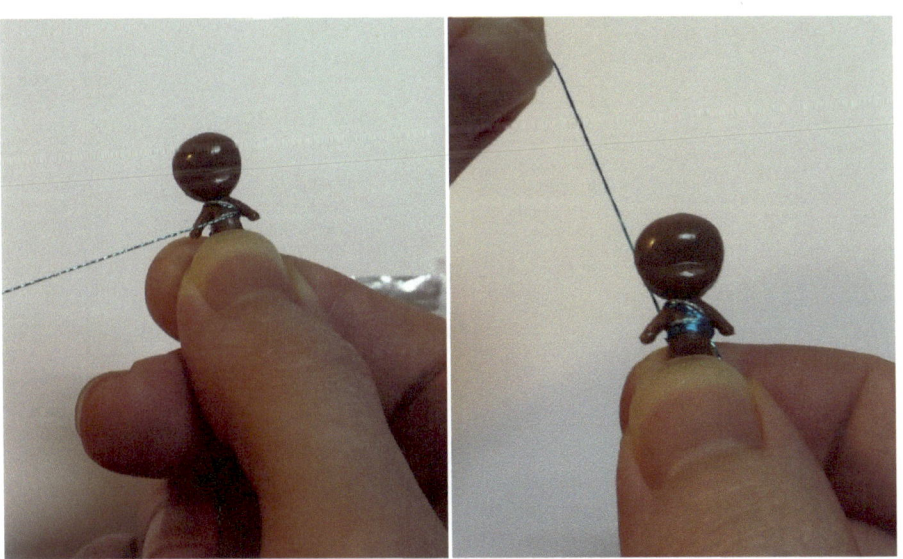

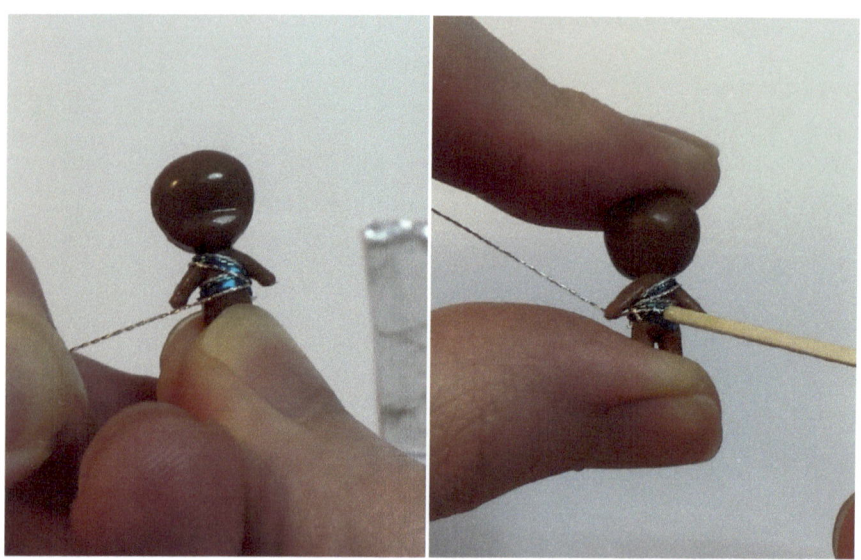

This costume top is secured with super glue.

The bottoms are started by securing silver floss with super glue and wrapping the floss around the legs once.

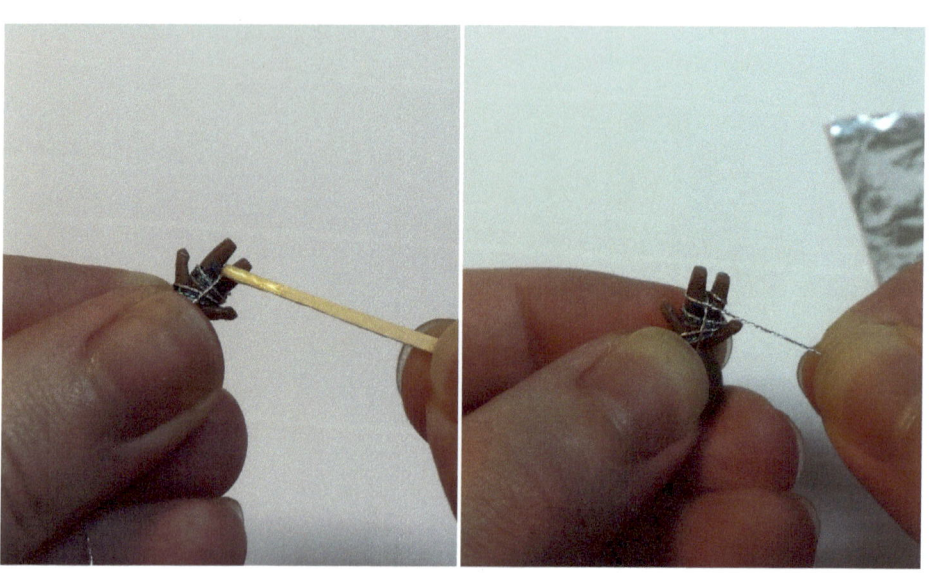

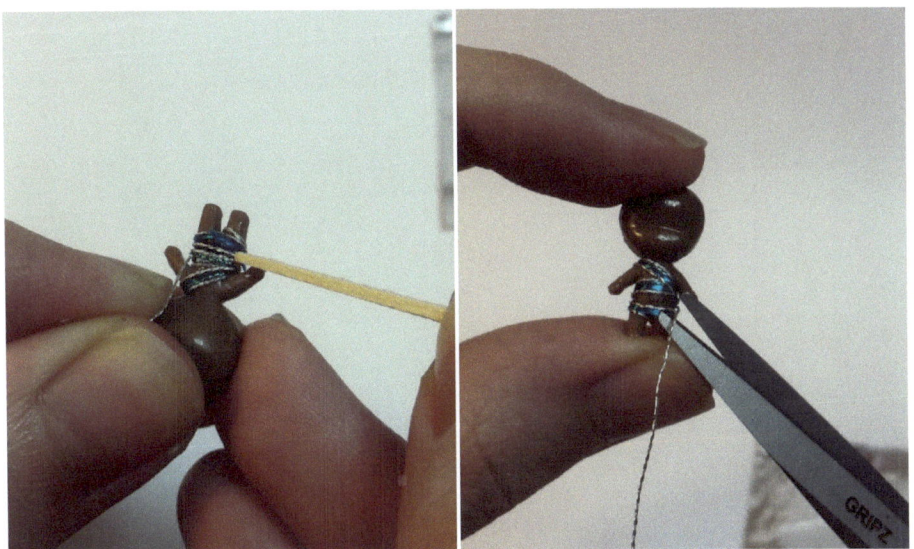

Wrap floss twice then once more with silver floss to complete the bikini bottoms. Secure with super glue. Trim excess floss close to the figure after the glue has cured about 30 seconds.

White floss is wrapped first in this design, then brilliant blue and back to white. Secure with super glue.

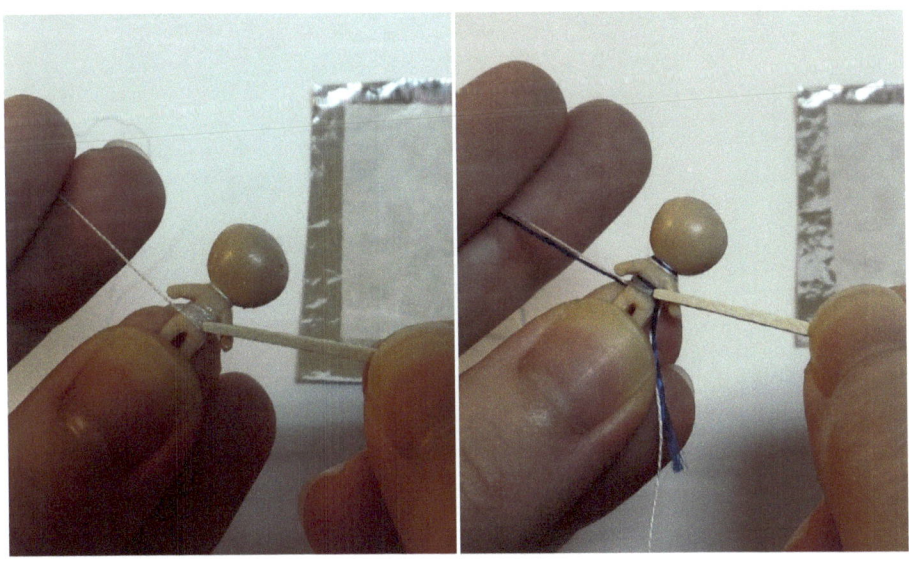

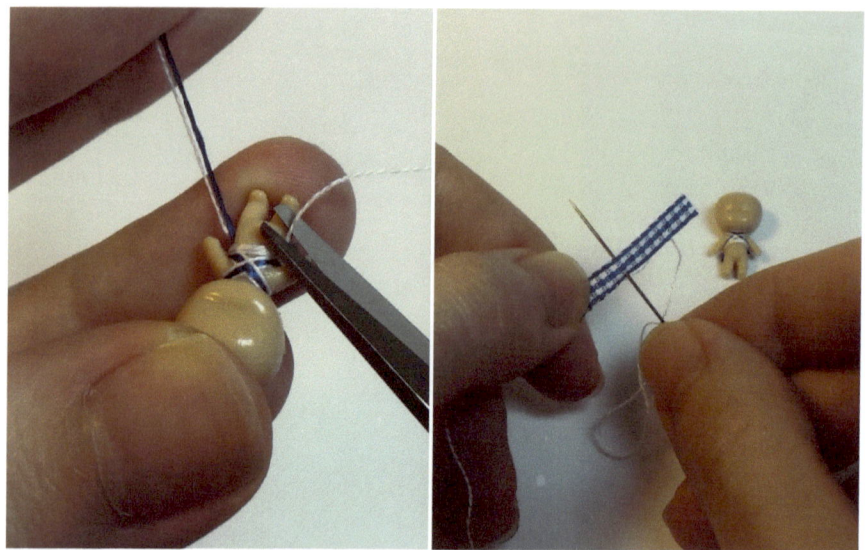

Trim excess floss after the glue cures 30 seconds. Stitch ribbon on one edge and wrap the ribbon around the figure, creating the skirt portion of the costume design.

Again, trim all excess floss flush to the costume.

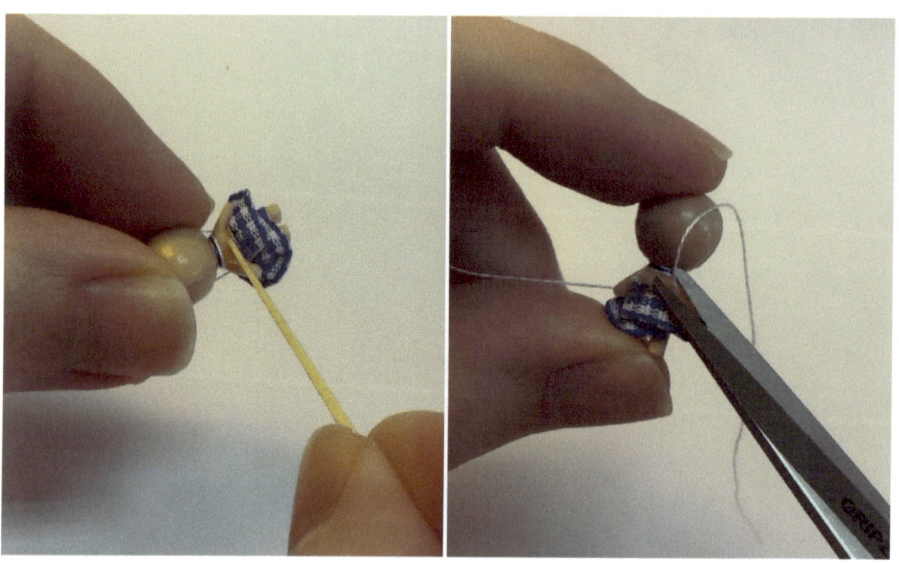

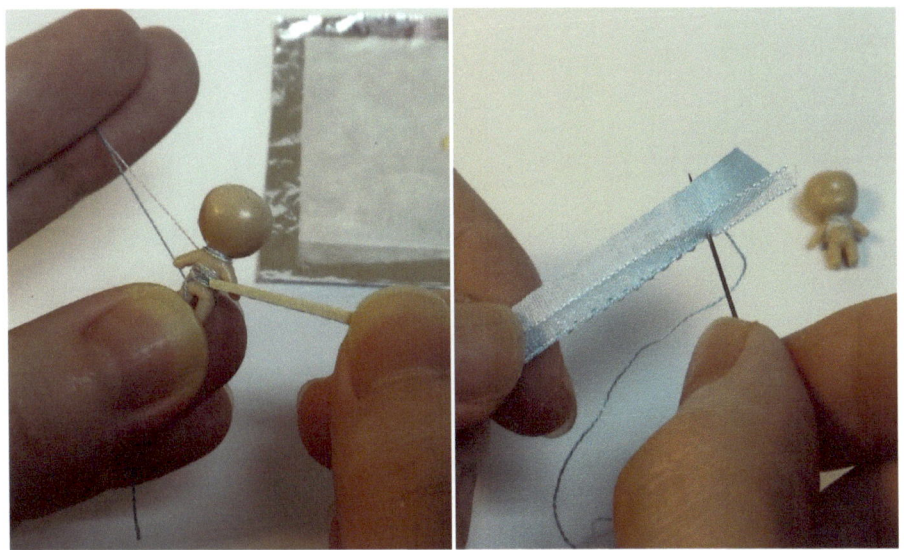

Iridescent and pale blue floss is wrapped around this model and secured with super glue. Pale blue silk and nylon ribbons are stitched up one side and pulled gently to create a full skirt.

Super glue is applied to the back of the skirt portion to secure it to the model before and after wrapping.

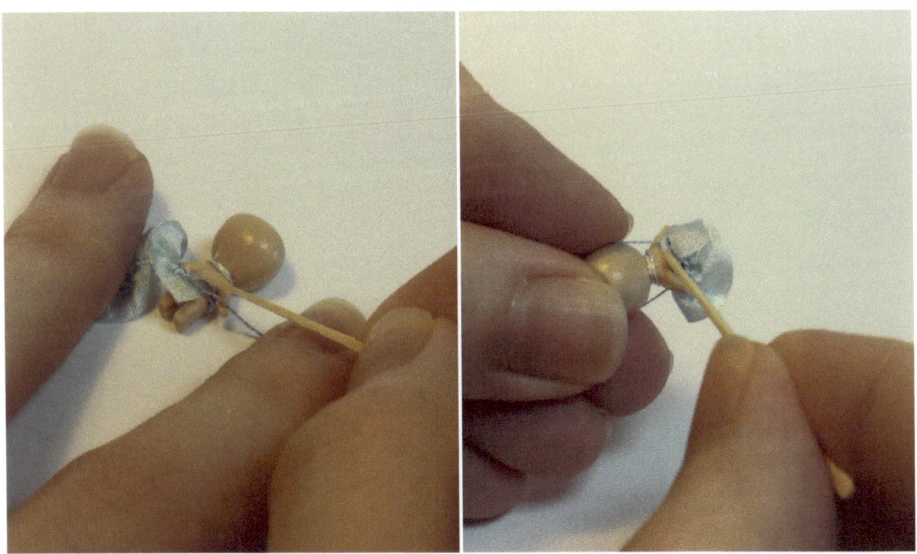

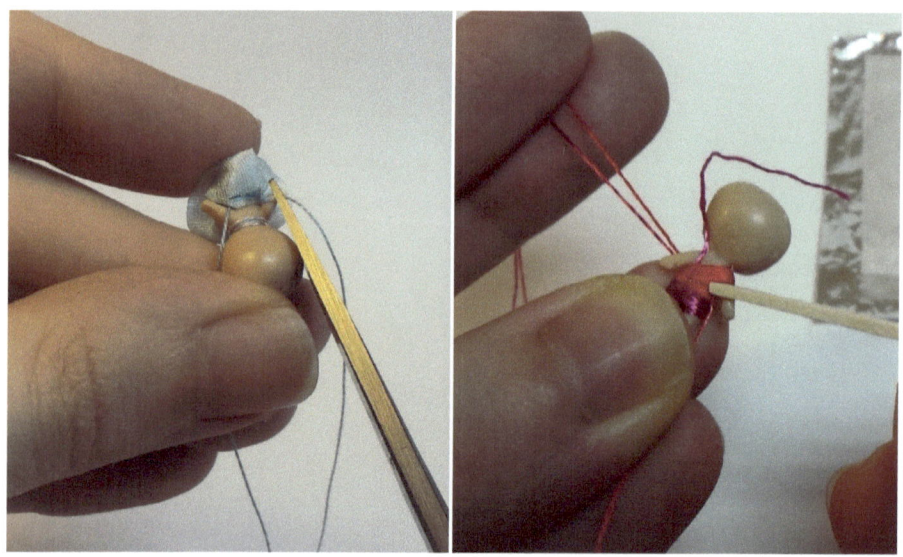

Trim excess floss flush to costume. Wrap coordinating colors to form an asymetrical costume top.

Stitch contrasting nylon ribbon and gather to create a short, full skirt to this bright costume.

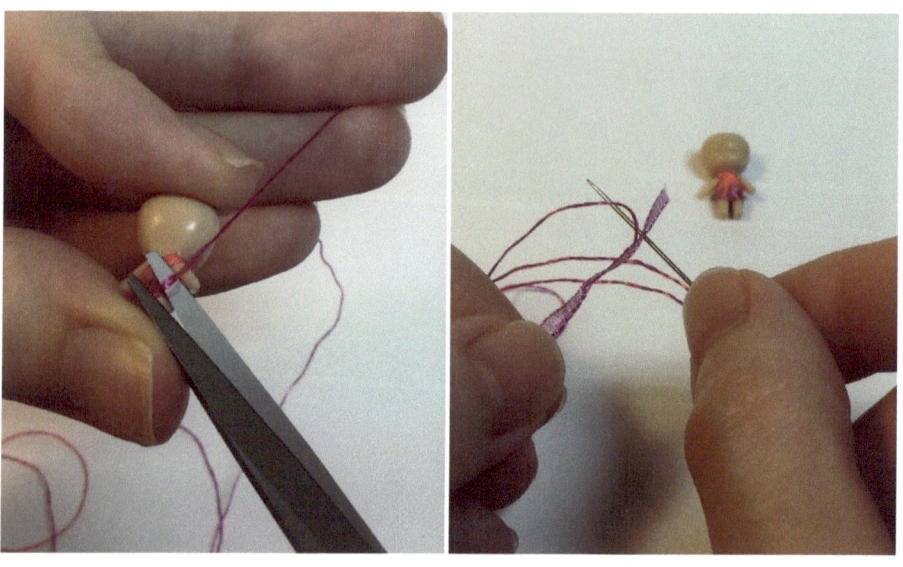

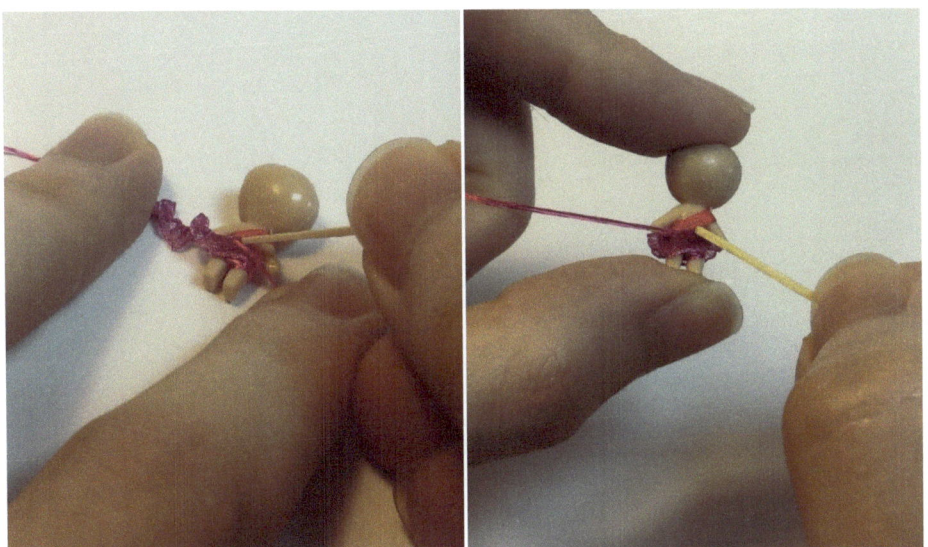

Wrap the skirt and secure with super glue and trim flush to costume.

Brilliant blue and red are wrapped and secured with super glue and trimed flush when cured.

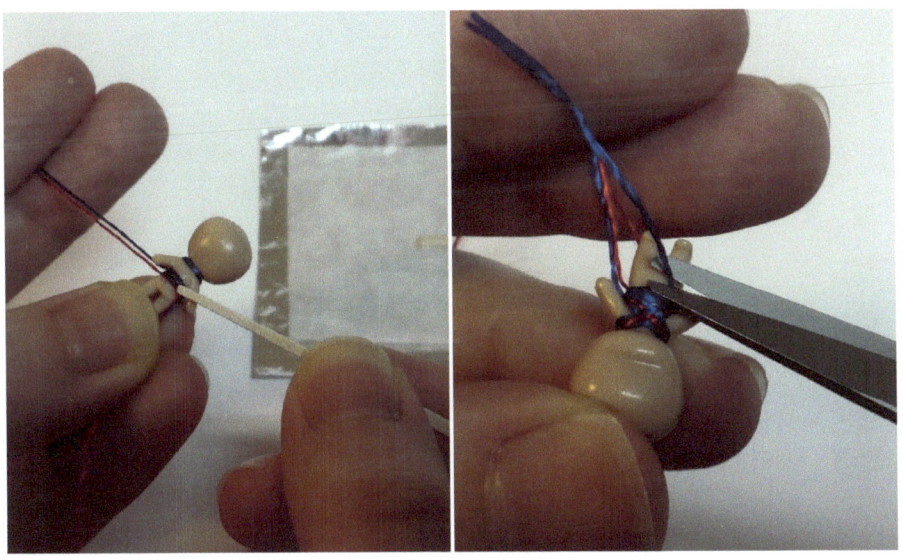

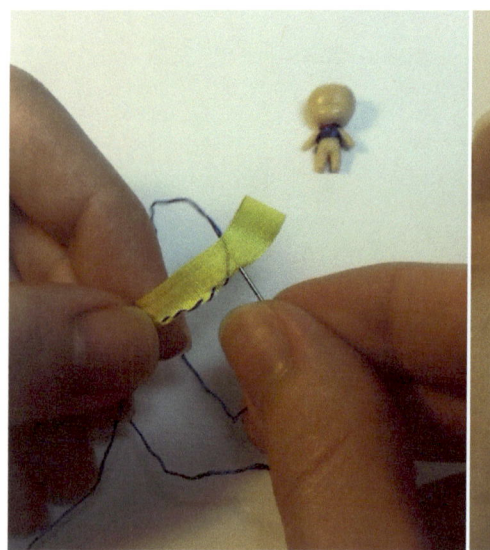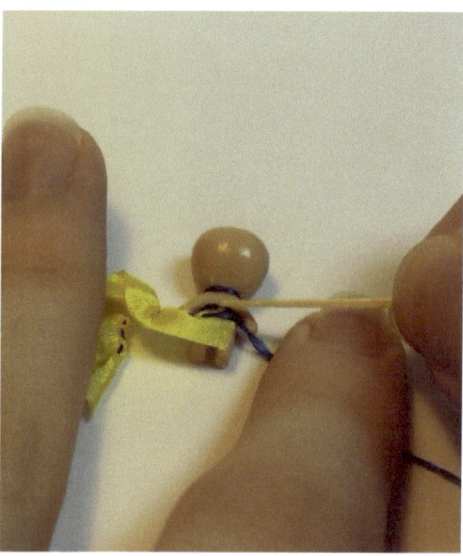

With this costume, I chose to use a contrasting colored floss in comparison to the skirt of the costume instead of the same color because as the silk ribbon is gathered and wrapped, it blends in with the rest of the costume. Allow the super glue to cure about 30 seconds before trimming flush to the costume.

Iridescent floss is secured after the top of this ballerina costume is tied on.

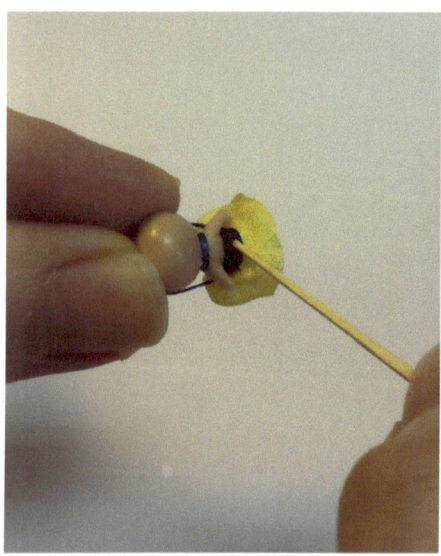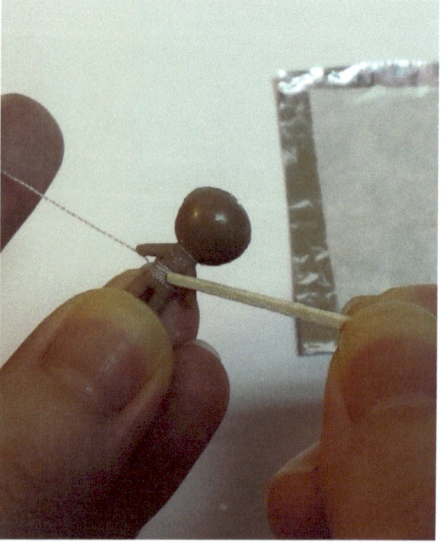

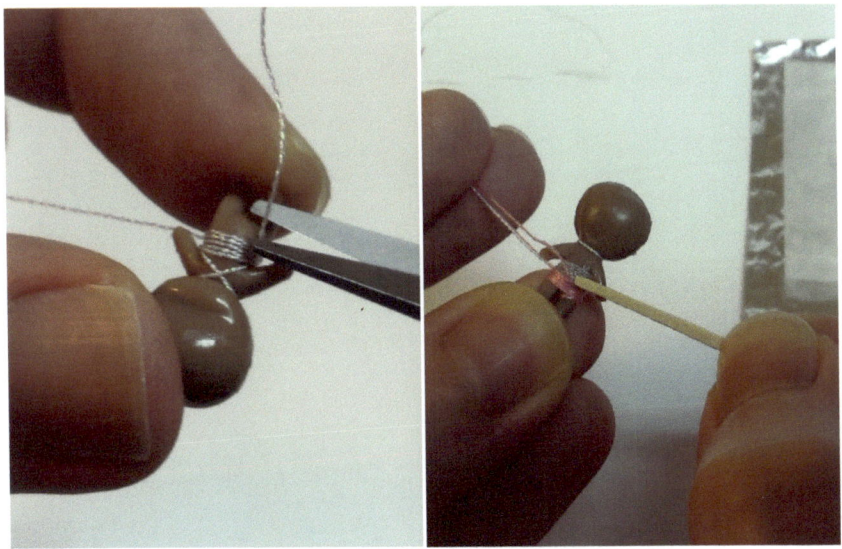

Trim excess floss flush to costume and add complimentry shade of pink floss to complete this step. Stitch one side of sheer pink nylon ribbon and gather to create a full tutu skirt.

Wrap the ribbon around the model, secure with super glue and trim flush.

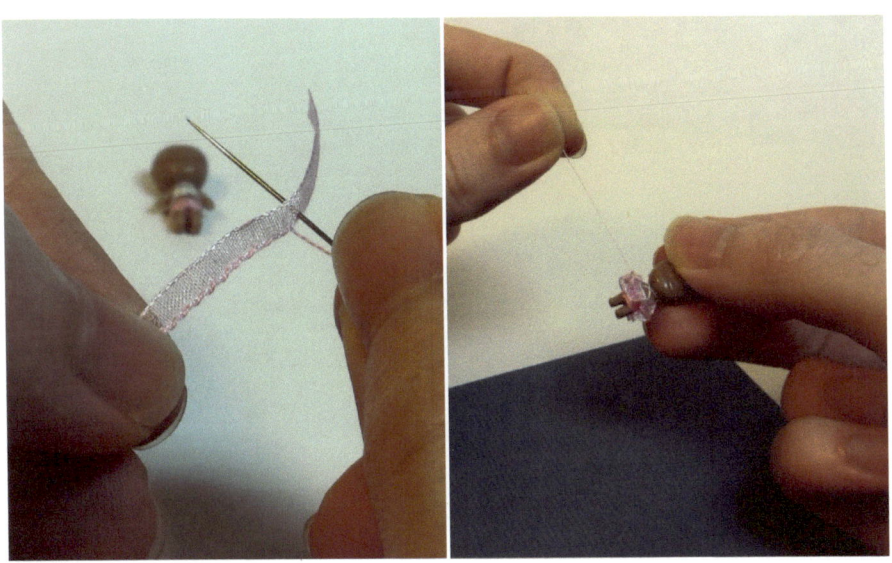

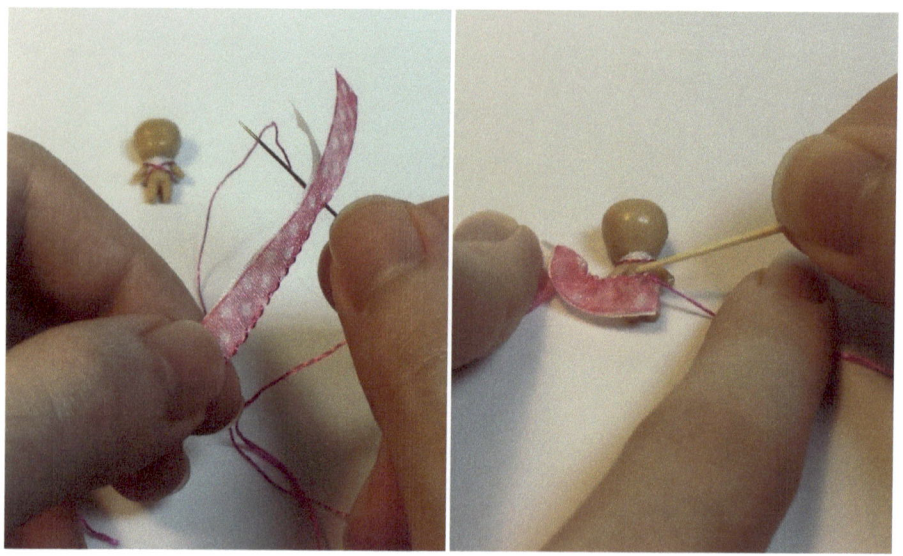

After the top is tied and secured, stitch a silk ribbon and nylon ribbon together on one side. Pull to create a full skirt and secure with glue then trim flush.

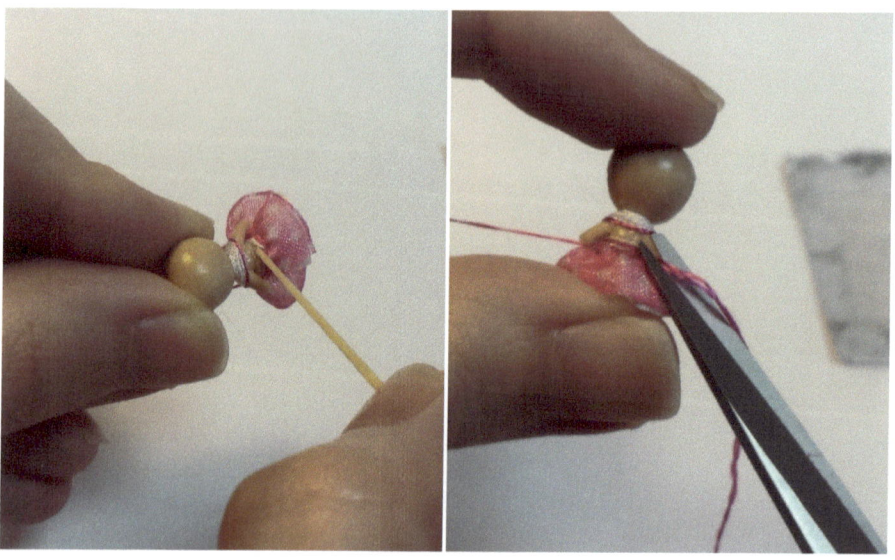

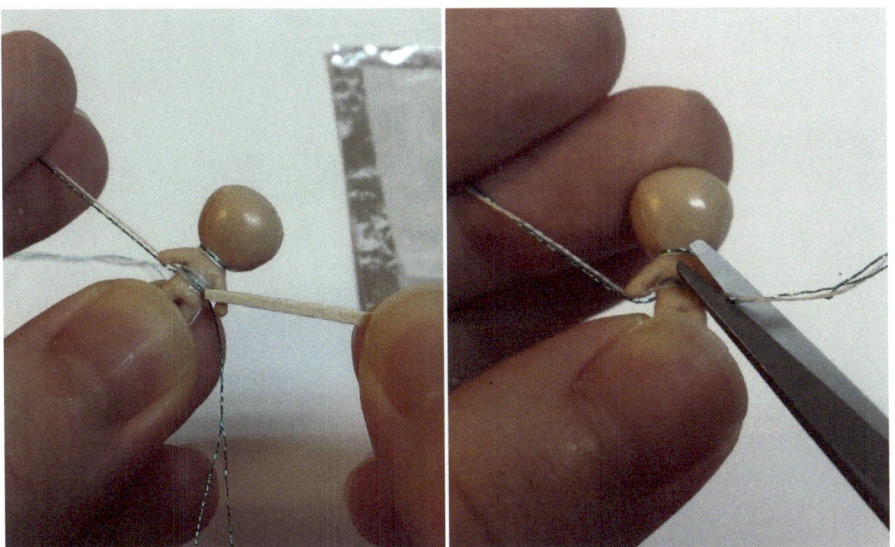

In this example, I used iridescent and metallic floss to add shimmer to the finished costume.

Secure with super glue and finish wrapping the skirt onto the model.

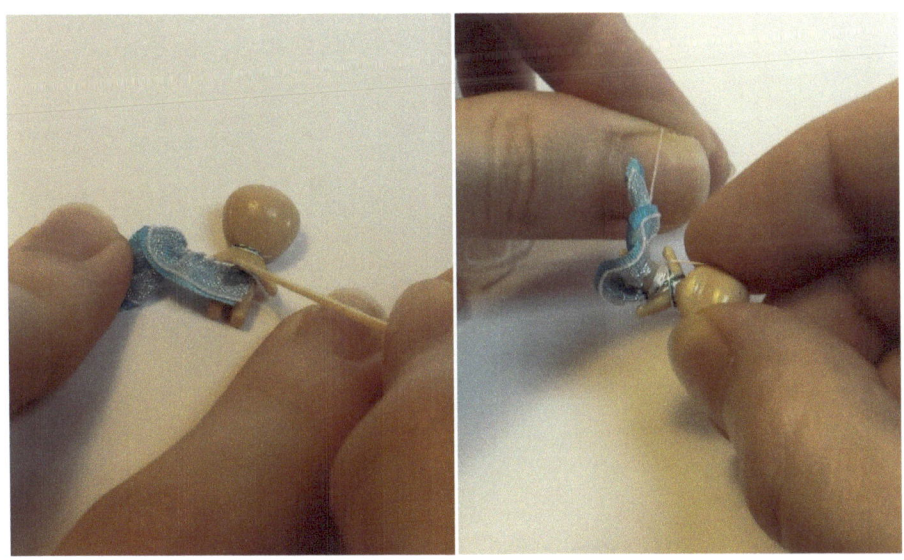

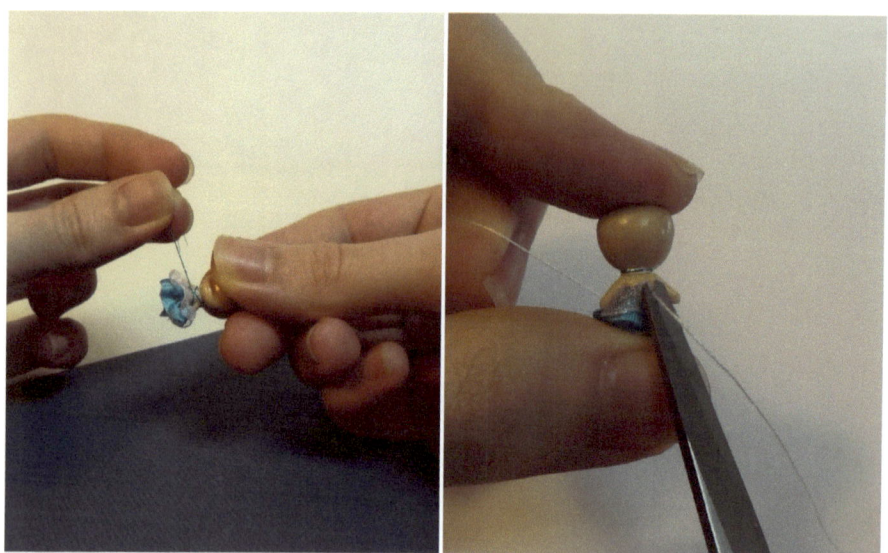

After securing the last layer with super glue and allowing it to cure, trim excess floss flush to costume.

If the figure will be wearing pants, apply acrylic paint from the mid torso to the feet and set on wax paper to cure for about an hour before adding additional layers of costume.

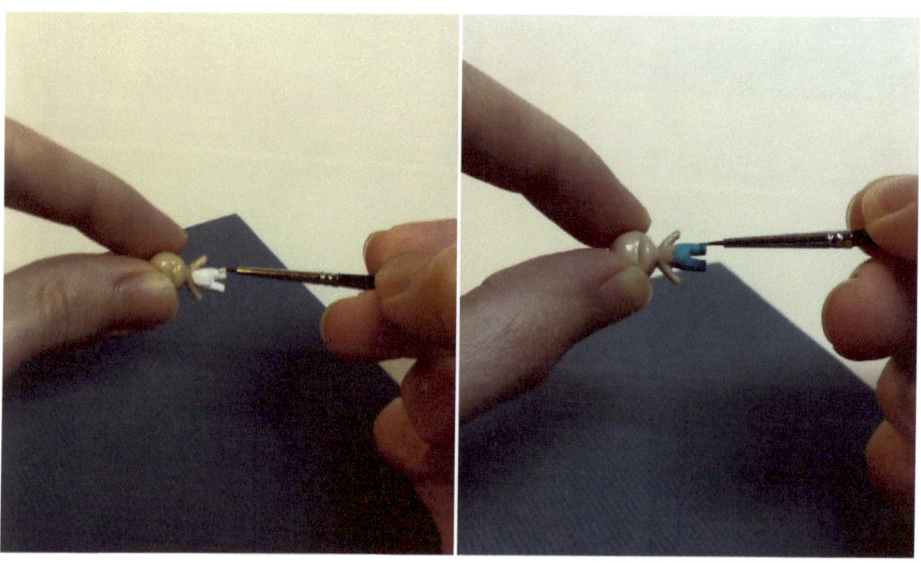

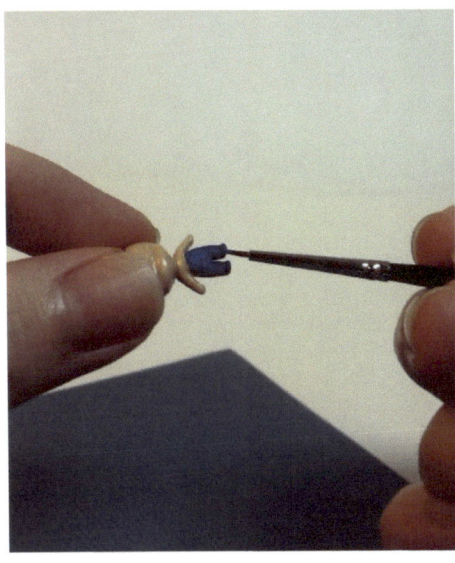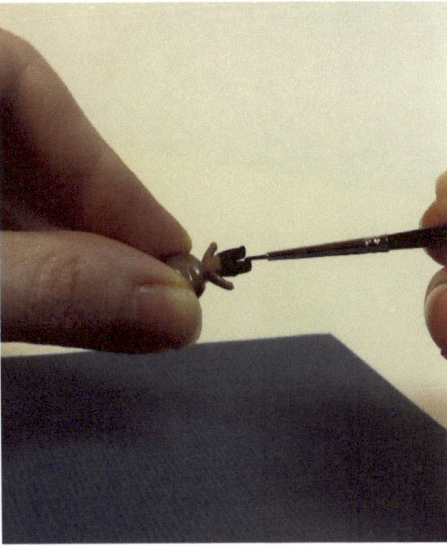

If the doll will be wearing a body suit, apply acrylic paint to the entire body, taking care around the neck line and avoiding the hands and allow to cure for at least an hour before testing with gentle touch to see if it is workable. Cure time for acrylic to urethane varys according to temperature and humidity and consistancy of the paint.

Some costumes require layers. I start with matching top and bottoms.

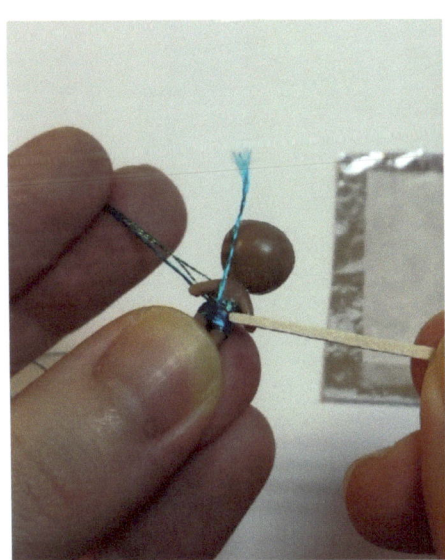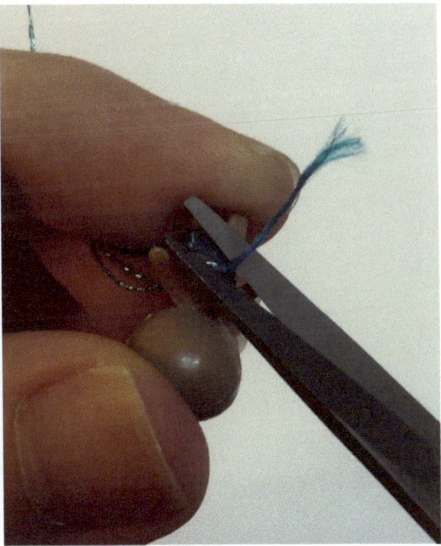

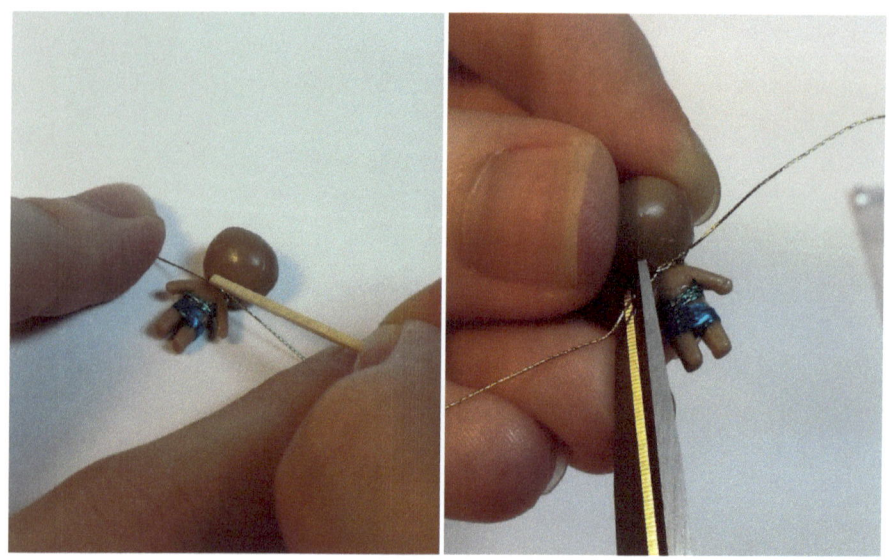

Secure floss with super glue and trim excess.

Use sheer knit fabric to create "harem pants." First secure with glue, wrap without pulling and glue gold floss at this step.

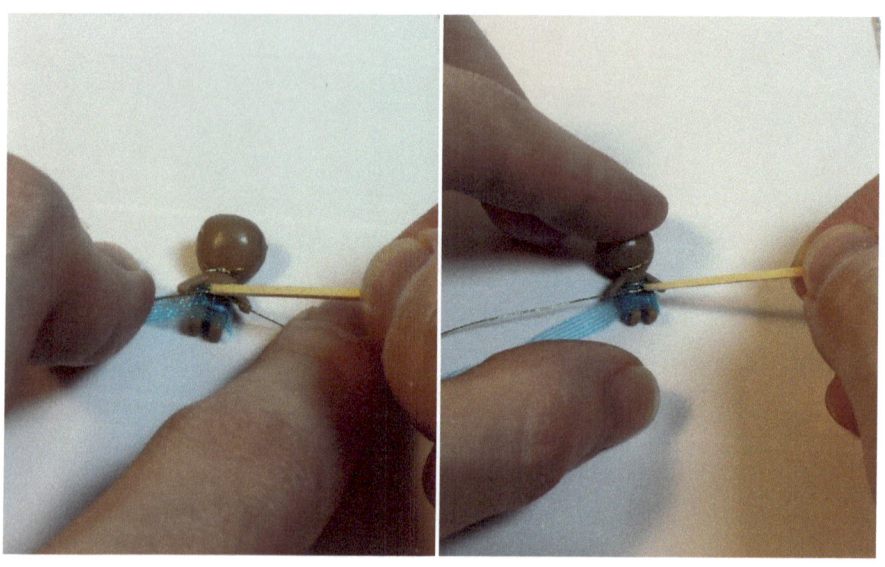

38

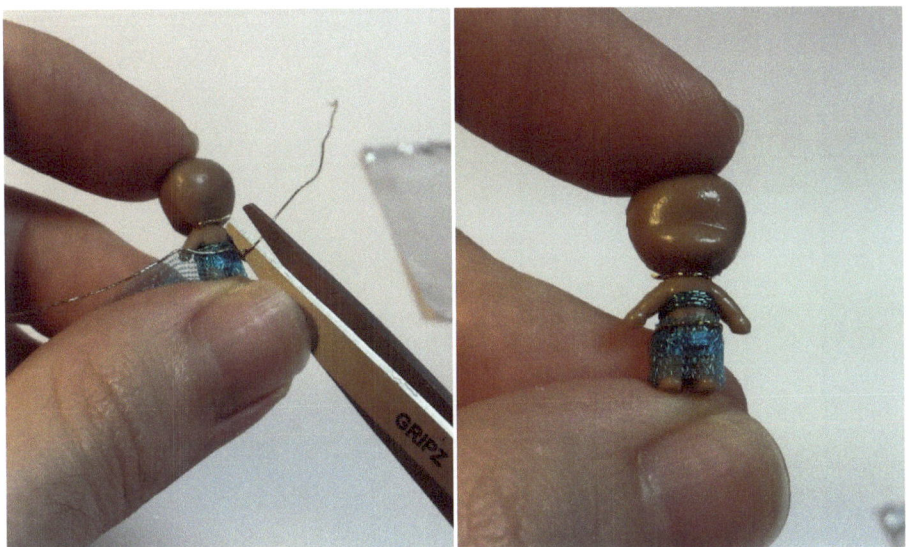

After the glue cures, trim all strands of floss flush to the costume. This is the result.

This design needs a single strand to imply the first layer of a kimono. Complimentary shades of floss and silk ribbon add to the effect.

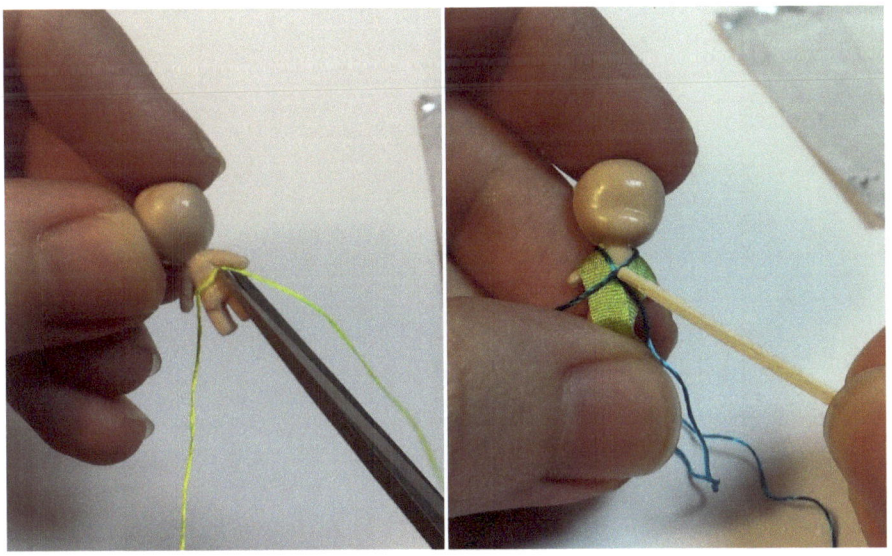

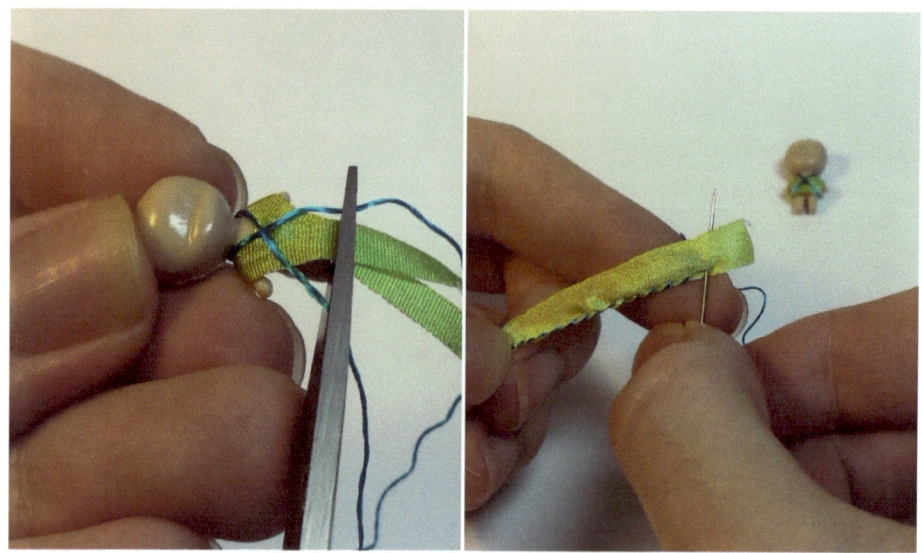

Trim excess fabic and floss. Stitch one side of silk ribbon to create the skirt portion of this costume.

Secure with glue, finish wrapping and add the wide belt with another shade of silk.

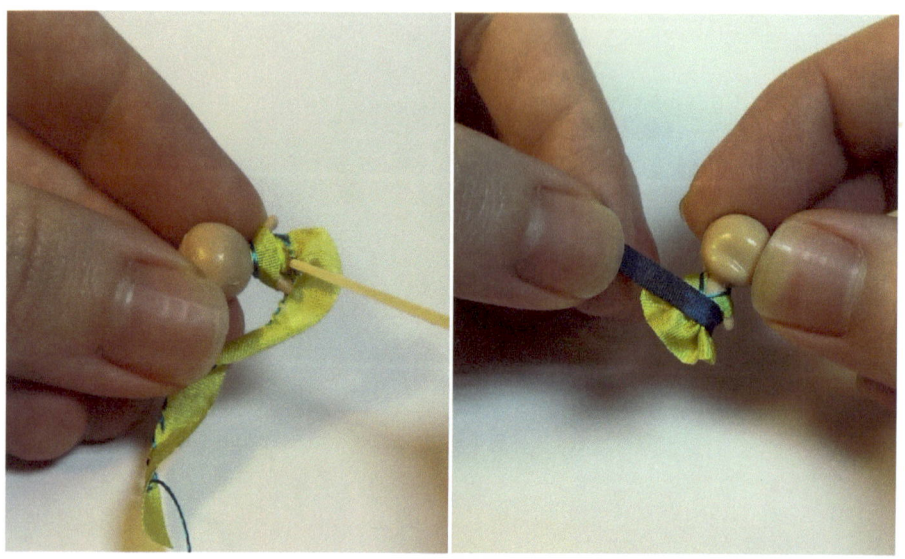

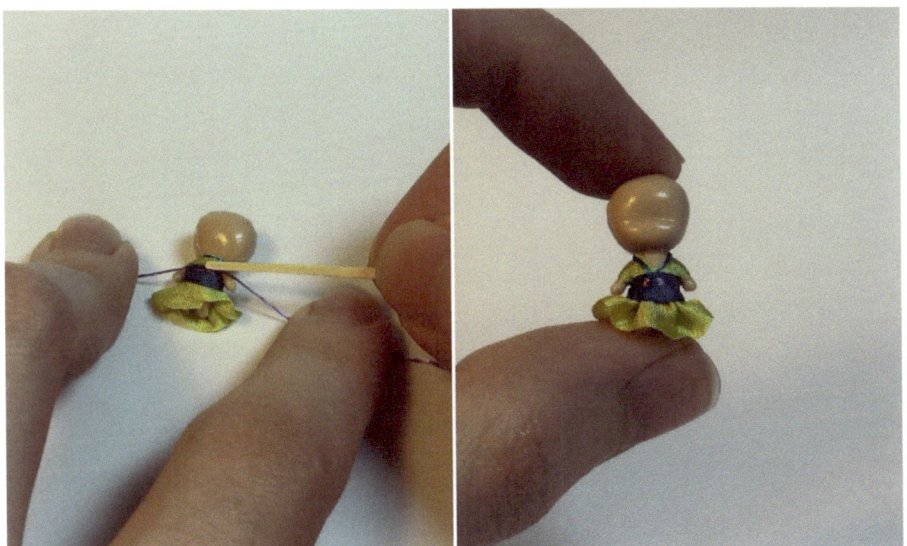

Secure and trim final shade of floss to create a six color, layered kimono costume.

This fairy costume starts with securing ribbon with super glue, wrapping and trimming excess.

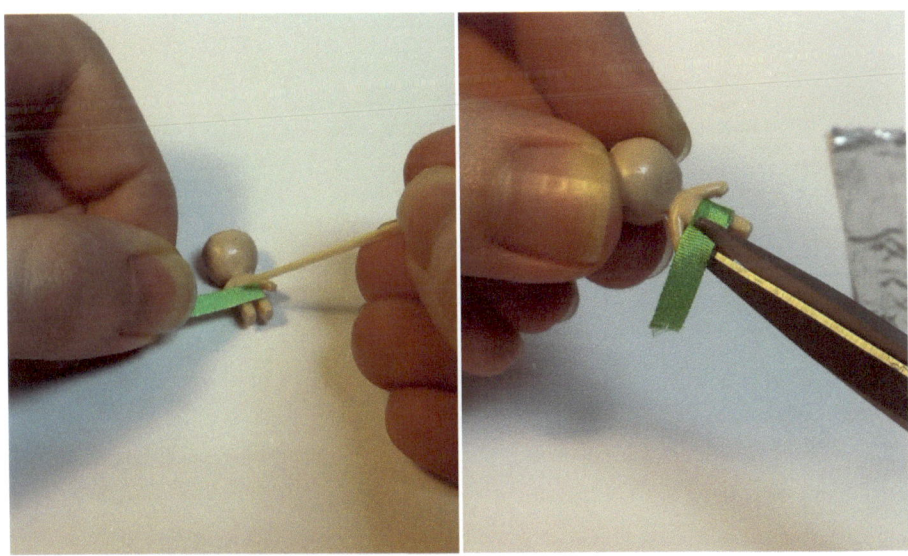

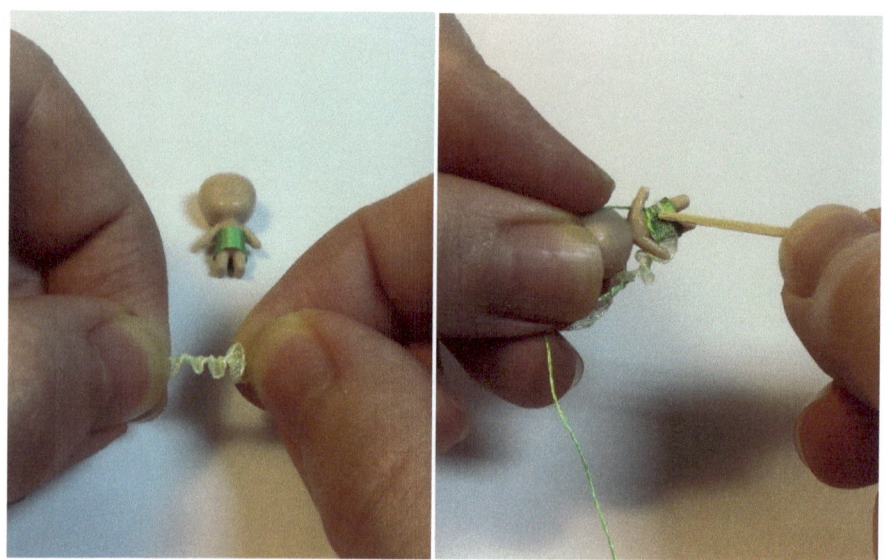

Stitch one side of ribbon to create the skirt portion of the costume. Secure with glue before and after wrapping skirt. Wrap remaining floss to create the top portion of the fairy costume.

Secure with glue and trim excess floss. There are many ways to design costumes for figures this size even with the constraints.

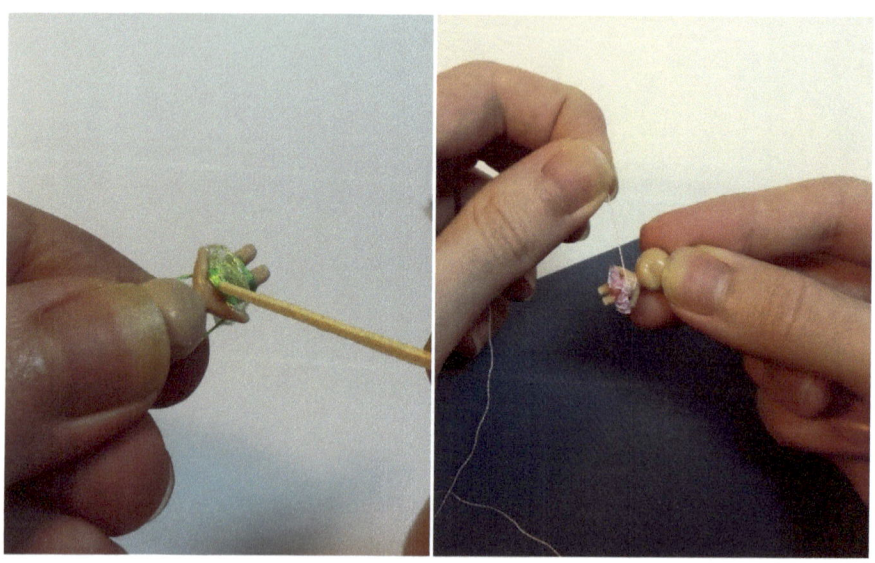

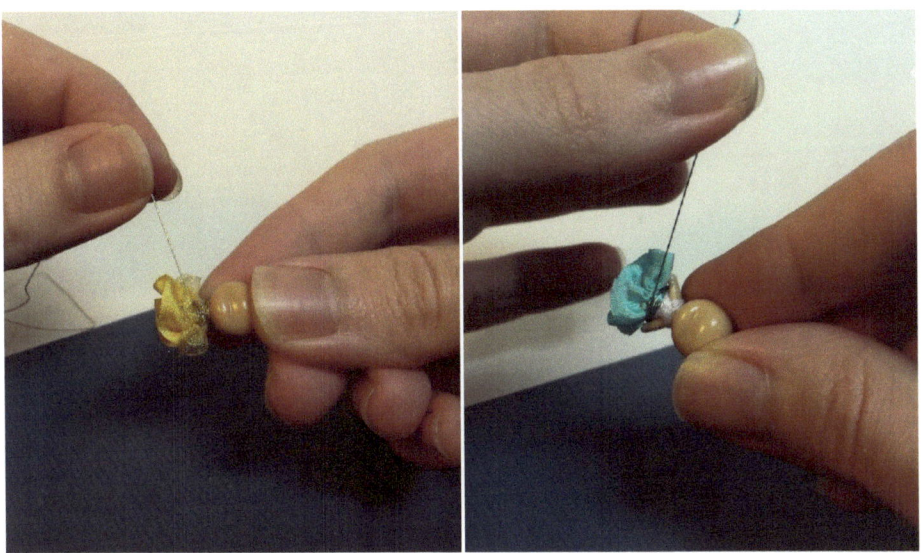

When I design costumes, I like to imagine the end product so as I add the layers, they compliment each other.

I think of the hair shade and well as accessories that might complete the costume ensemble.

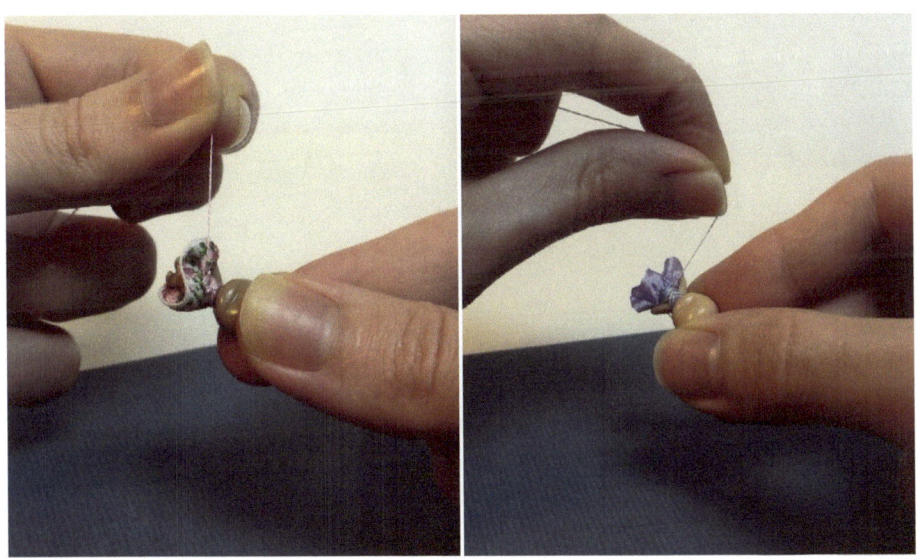

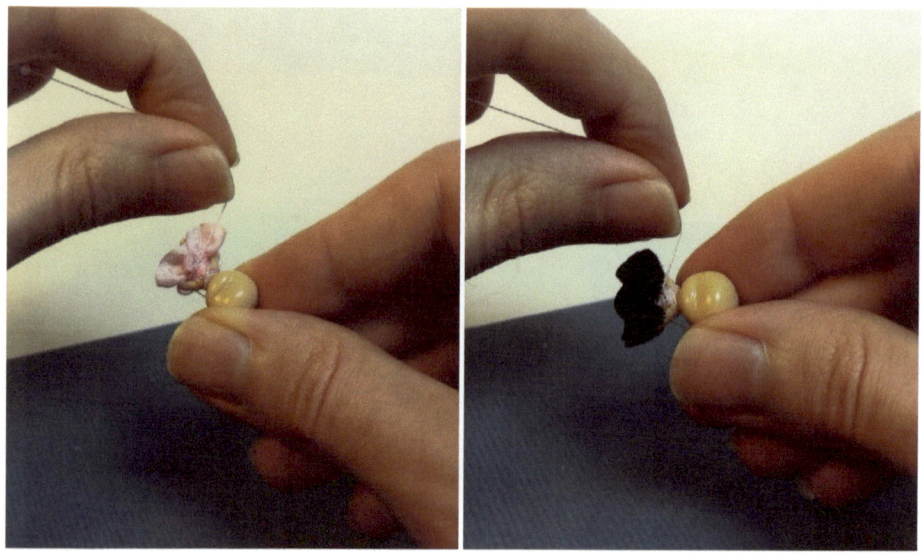

Another feature to consider is the eye shade when making the determination to contrast or compliment the elements that is chosen for the final product.

Costumes can be created to appear as pop culture icons or you may choose to create something new.

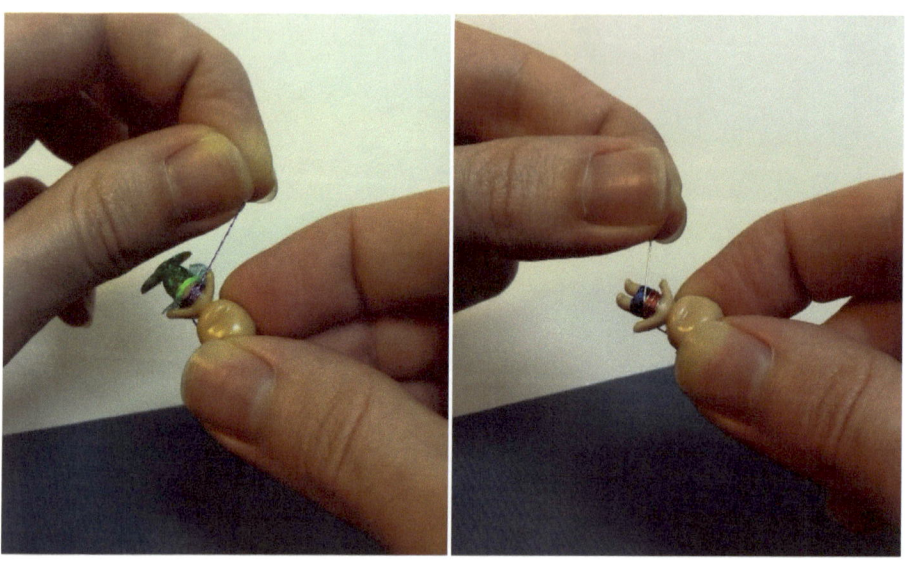

44

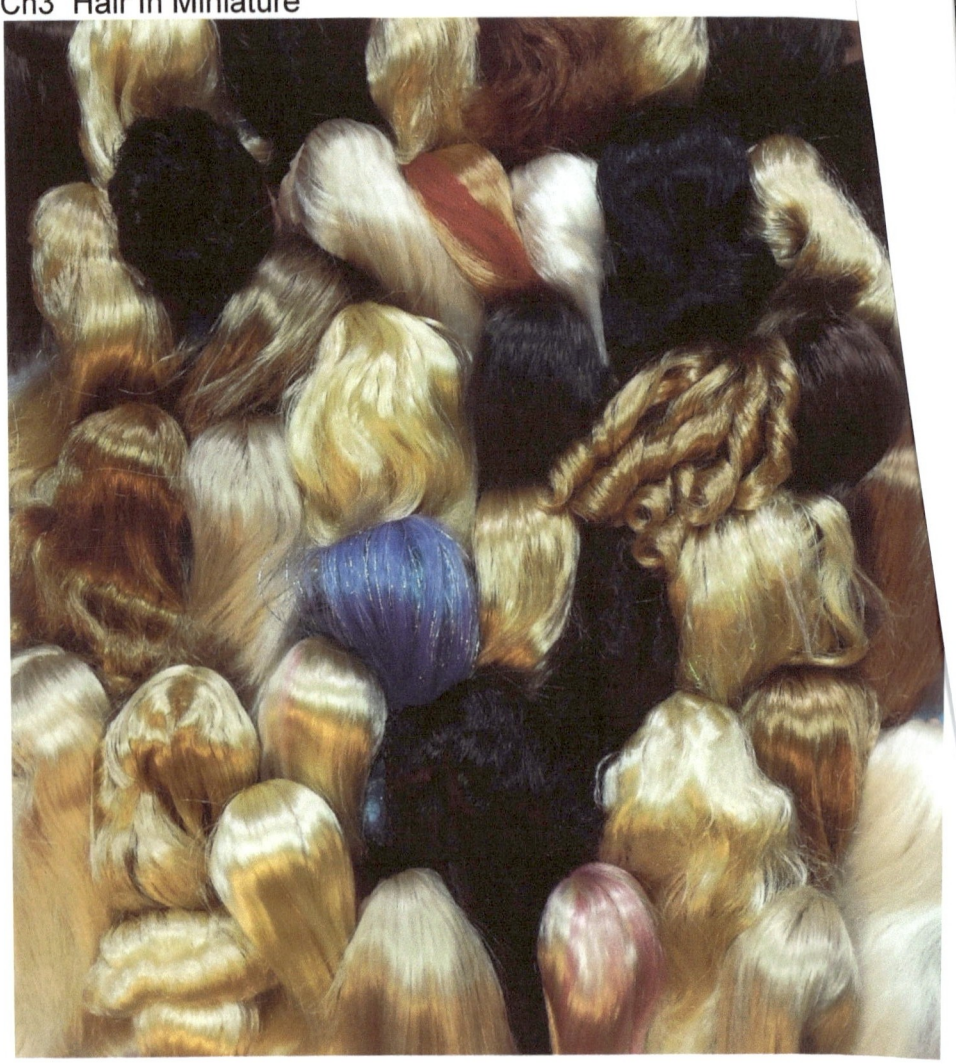

In addition to the tools needed in Ch2, you will need;

A quality pair of hair cutting shears, hot glue gun, glue sticks, silicone tools, alcohol, shampoo, dish detergent, glasses, towels and a tall sided plastic container, paper towels, nylon doll's hair, dolls brush and regular sized comb, bamboo skewer ends, first aid kit for cuts, burns and punctures. You will need to wash your hands often.

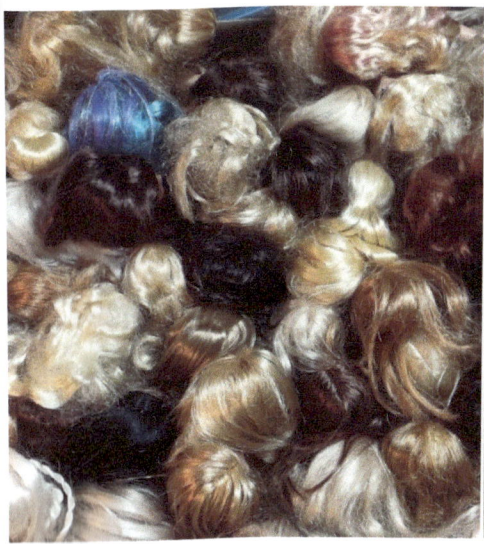
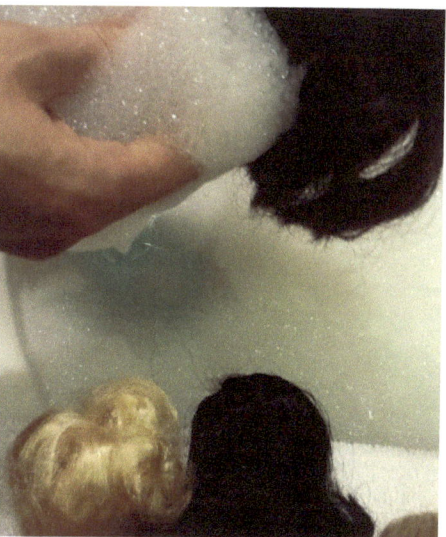

New locks of doll's hair can be located in speciality stores or online. It is a little costly but it is ready to use and available in assorted colors. Hair from new dolls are often contaminated with industrial grease from machinery that is used to stitch the hair plugs into place.

Factory hair-spray is sometimes applied to doll's hair to hold strands into place and secured with tiny rubber bands with the many new hair designs and types marketed today. All of which needs be removed carefully to avoid permenantly crimping and damaging individual nylon strands and to remove oils, prepping nylon to use.

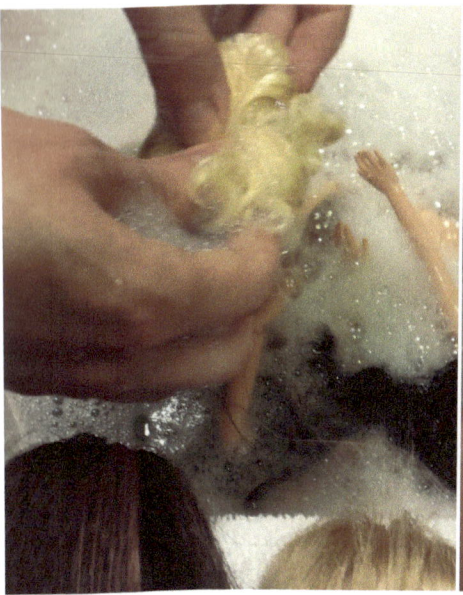
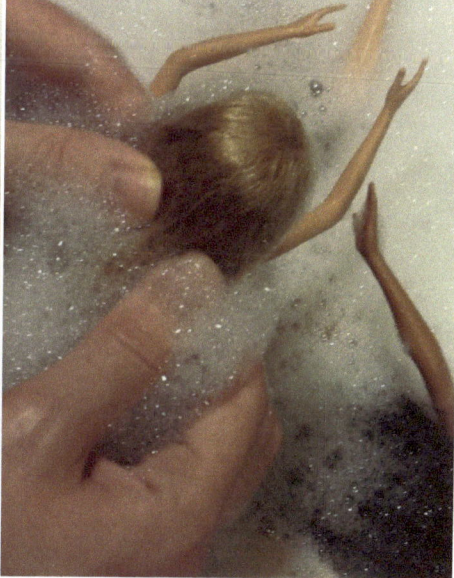

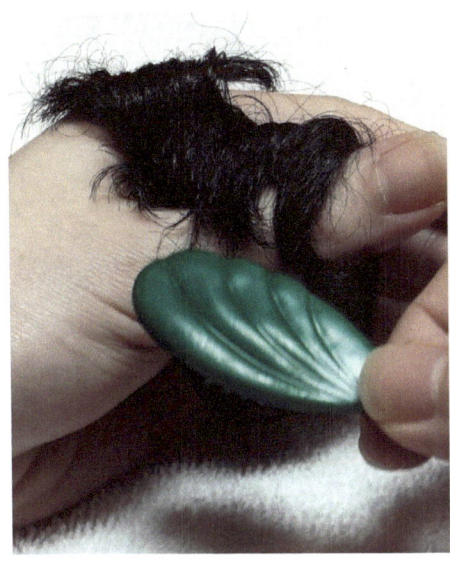
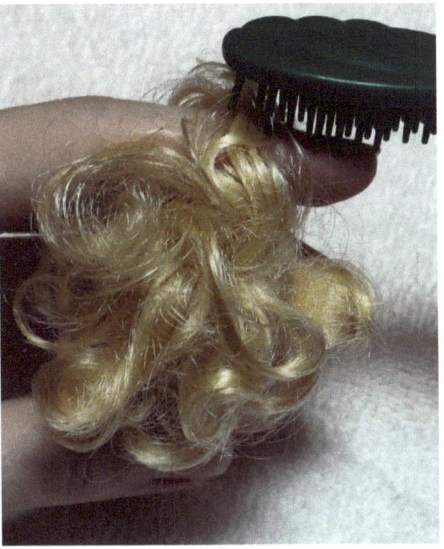

New and used doll's hair should be washed carefully and dried thoroughly before utilizing. I recommend a gentle shampoo to remove dirt and light oils. As the hair is drying, I comb it smooth whether into curls or straight because the nylon holds it's shape well after drying. Terry towels helps to wick away moisture. Inspect the hair when it is completely dry for residual oils from industrial application. If there is none, then the hair is ready for use.

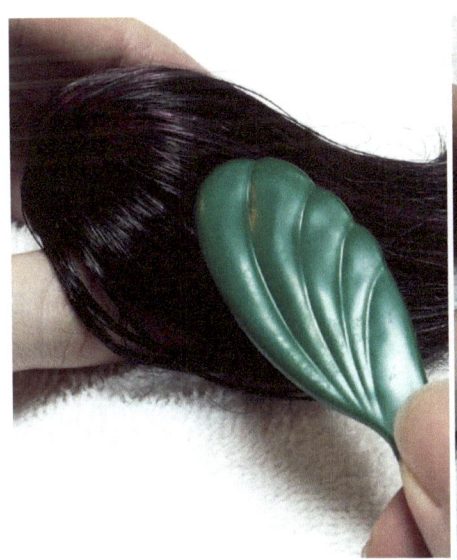
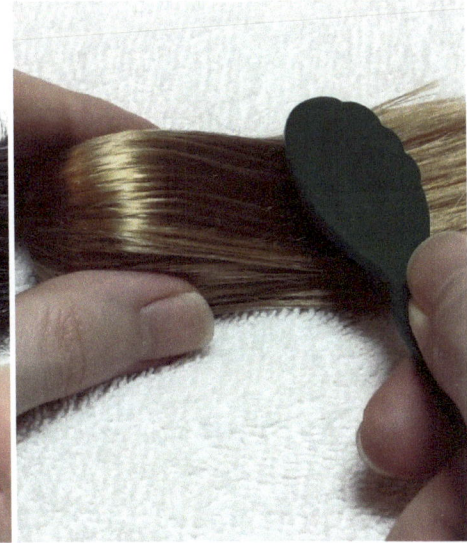

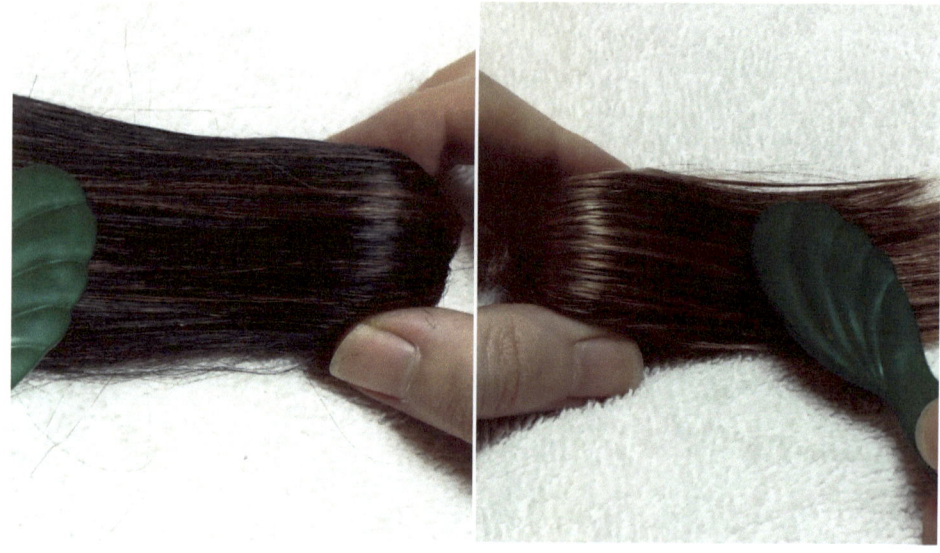

If some oils remain, these dolls should be cleaned with a mild dish detergent at this stage to strip away these residual oils.

After air drying a second time, inspect the hair for any remaining oils.

These side-by side comparisons illustrate the difference in appearance to greasy as opposed to clean and dry.

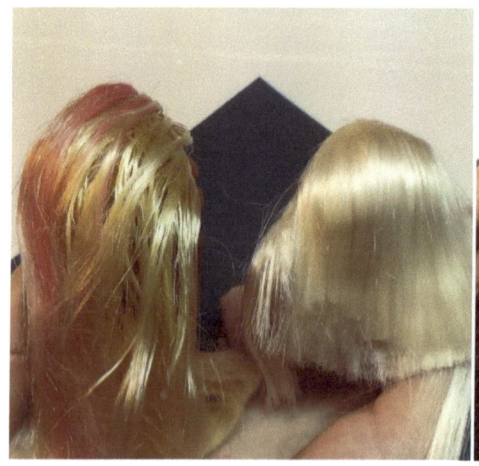
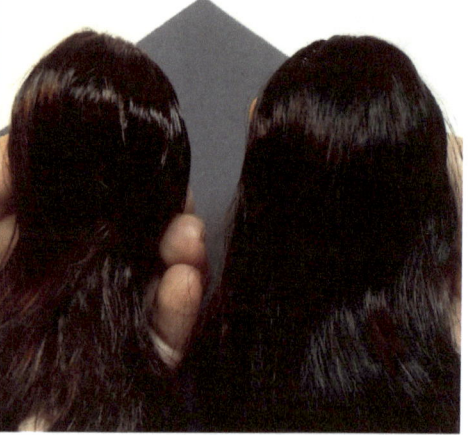

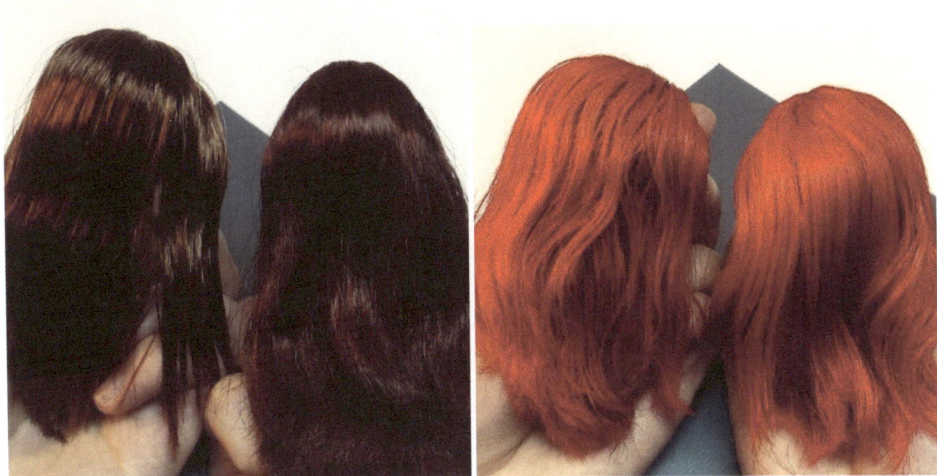

If dish detergent did not remove the oil, you can try rubbing alcohol to strip this toughest grease left by the manufacturing process.

In these examples, you can see the difference between the clean, dry hair and nylon with residule oils in varying degrees, from enough to cause the nylon to appear shinier than usual to so laden with grease, the hair sticks together and feels sticky or stiff to the touch.

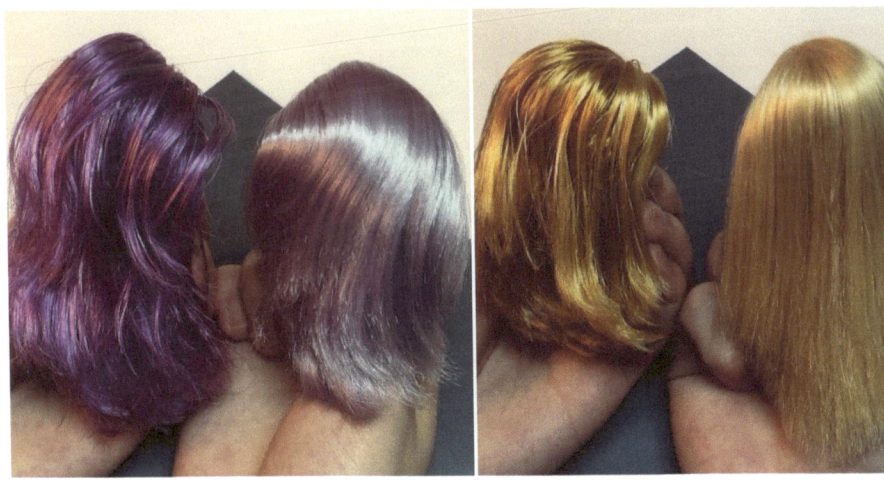

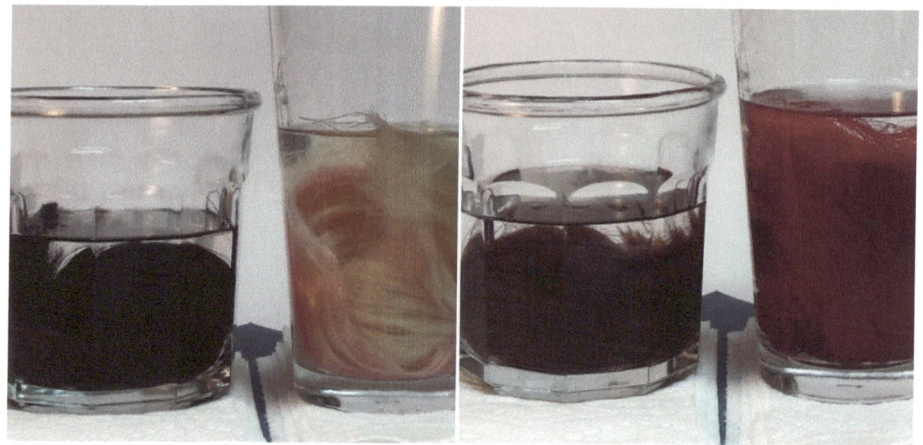

Soak the nylon in alcolol for up to an hour as needed. Rinse with warm water and wash again with mild shampoo. After hair dries completely, inspect it again for any remaining oil.

The process of cleaning nylon doll's hair is a little destructive and you should test strands with new cleaning methods in case the hair is more fine, requiring greater care.

At this stage if there is grease left, I must make the decision whether or not to invest in further soaking the hair in alcohol baths. If the hair is a unique texture or color, that is enough to justify soaking again but use care not to damage the nylon in the process.

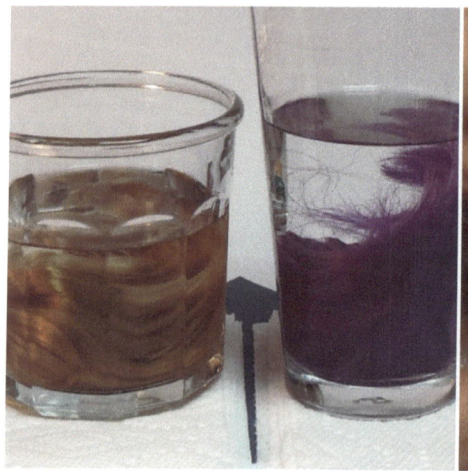
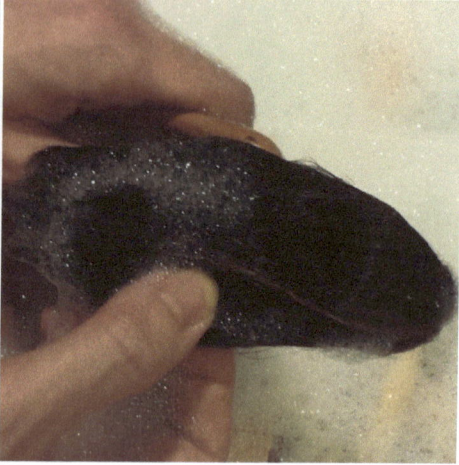

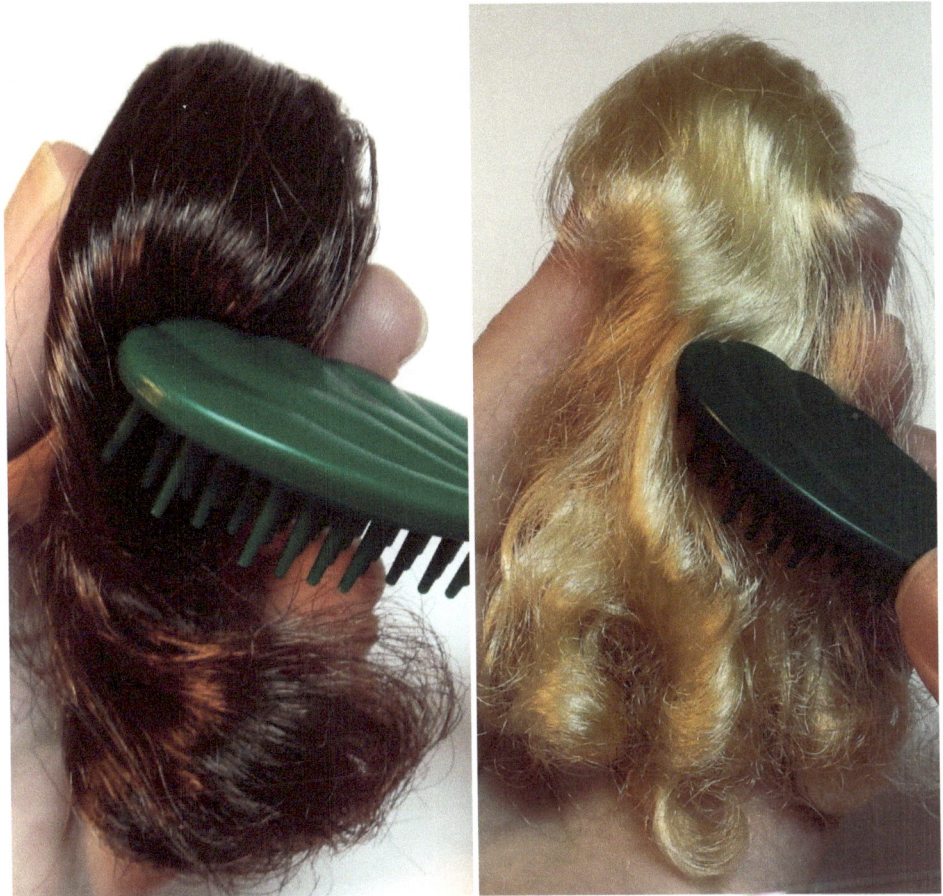

Used dolls sometimes have a tendency to have it's hair already cut by aspiring hairdressers but that is not a problem when recycling doll's hair. Comb or brush the hair in advance to smooth the fibers out.

Wash and dry your hands often while working with clean hair. Place the prepared hair onto a clean surface while you are working with it. Store completly dry hair in seperate plastic bags in order not to damage or tangle the fibers from friction.

If the hair has any moisture left, it can cause problems while in storge. Allow hair to dry for 48 hours to ensure the lowest moisture level before containing.

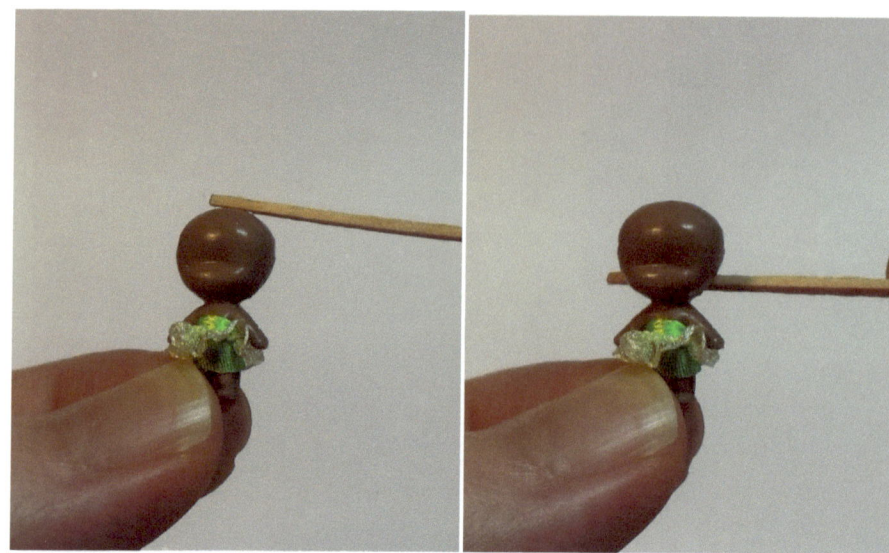

Prepare the heads of the urethane doll with super glue. I coat the surface that I want the hair to adhere to. This hairline should be similar to a person's natural hairline.

Allow the super glue to cure for about a half hour before advancing to the next step. It is advised to lay the figure onto wax paper, glue side up, that it might not stick to surfaces before drying completely.

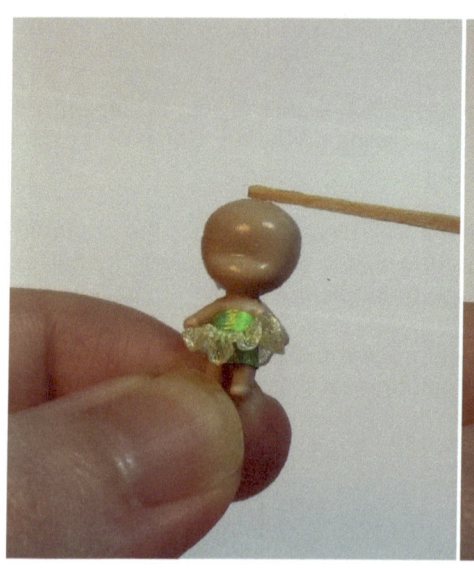
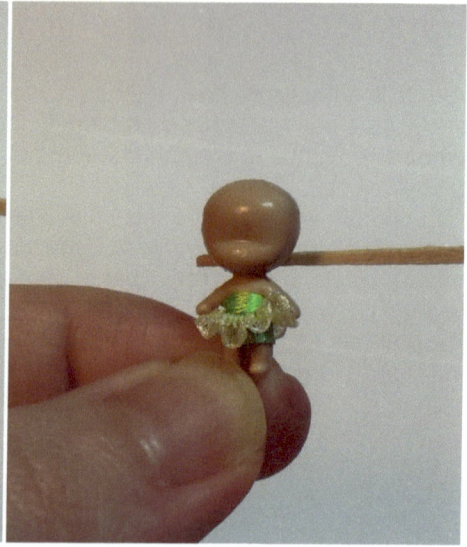

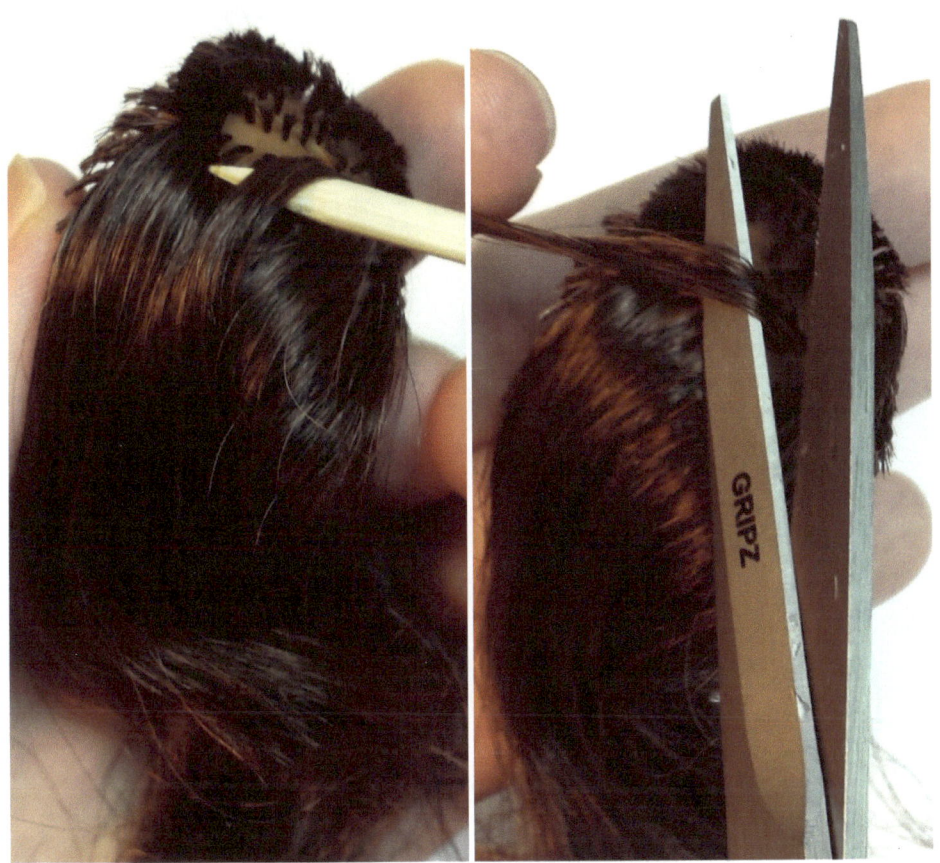

Use a bamboo skewer end to seperate a measured quantity of plugs of hair at a time and cut from the head. Trim the hair to desired length with quality hair cutting shears.

Be certain the cut is even. This will be the end that will be applied onto the doll's head.

When triming the hair length, keep in mind the final out come of the hair design. If the hair will be falling naturally, I apply the hair that direction. If it is to be styled into ponytails or into a complex design, it is necessary the hair is attched to make the design possible.

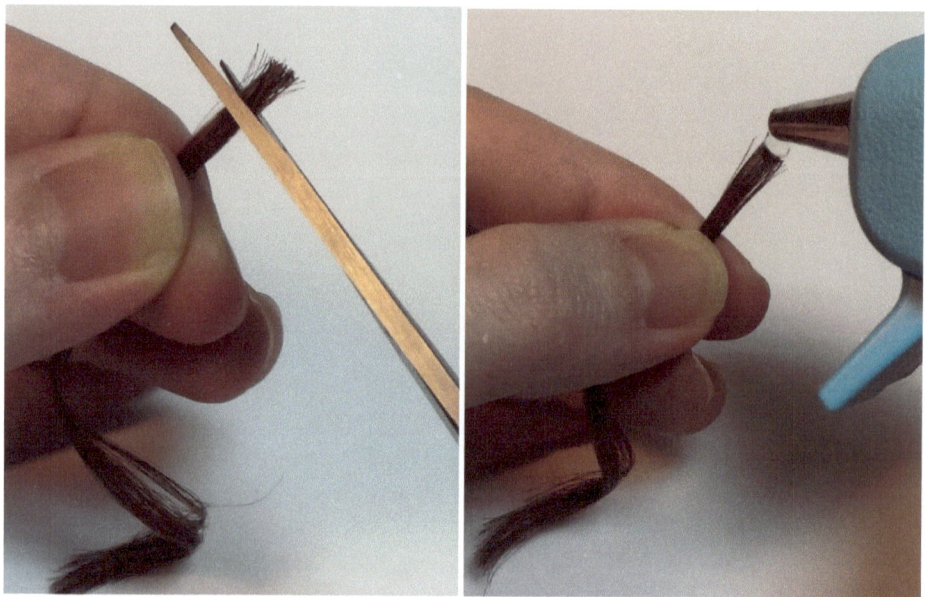

Apply a bead of hot glue onto the hair and secure to the head of the doll using a silicone cube tool, pressing in the direction you wish for it to fall. Repeat this process, starting in the back, working to the front of the doll's hairline.

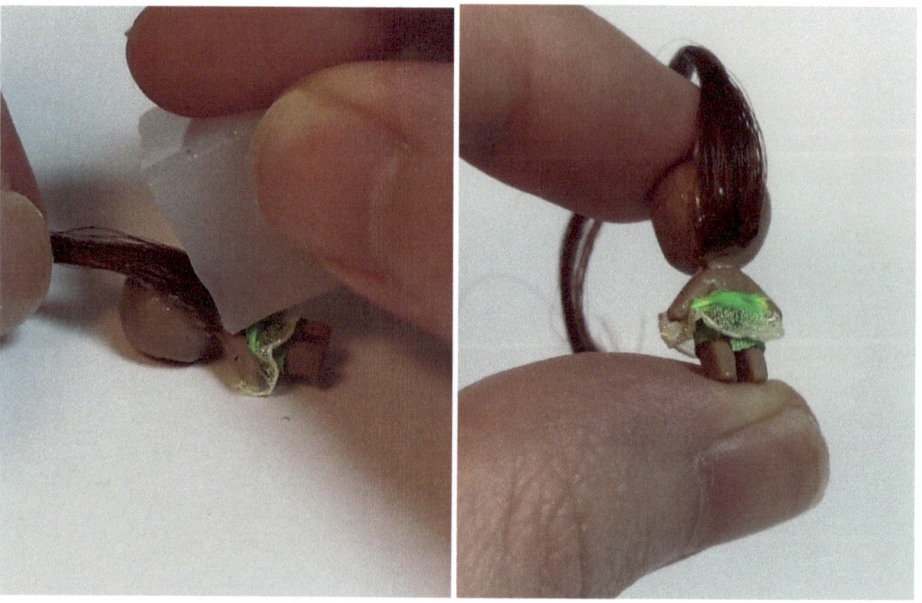

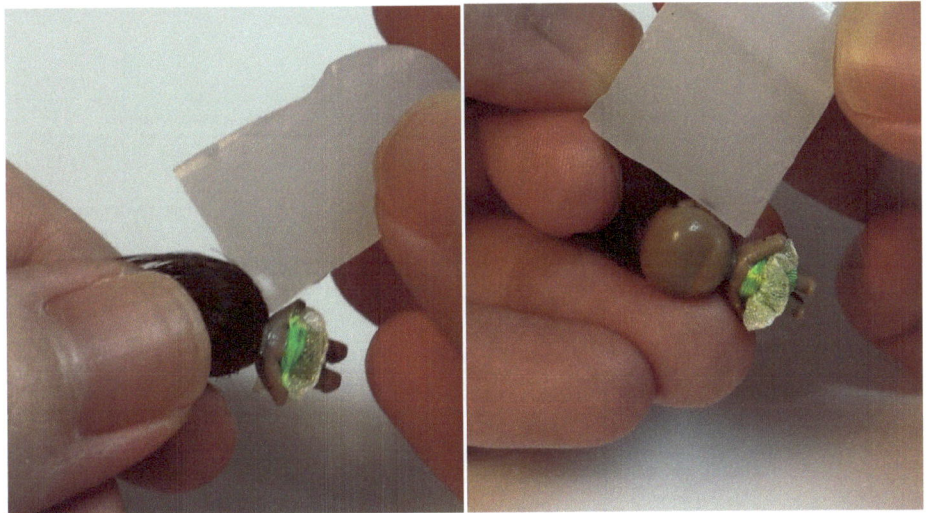

Repeat the gluing process to attch sections of hair. Pictured is the application of the right then left. This is the result.

I am showing the same process with a different shaded hair color so if a step is not clear in the photograph, I am providing two sets of examples so nothing will be missed.

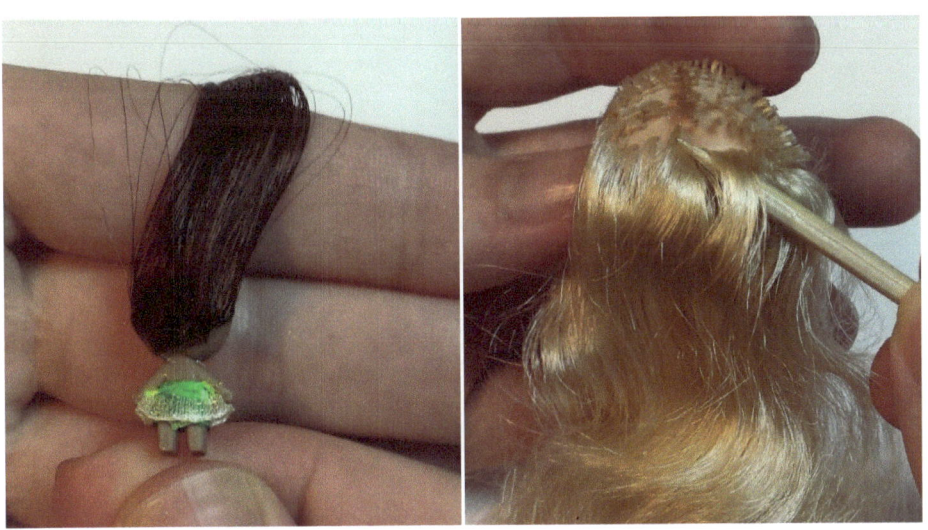

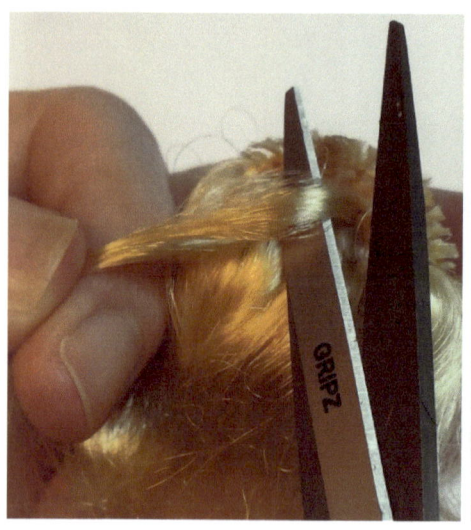 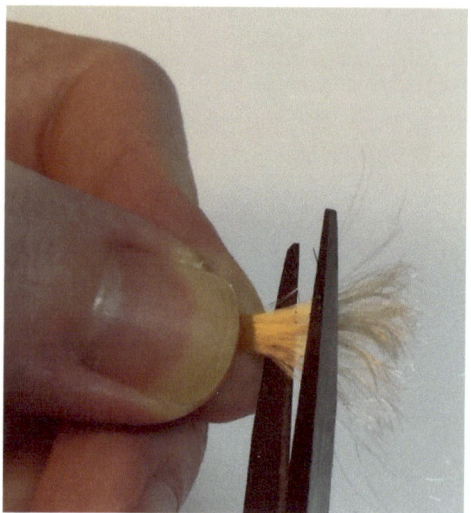

This is the second examples of cutting, trimming, gluing and using the silicone tool to press the hot glue into place on the doll's head.

Silicone can withstand temperatures up to 400 degrees making this ideal in the application process.

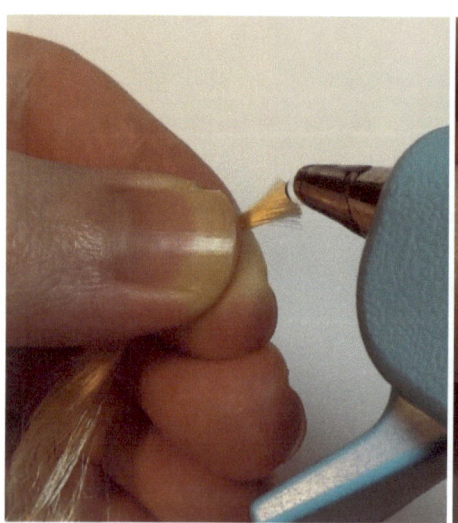 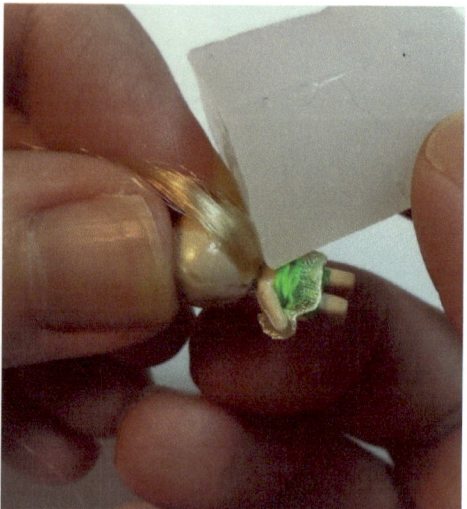

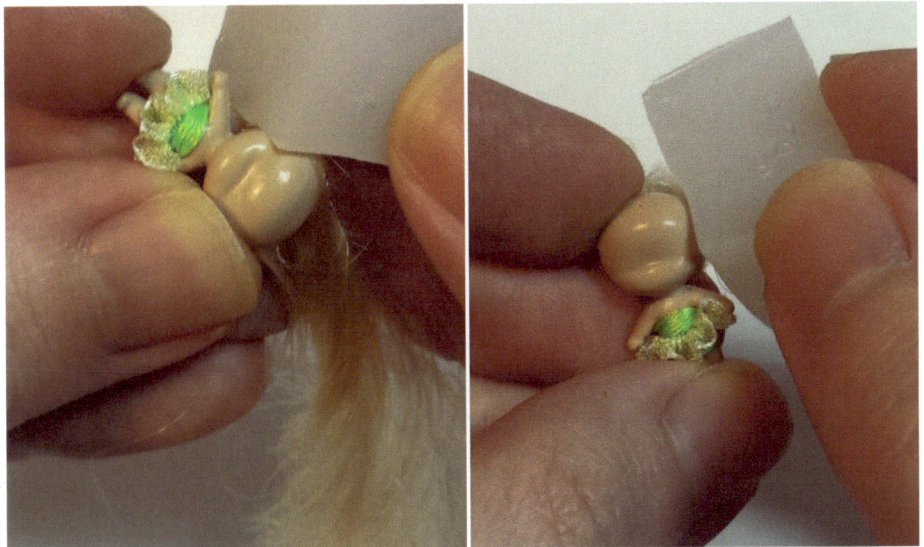

After pressing the hair into place on the right and left sides like the first example, we progress onto applying the "bangs."

This is applied in a forward position, originating beyond the center of the head.

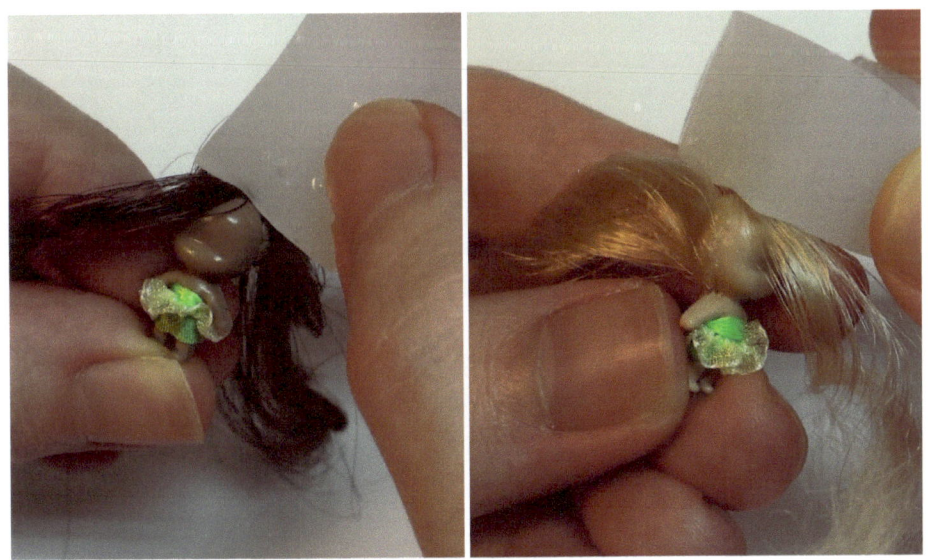

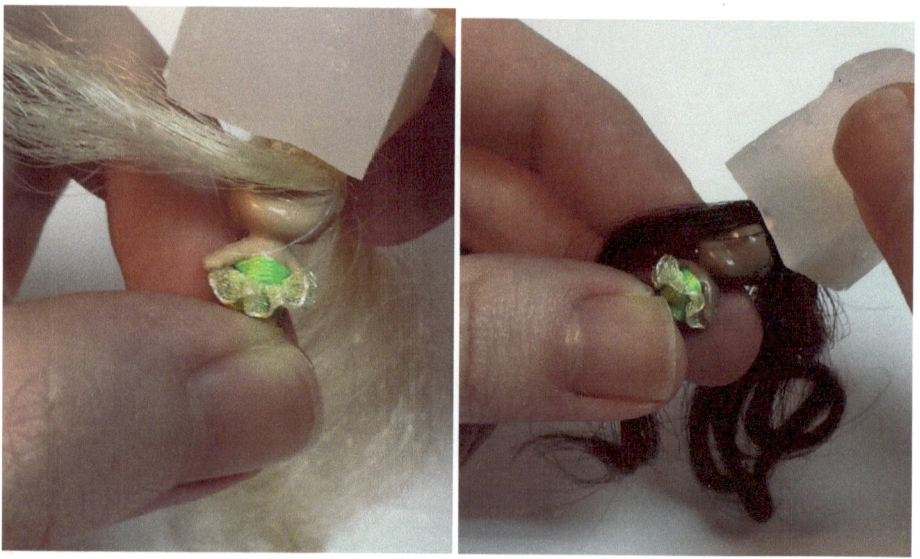

The top portion is applied and pressed onto the head, creating a "part" where the hairline meets the bangs.

Use floss to create a ponytail and apply super glue to secure it.

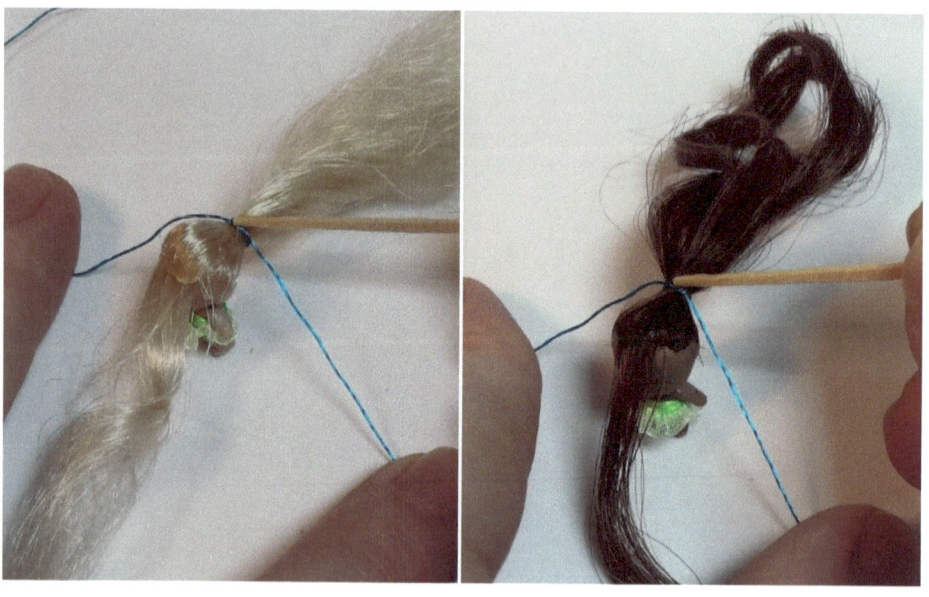

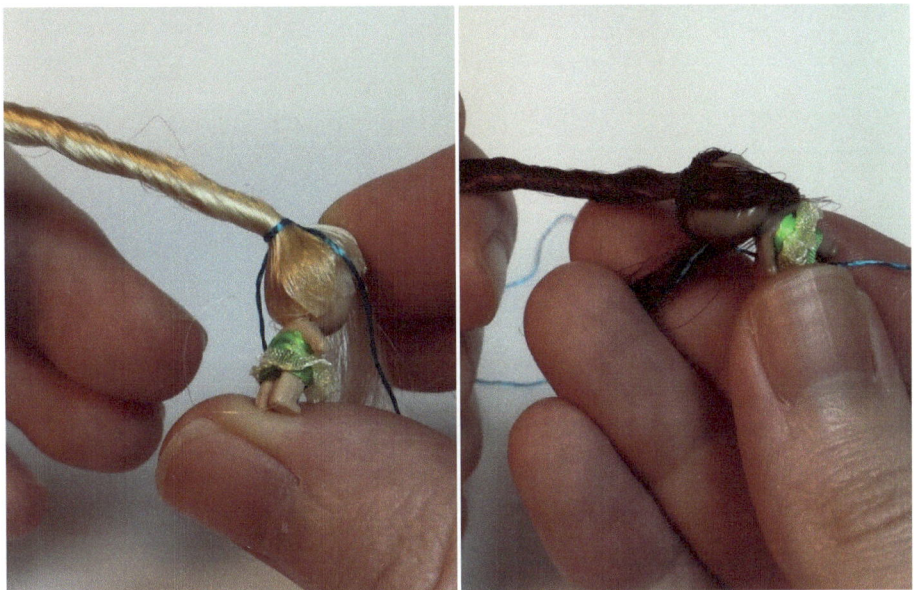

After the super glue has cured for about 30 seconds, twist the ponytail and allow it to flip into a small bun.

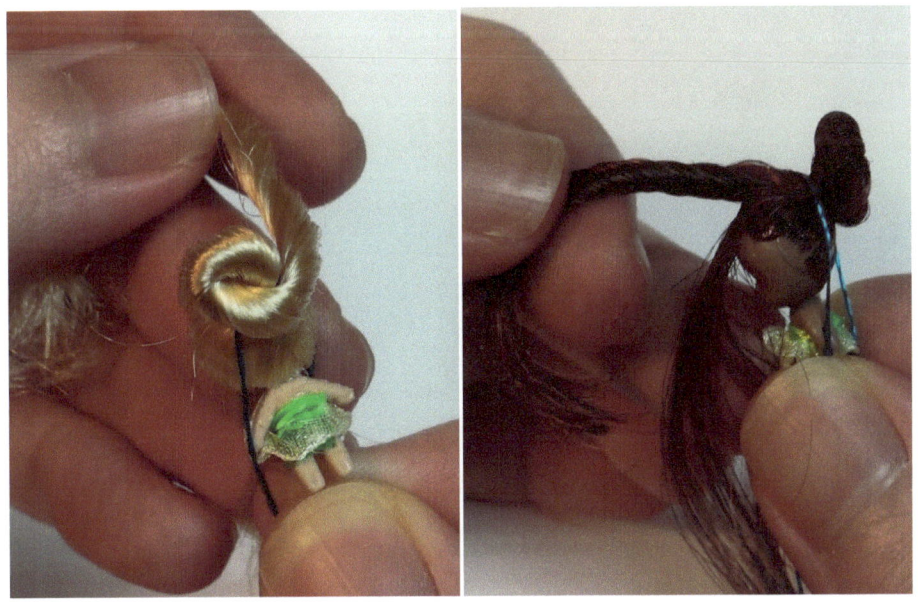

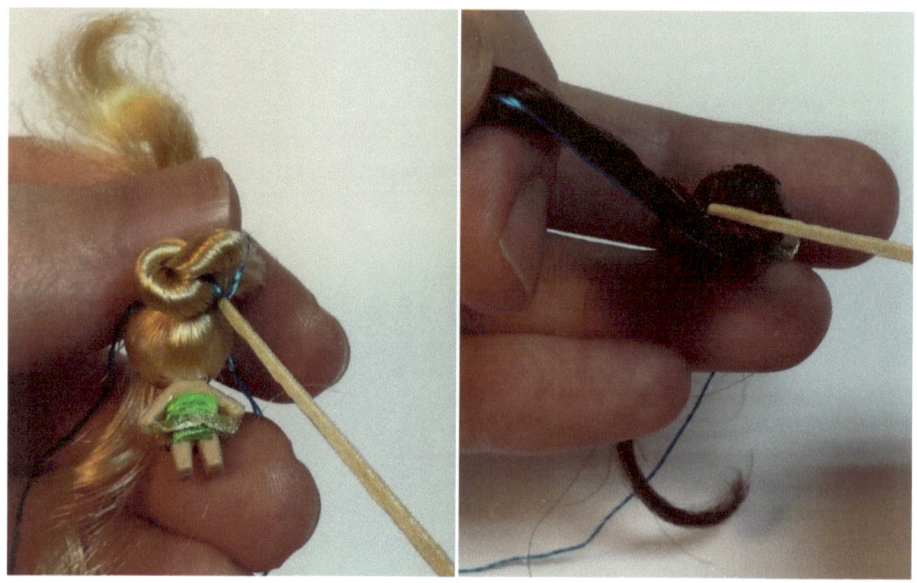

Use the end of the floss to wrap around the hair close to the ponytail base and secure with super glue.

Trim hair ends close to the base of the secured bun.

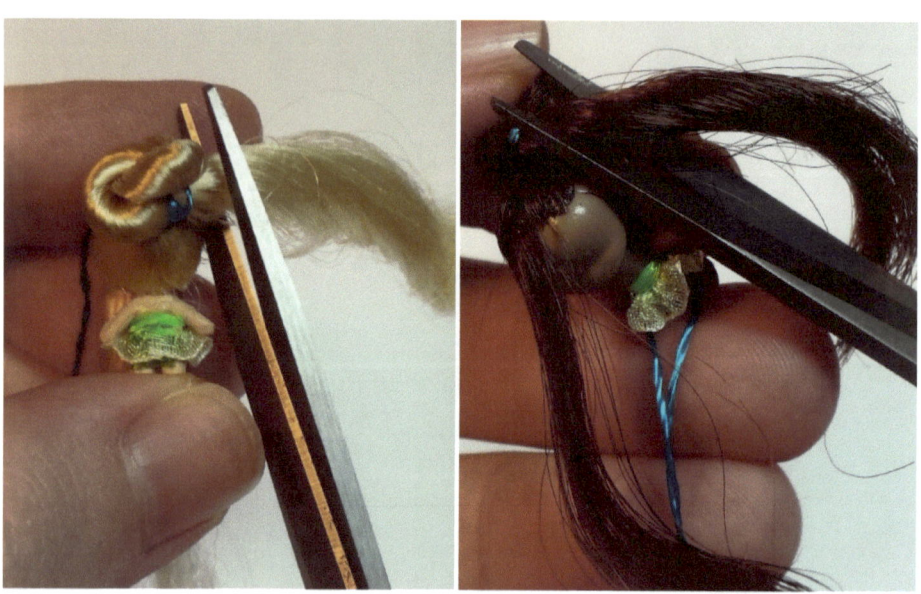

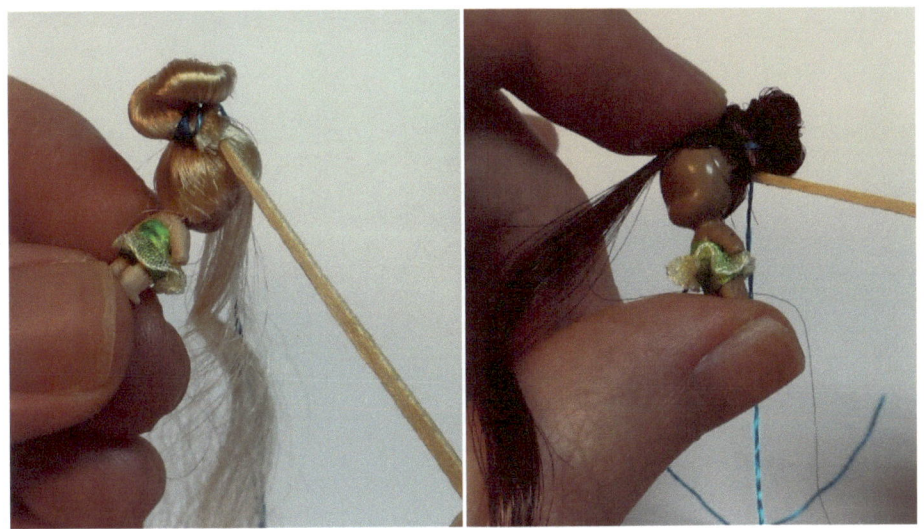

Apply super glue to the hair near the base of the ponytail and press it into place.

Repeat this step around the bun as necessary.

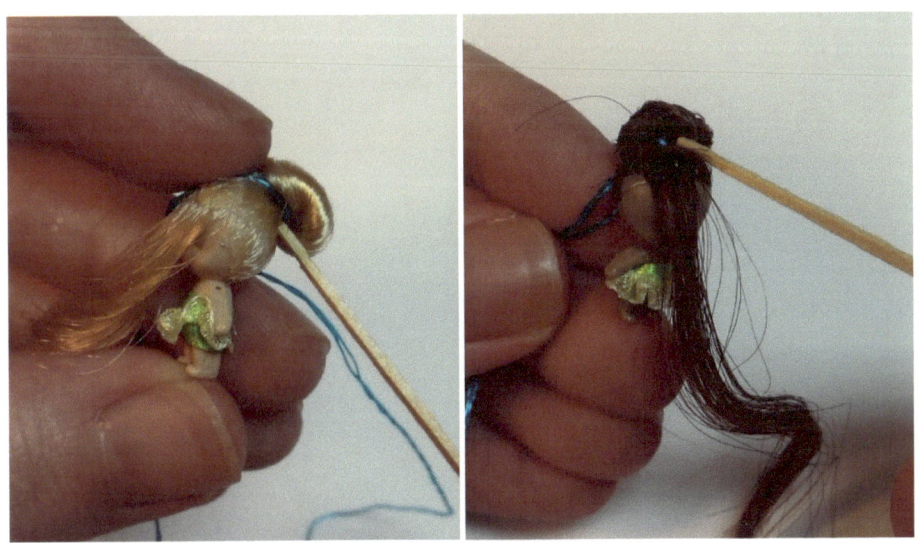

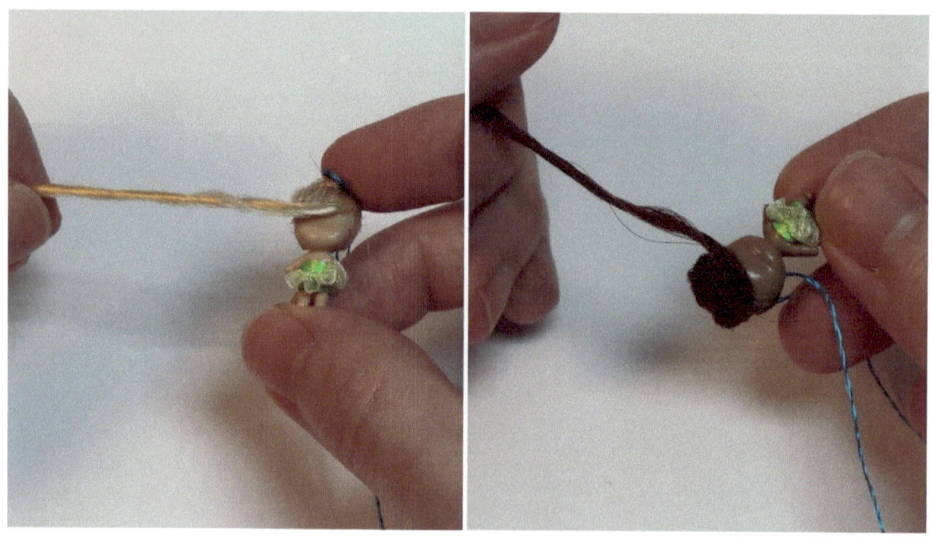

Twist the remaining front section of hair and wrap back, creating twisted "bangs."

Secure with super glue.

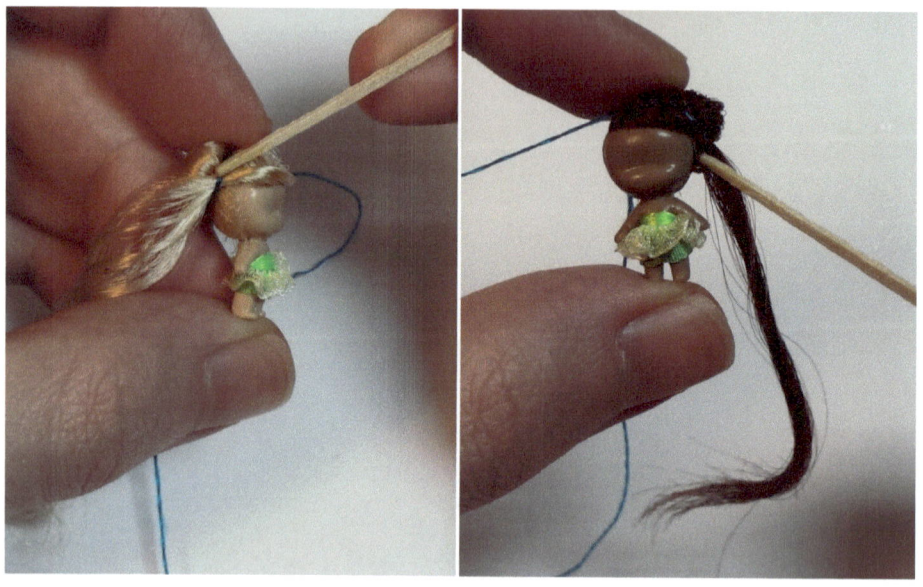

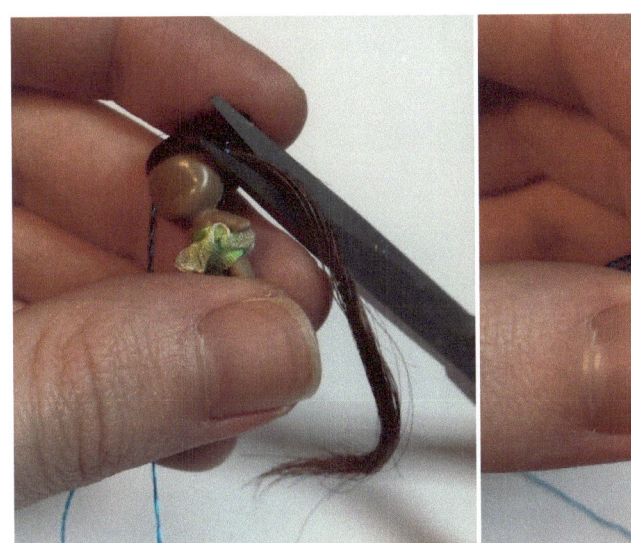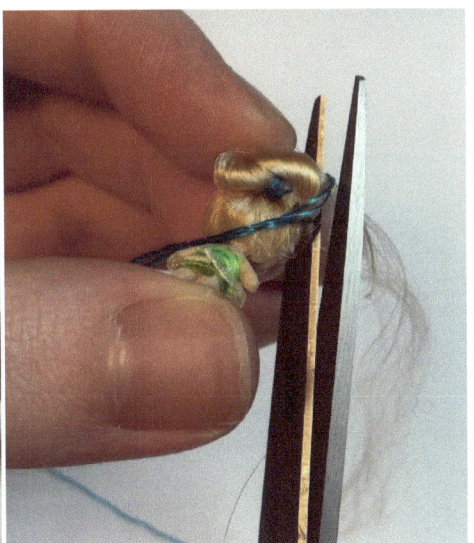

Trim the hair almost flush to the floss.

Add a second, complimentary shade of floss and tie a loose knot around the bun.

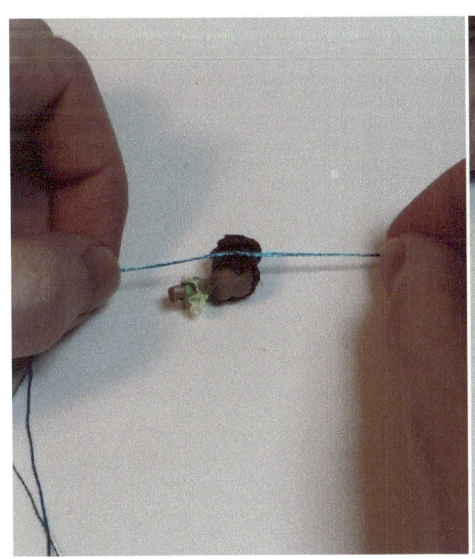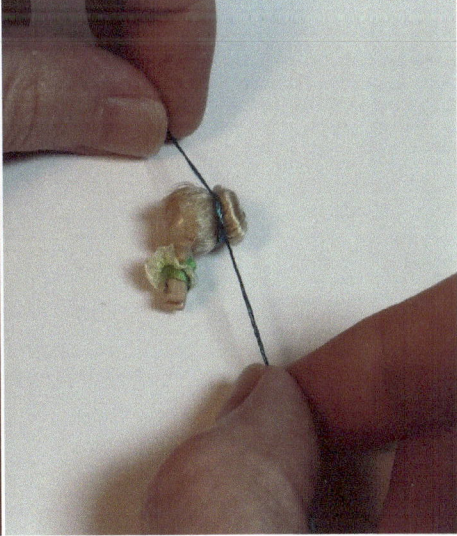

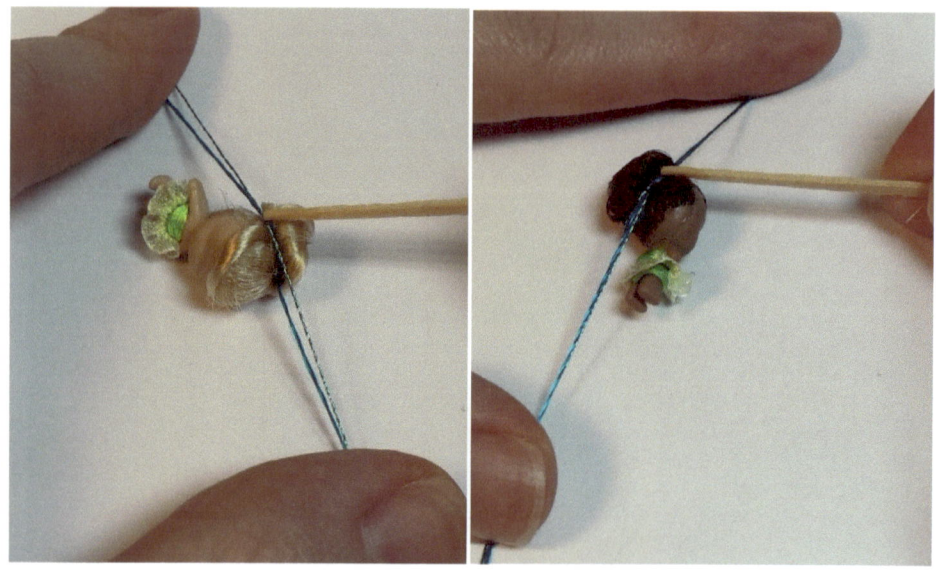

Secure the loose knot with super glue.

After the glue has cured for about 30 seconds, tie a bow.

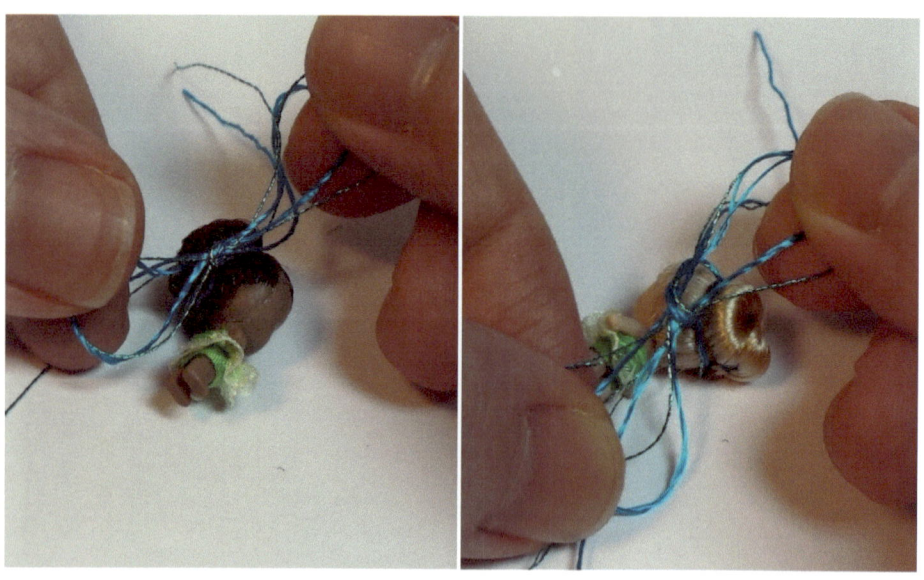

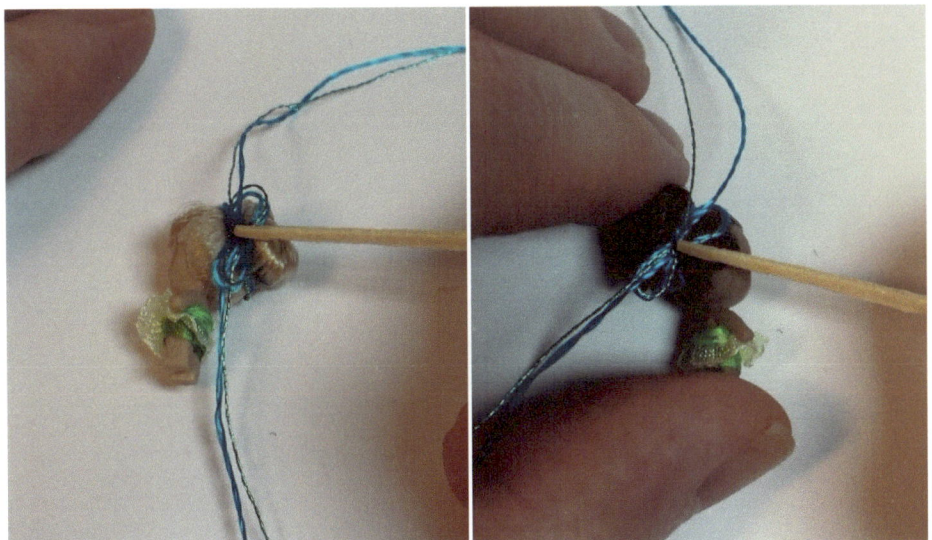

Adjust the bow size down to scale and secure it with super glue.

Trim the floss ends of the bow to size.

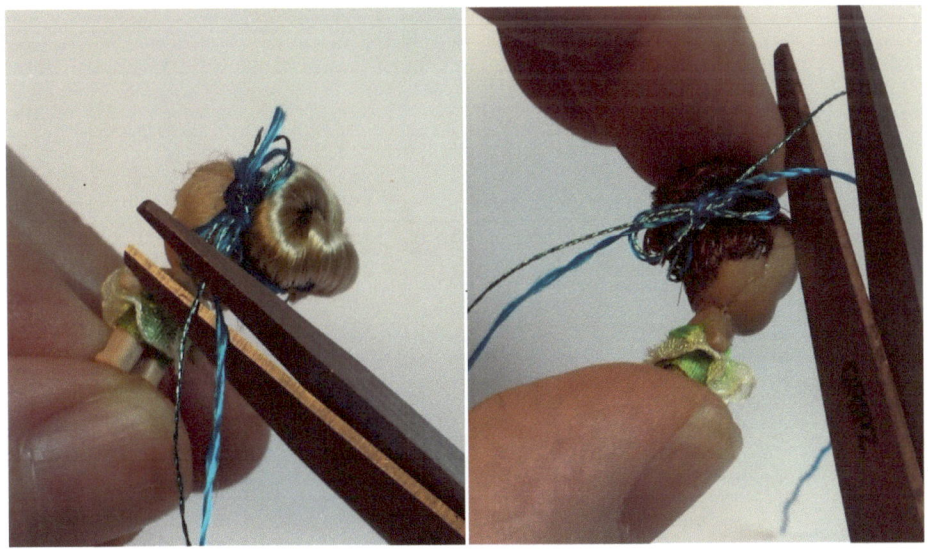

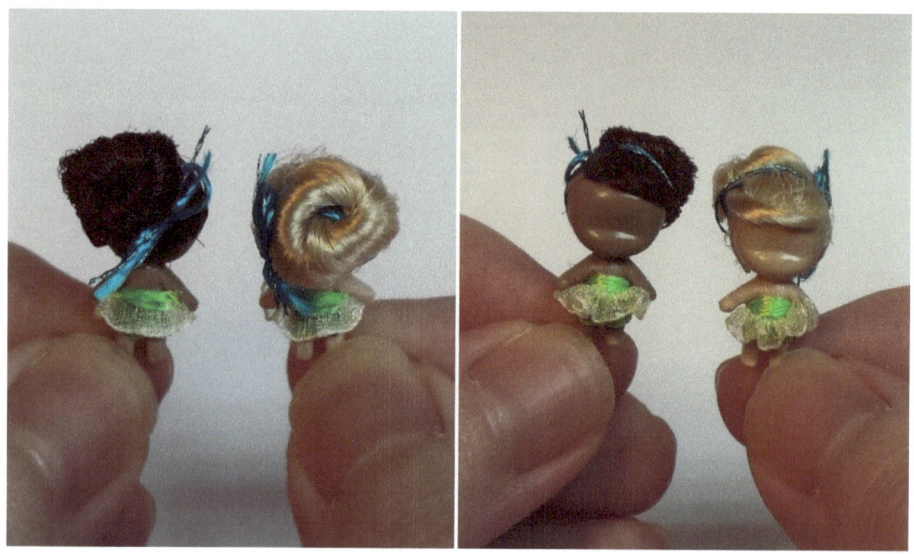

This set of isometric views shows how the finished result of this hair design appears.

You can use the basic idea of the bun hairstyle and use plaits and add curls and decals and colored floss.

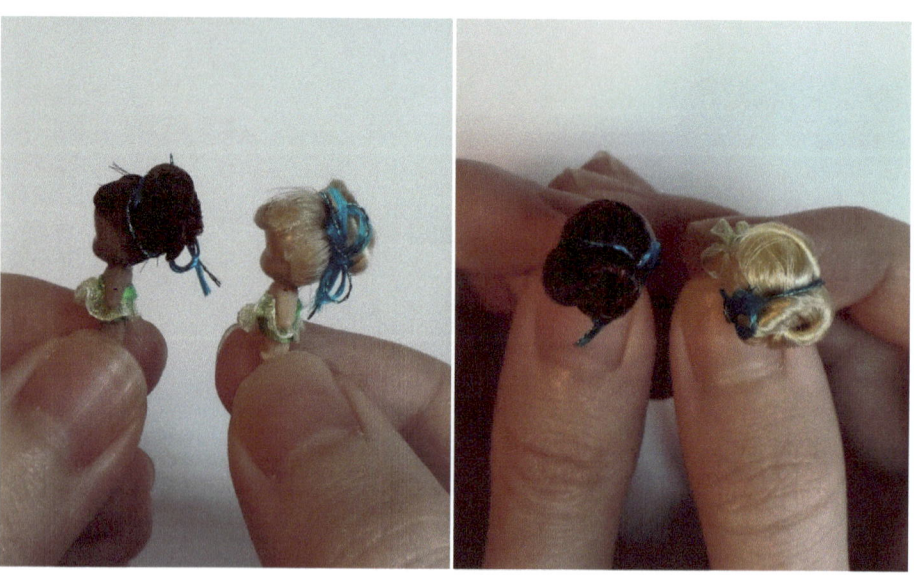

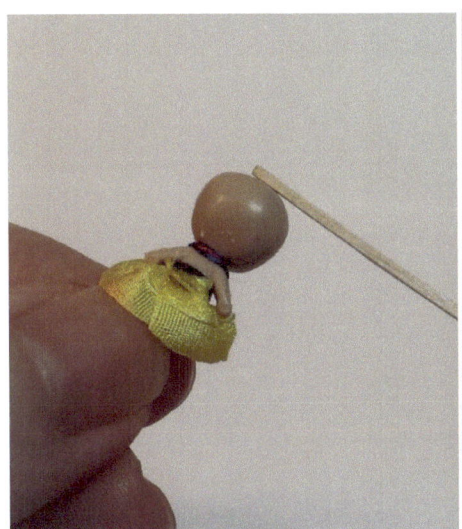 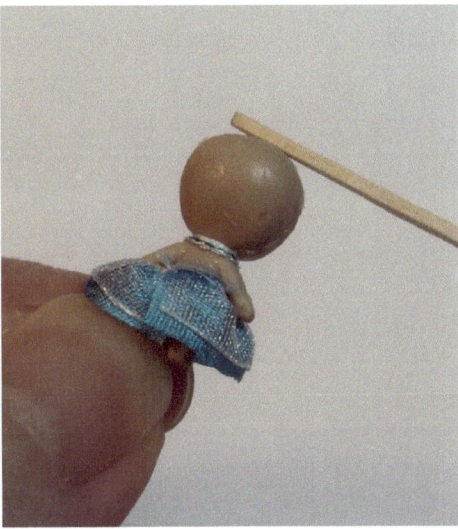

This next hairstyle is prepared the same as the first set with applying super glue to he portion of the head that is to become the scalp.

Start with the top and apply to the bottom of the hair line.

Allow the super glue to completely dry before advancing to the next step of application.

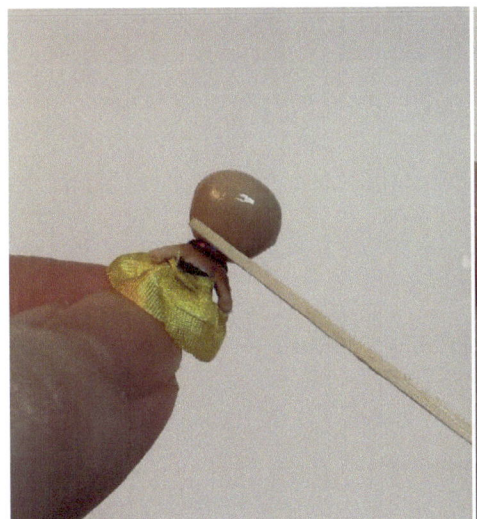 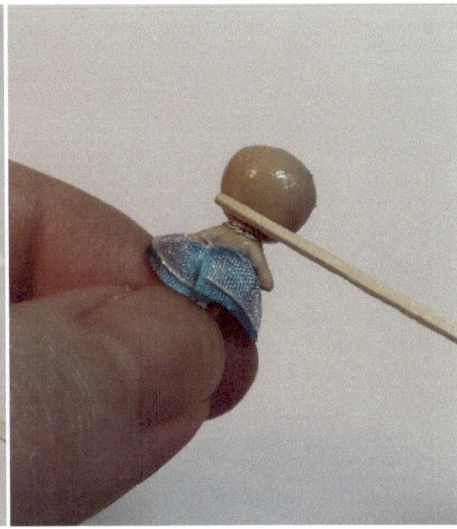

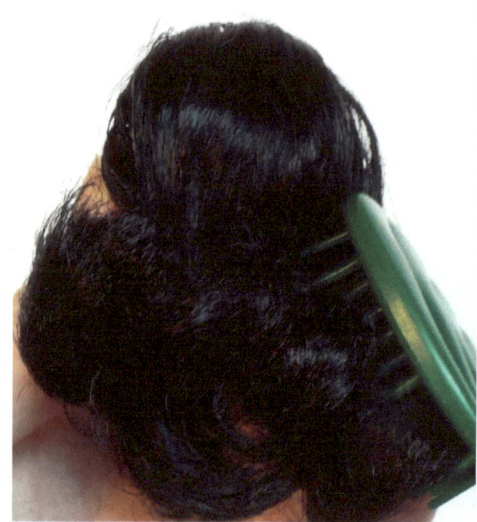 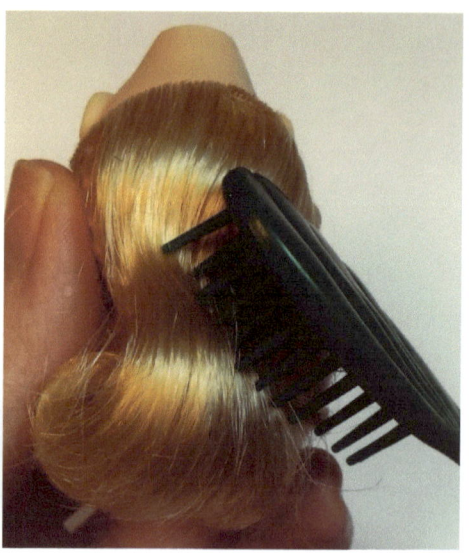

While the super glue cures, take this time to prepare the nylon hair. Inspect the hair for dirt and oil that might have been missed in the cleaning process.

Brush or comb the nylon strands with care to smooth and not to break them.

Section off hair plugs for use with bamboo skewer end.

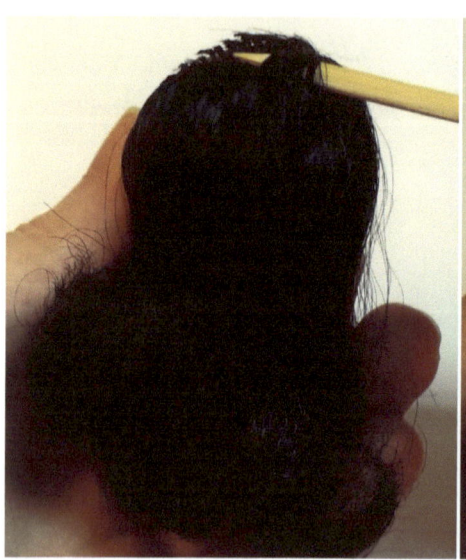 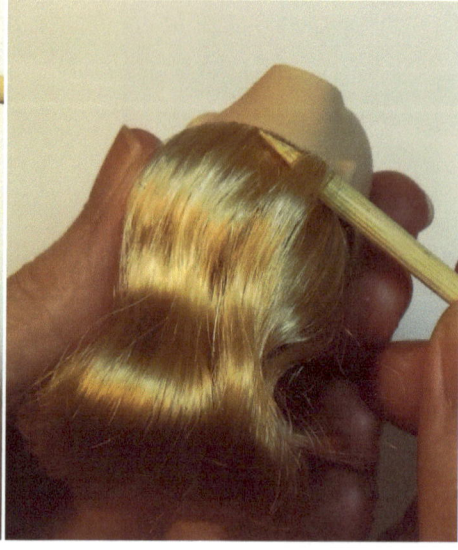

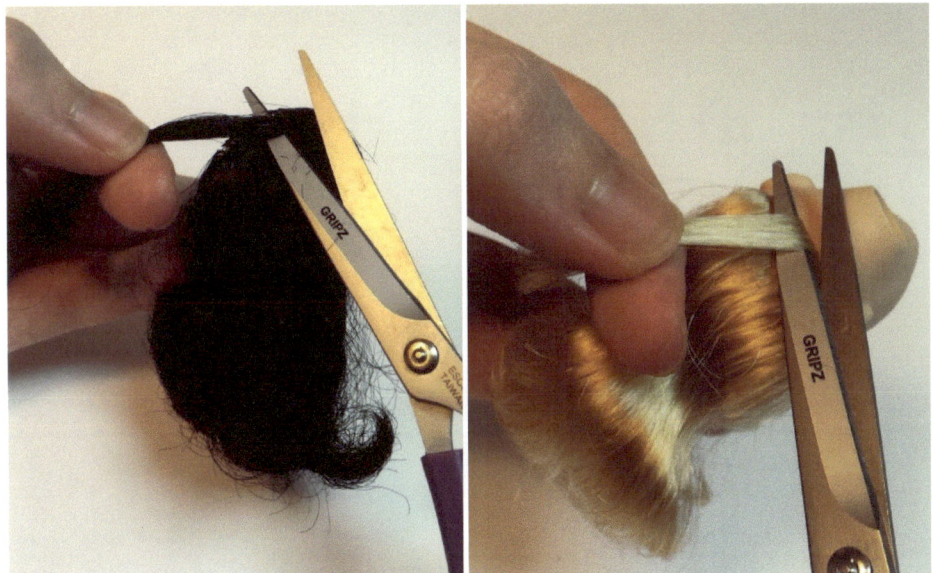

Trim off sectioned hair strands.

Apply a small bead of hot glue to the end.

Observe how the different kinds of nylon hair reacts to the heat from the glue. Some hair is more heat sensitive than others.

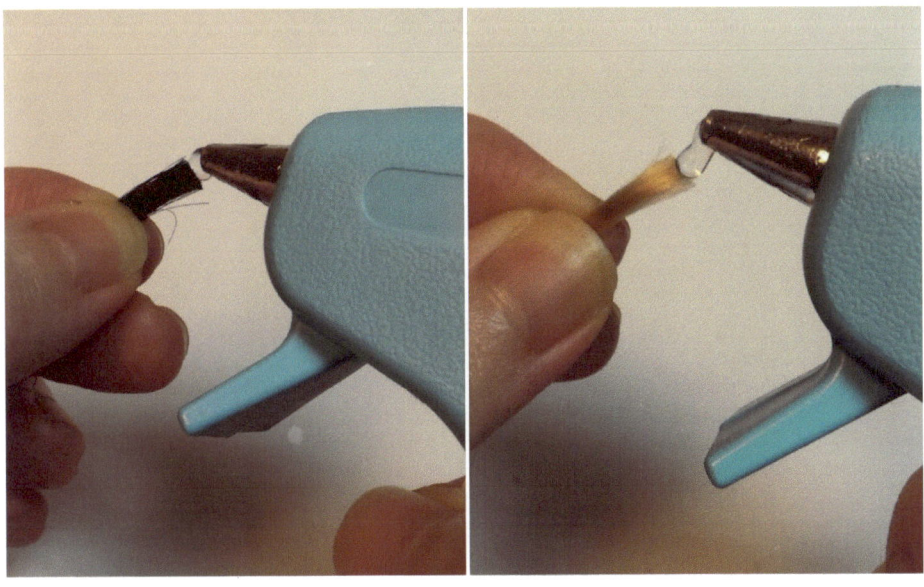

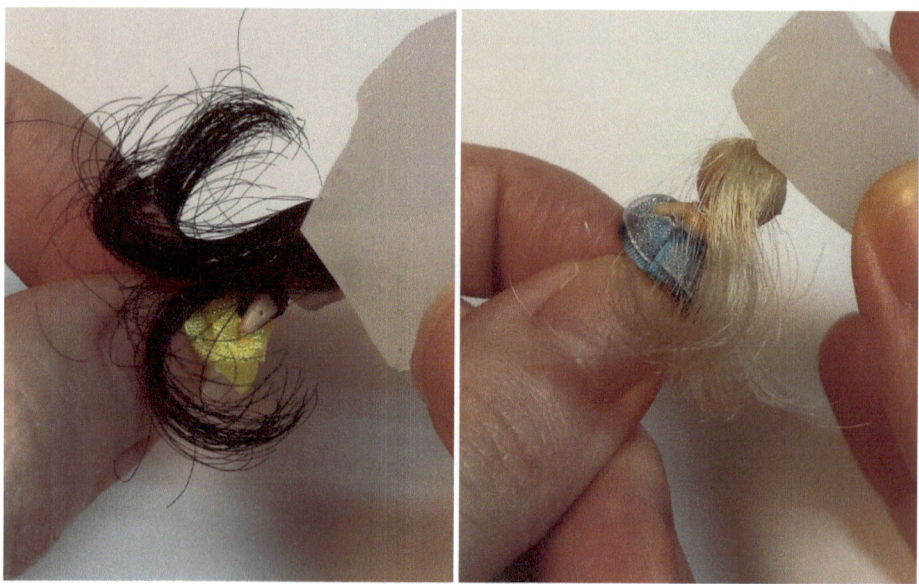

As you press the hair into place, keep in mind the way the hair needs to fall.

The hair in these examples has texture that I will incorporate into the end design.

As pressure is applied, start at the root ends and use a rolling motion to press the hair into place.

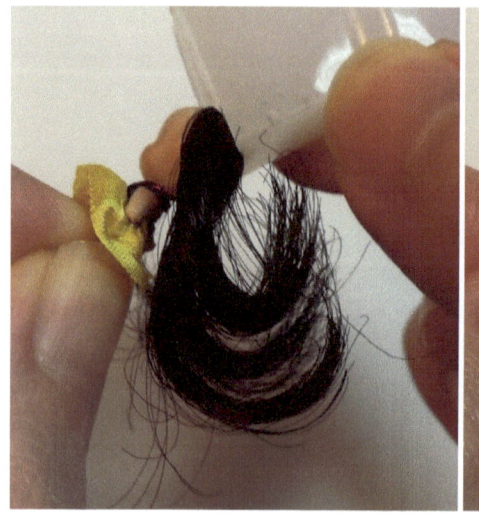 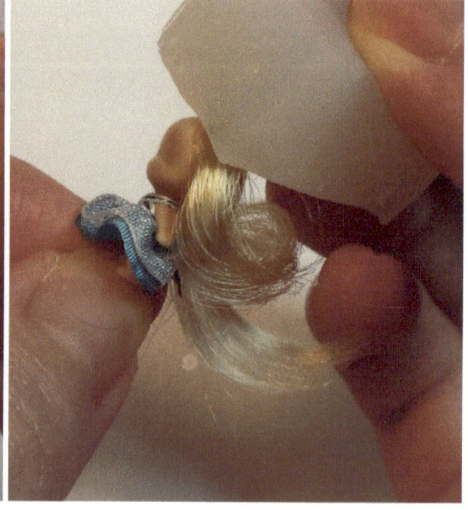

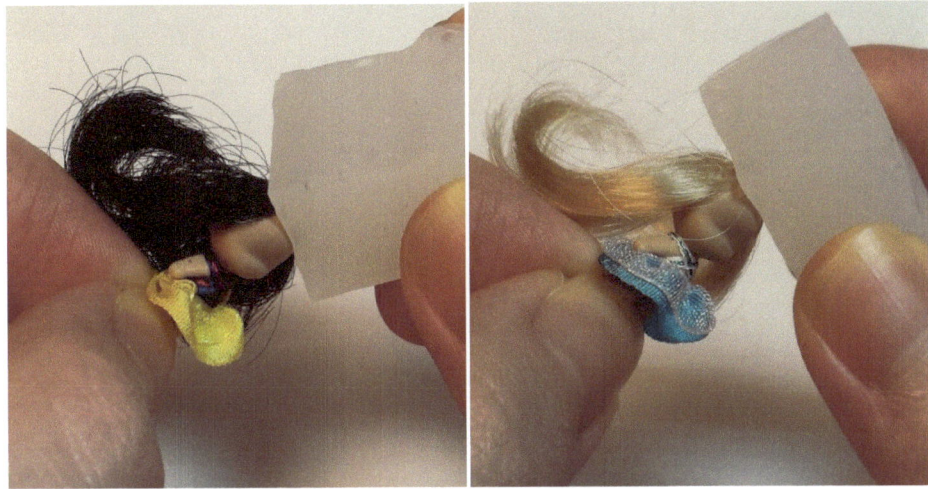

These illustrations show the right and left sides of the hair being glued into place. I note the direction the curl or flip and hair texture and use that in the design.

Start from the root ends and use a rolling motion to secure.

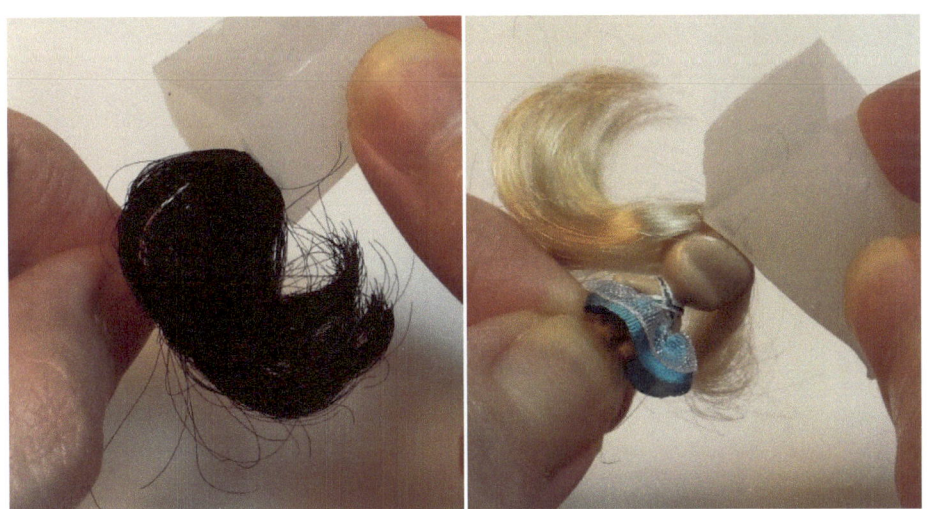

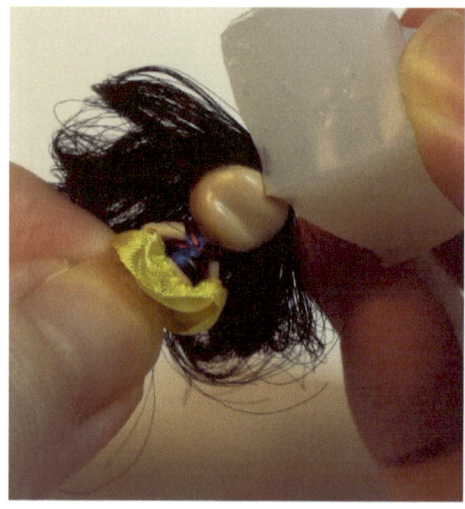 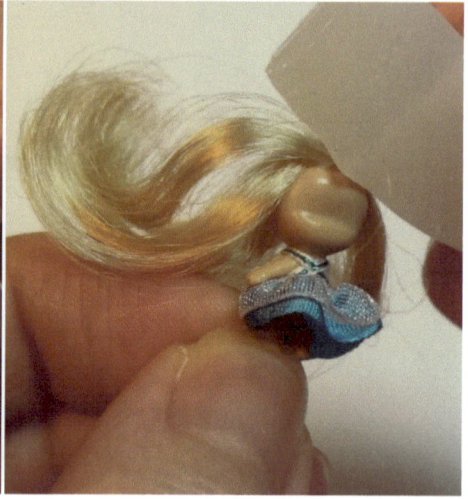

The top most back portion is glued on, then the small sections in the front is glued with the root ends meeting exactly in the center of the head for the best results.

As with gluing on the previous sections, use a rolling motion to glue these strands but be careful not to accidentally rub the strands before they cure as they could attach in the wrong place.

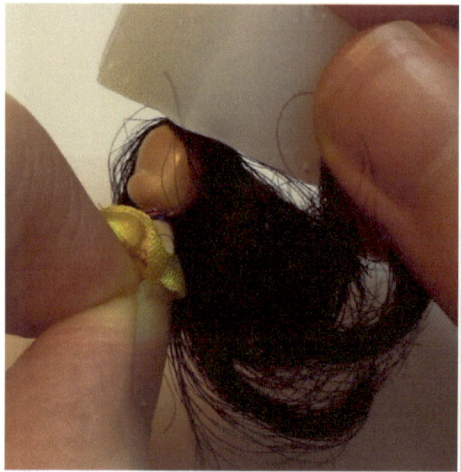 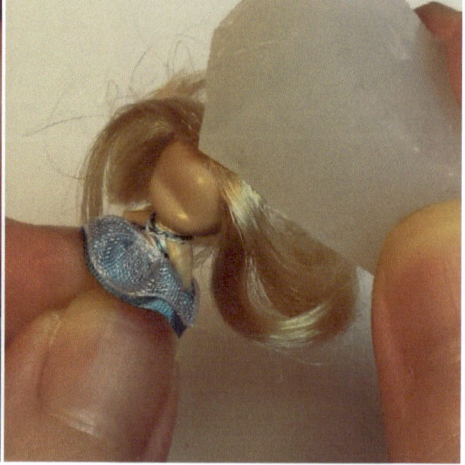

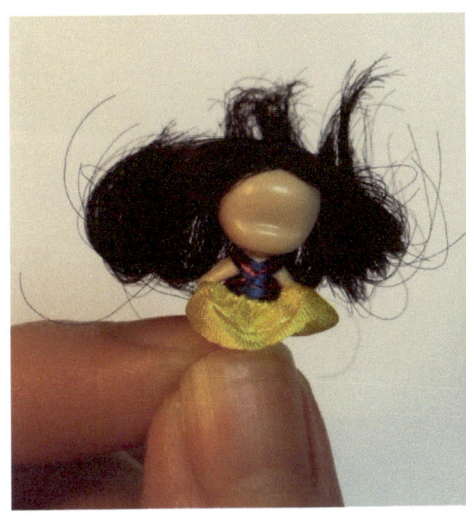 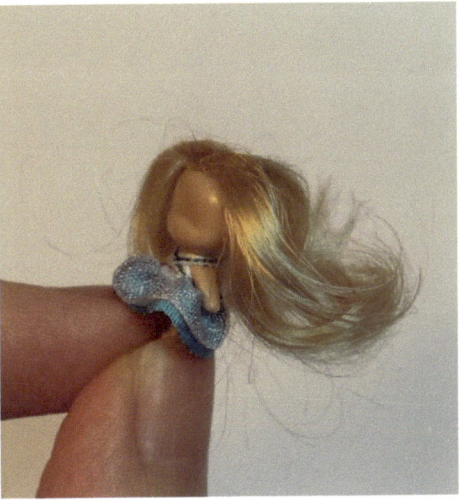

While in the process of gluing the hair into place, take care not to handle the costume. Over-handling can cause rips, wrinkles and unintended stains. Keep this in mind while working on each process.

Use two complimentary or contrasting strands of floss to wrap around the head of the doll.

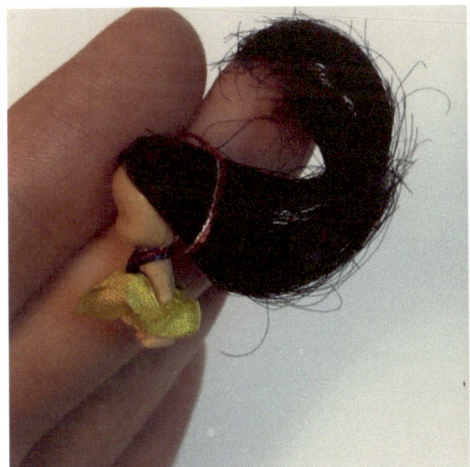 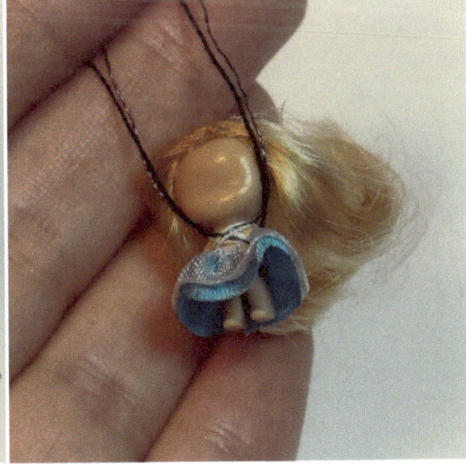

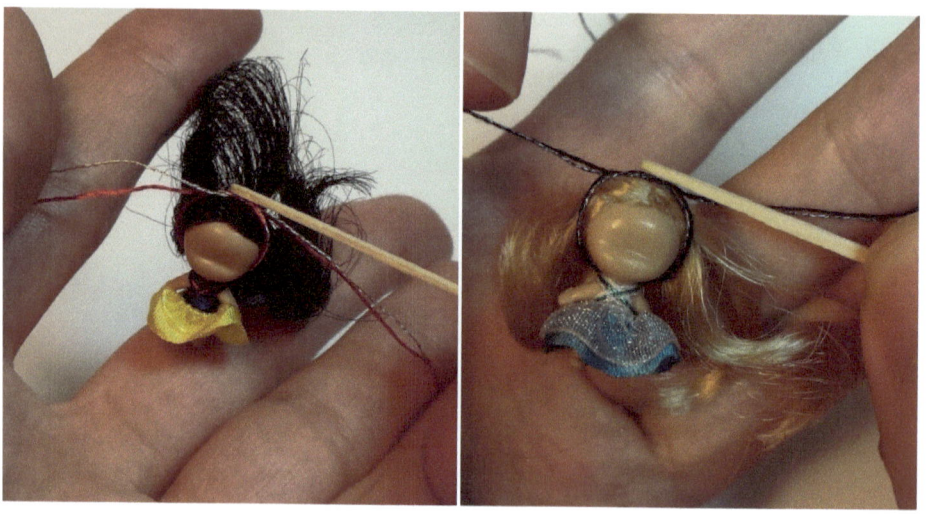

After tying the floss into a knot, secure it with super glue.

Allow the super glue to cure before tying the bow or the floss might stick where it is unintended.

Pull the strand ends to adjust the bow down to size.

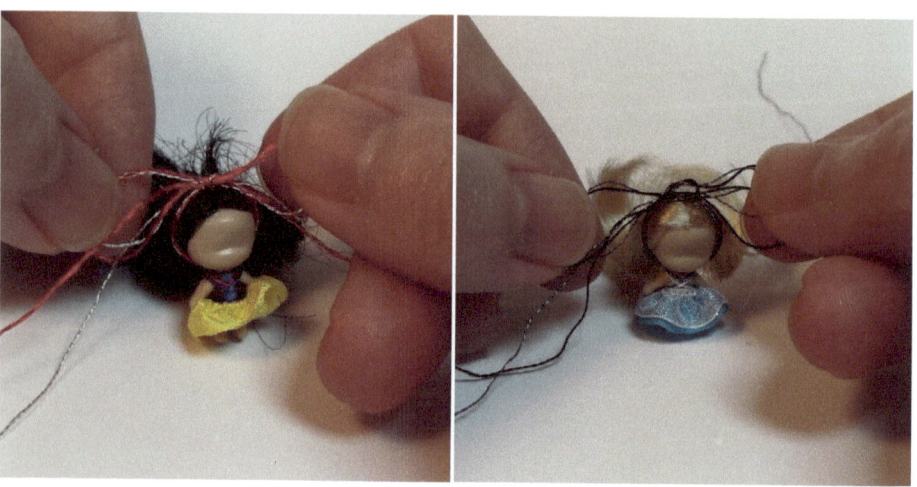

74

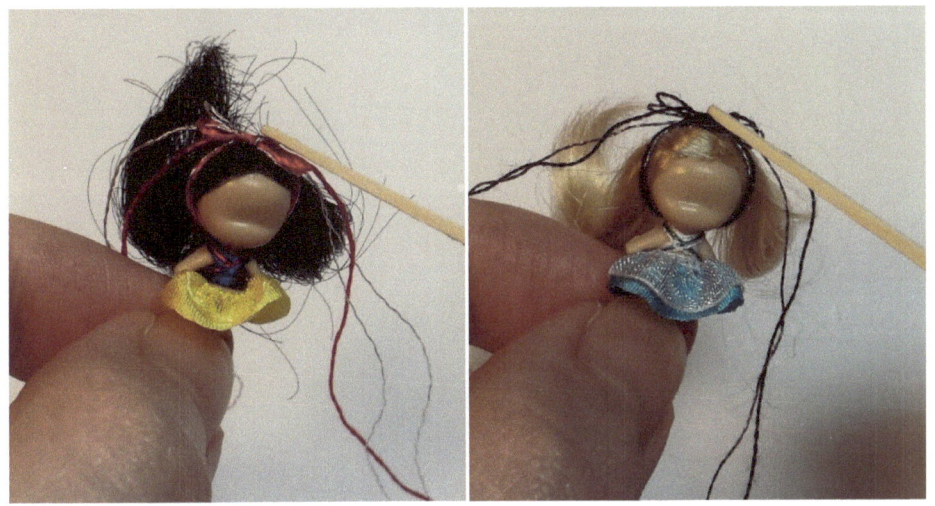

Secure the bow with super glue and trim the ends to size after the glue has cured.

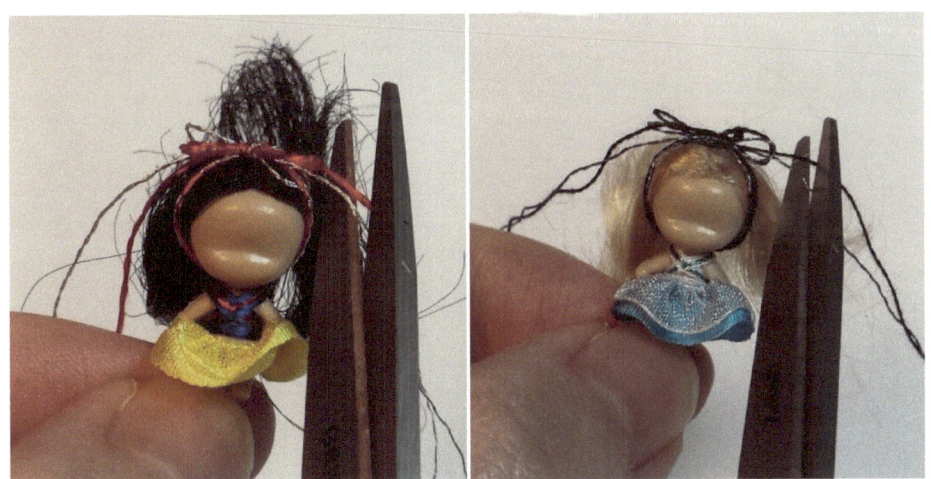

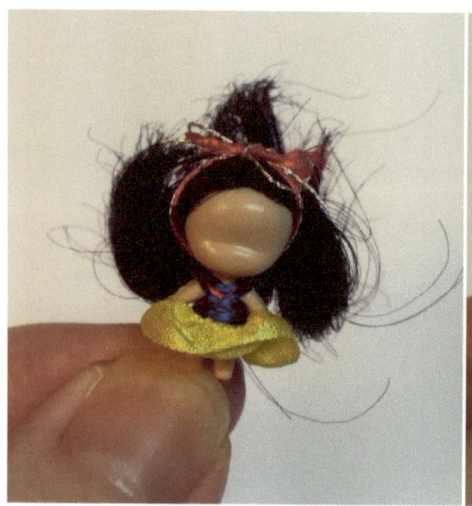 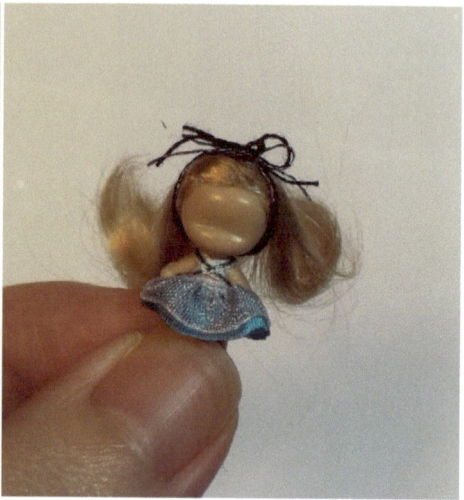

This is the end result of this hair design. Note how the front of the hair meets in the middle while the back falls strainght back with a flip in the ends.

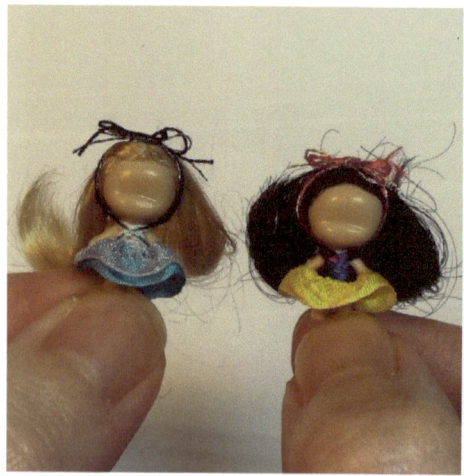 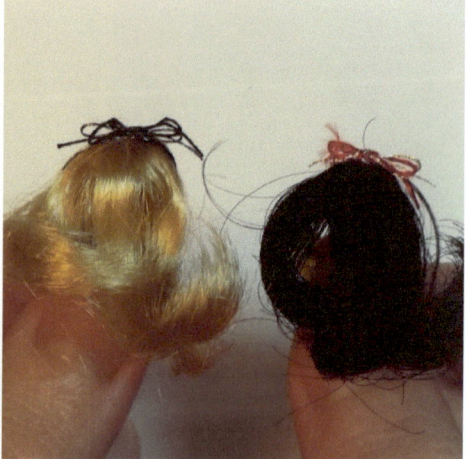

76

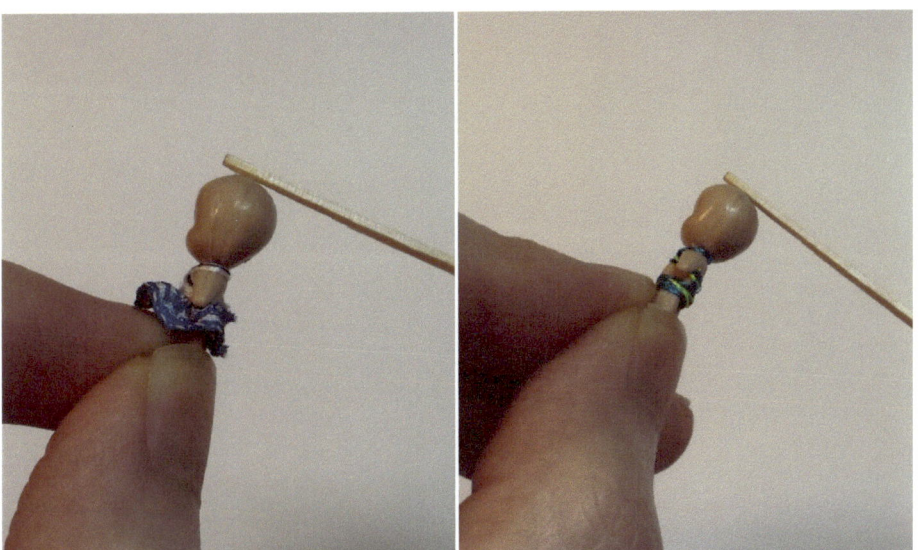

This hairstyle is prepped the same as the others with super glue on the scalp area of the figure.

Allow the glue to cure before advancing to the next step of applying the nylon strands.

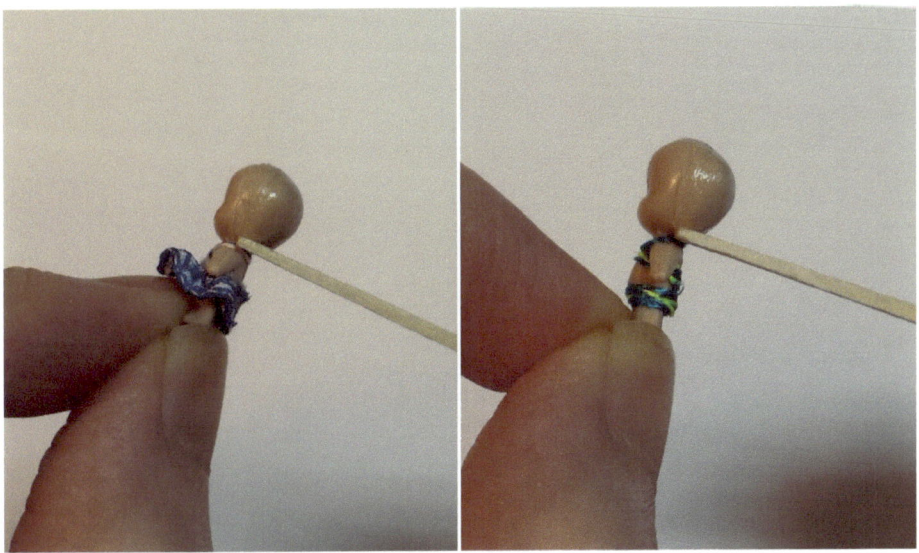

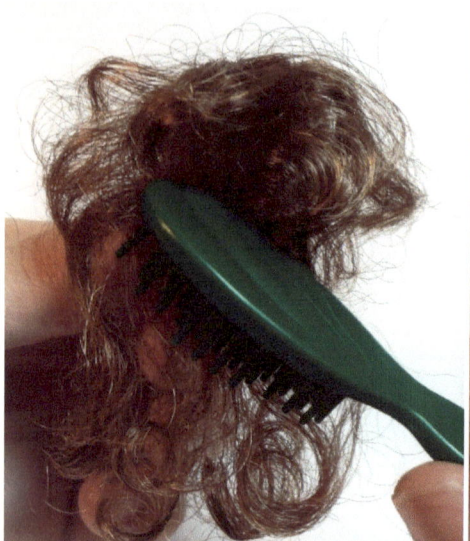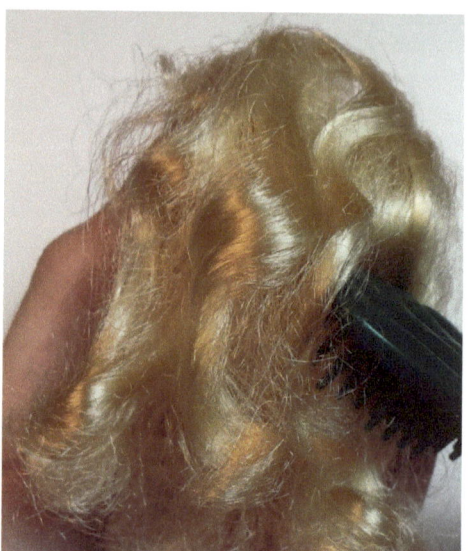

Brush or comb the nylon hair to smooth the fibers. Note the hair chosen for this hair design is textured with curls.

Section off measured hair plugs with a bamboo skewer end.

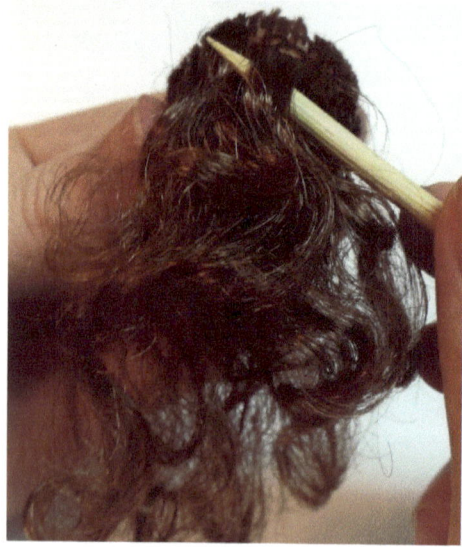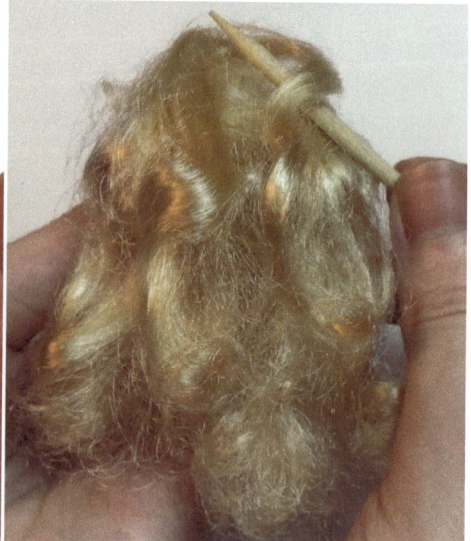

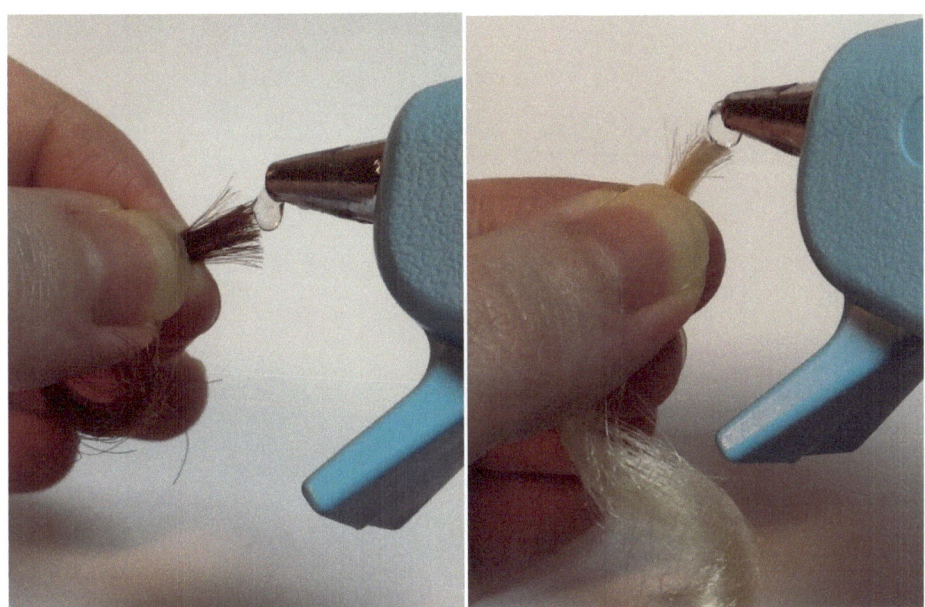

Apply a bead of hot glue to the root end of the nylon hair.

Quickly place it onto the doll's off center of the back of the head to create a part down the middle of the head.

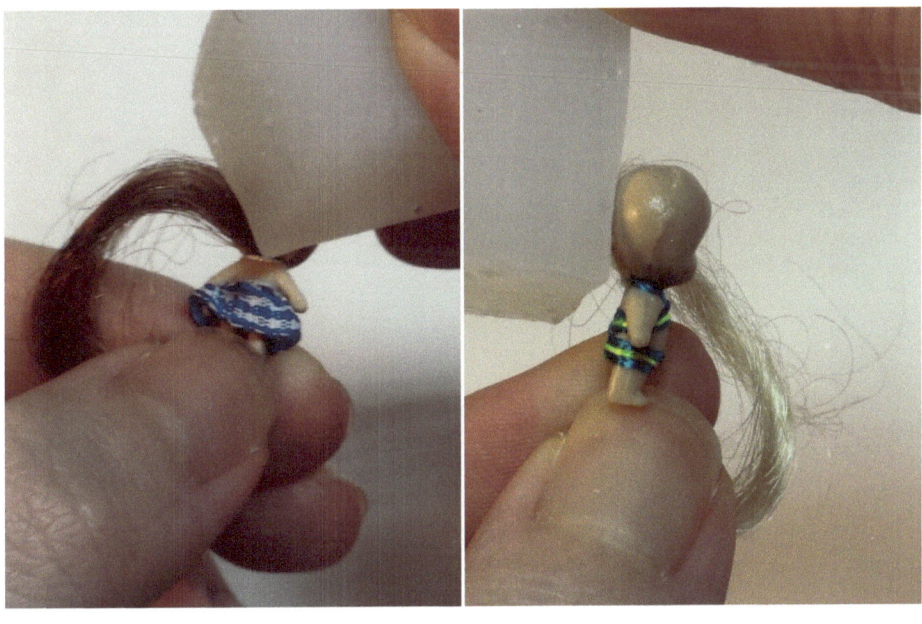

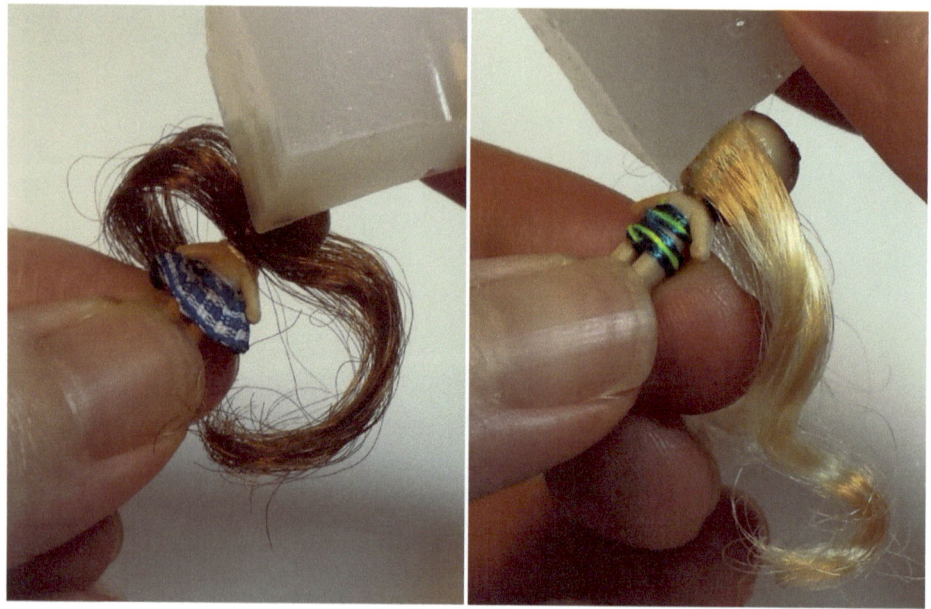

Apply the next strands of hair with the root ends creating a straight part line in the center of the back of the head.

Apply more strands off center to allow for a tiny bit of overlap to create a neat part.

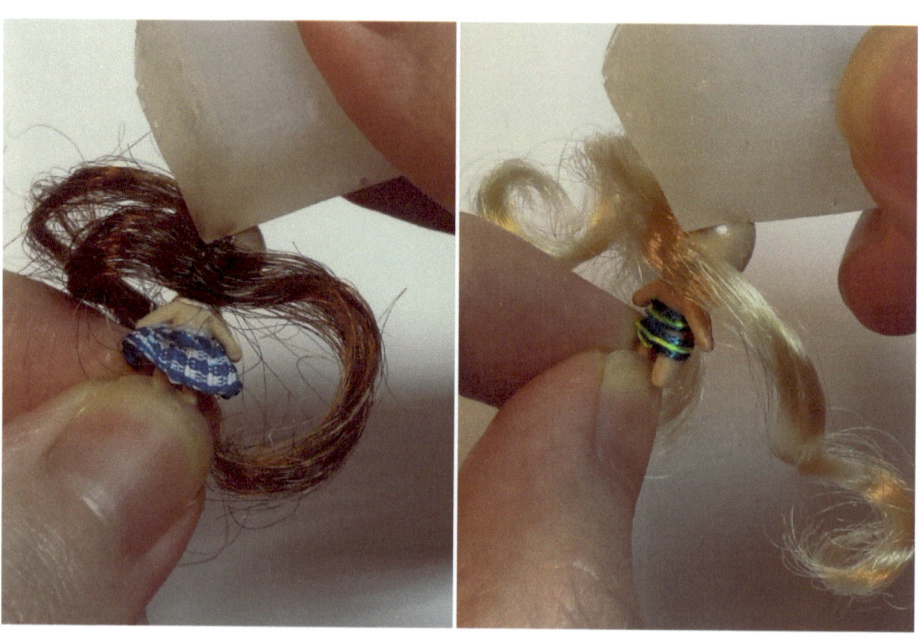

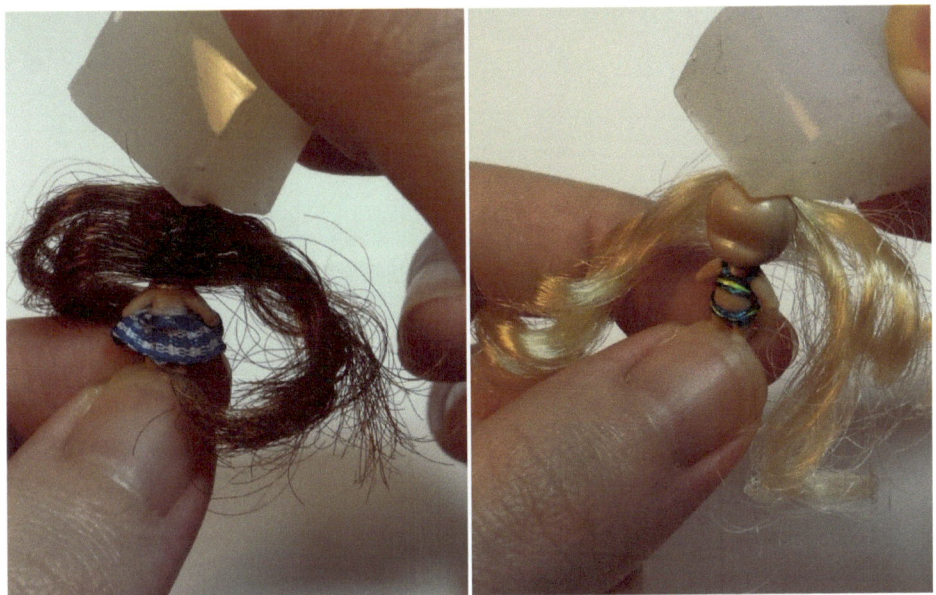

As you work your way up the back of the doll's head, be certain there is enough overlap of the root sections so not to leave a gap in the hairline.

Apply the front section with a rolling motion to match the hairline created with the super glue.

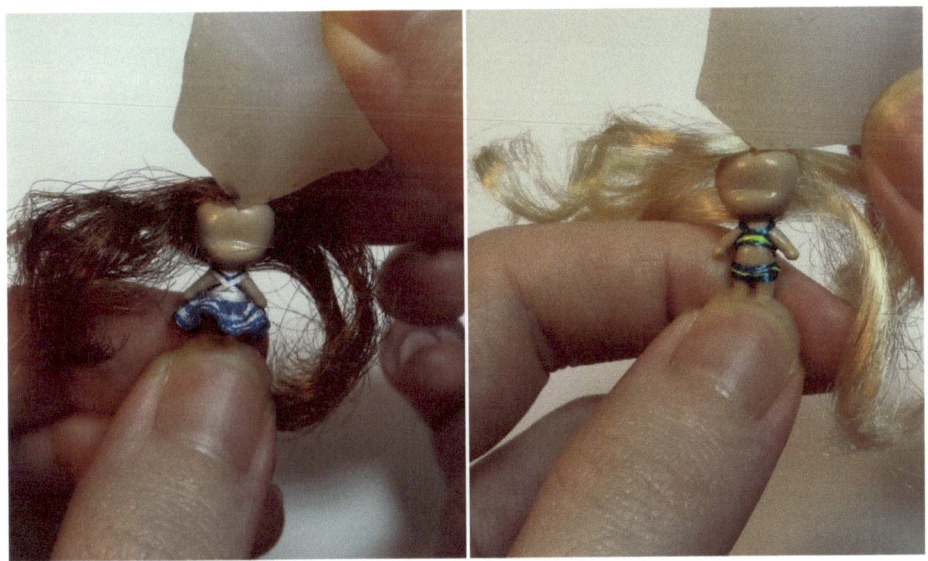

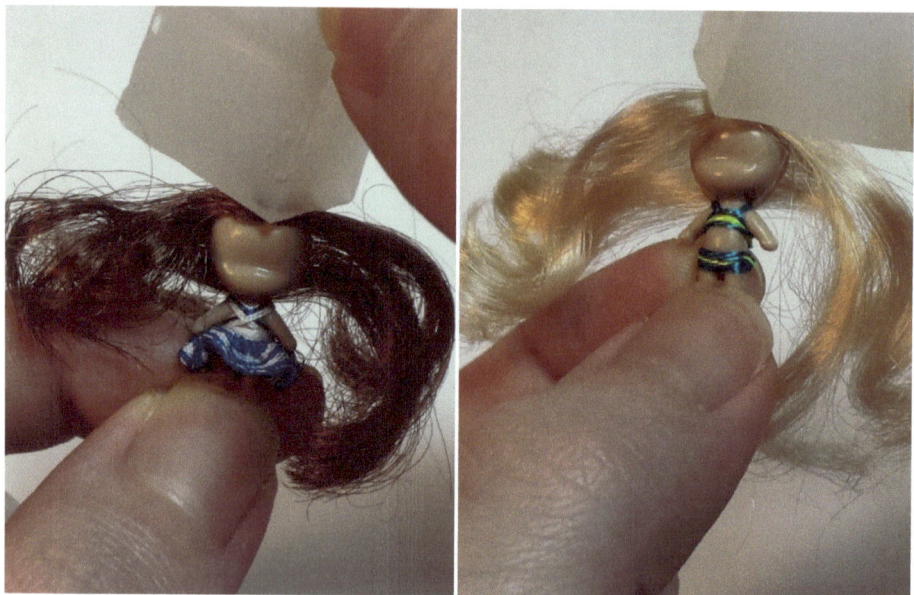

The last front section of hair is the most diffficult because it must match the other side. If the last section doesn't appear as planned, carefully tear it off the head, trim the glue end and re-apply. You have a few seconds after applying the hair with hot glue that it is easier to remove than after it has cured a few minutes. When the hair is satisfactory, add complimentary floss to create ponytails.

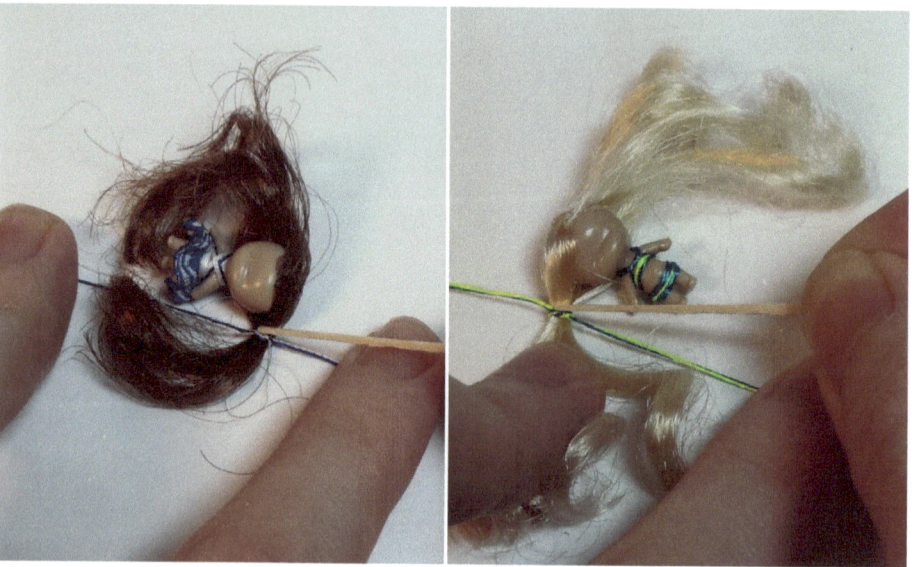

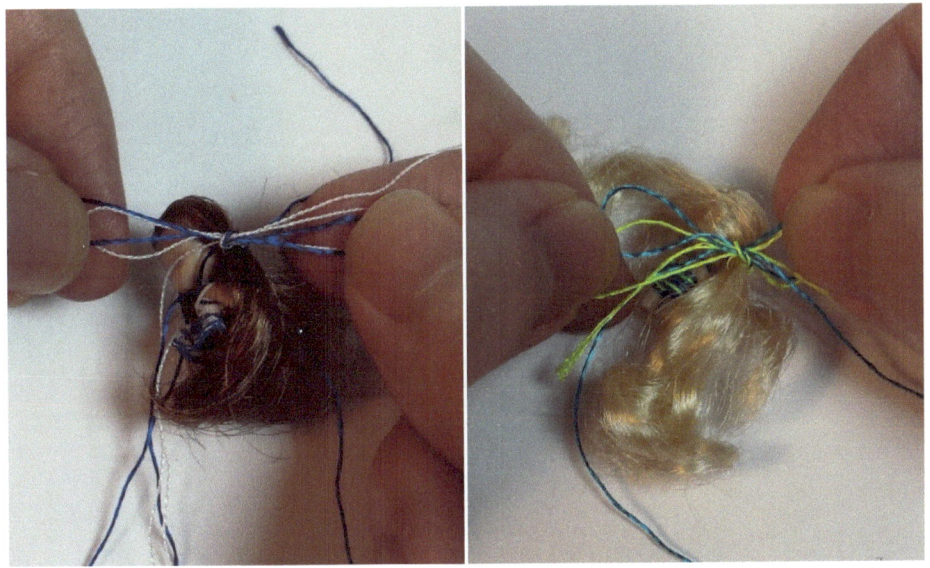

Tie a bow and adjust the size down to scale of the figure.

Trim the floss ends carefully. You can always trim more, but you can't trim less.

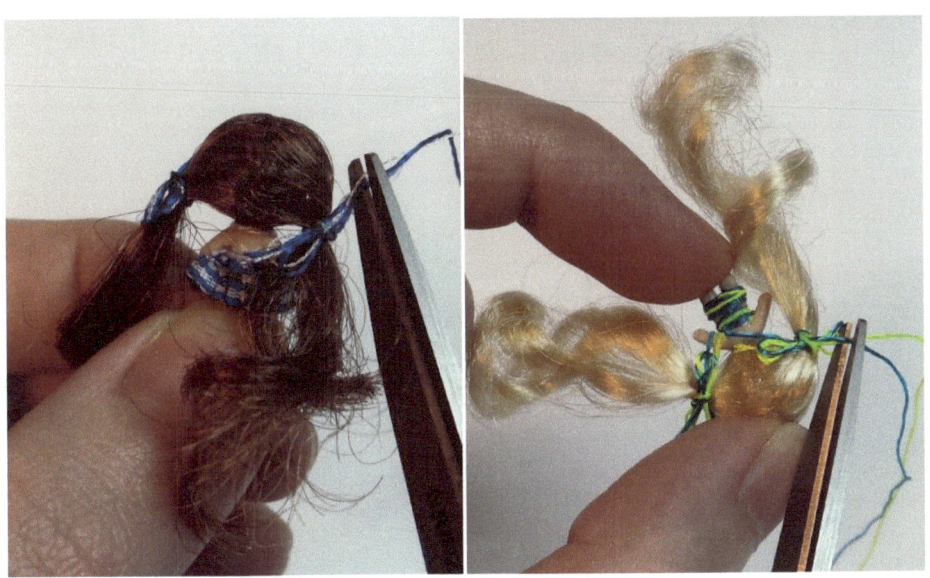

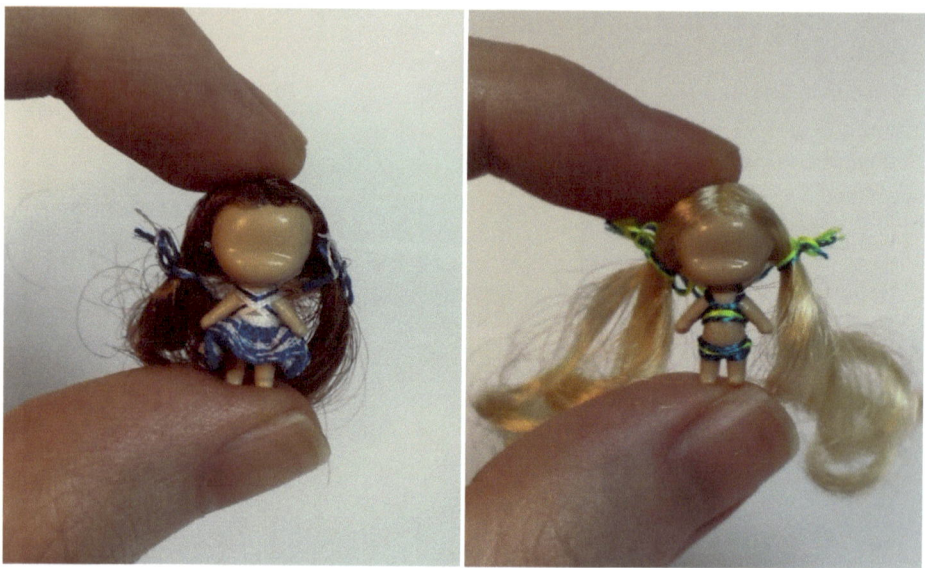

This is the finished result. Because of the small size, you might need a second pair of hands to hold the doll while working on small sections of hair. You can decorate with decals, flowers or bows and ties made from floss. Add head bands or crowns with glitter and jewels. The possibilities are only limited by your imagination.

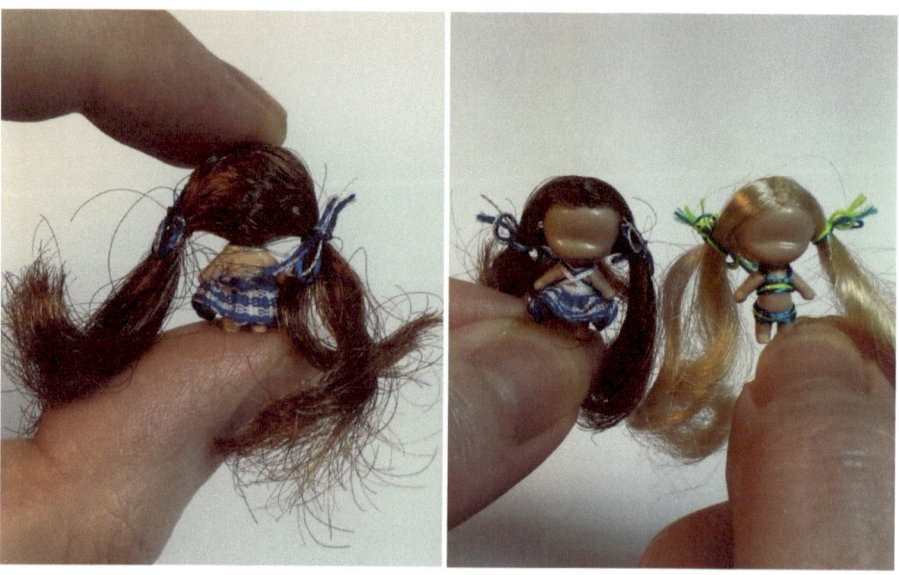

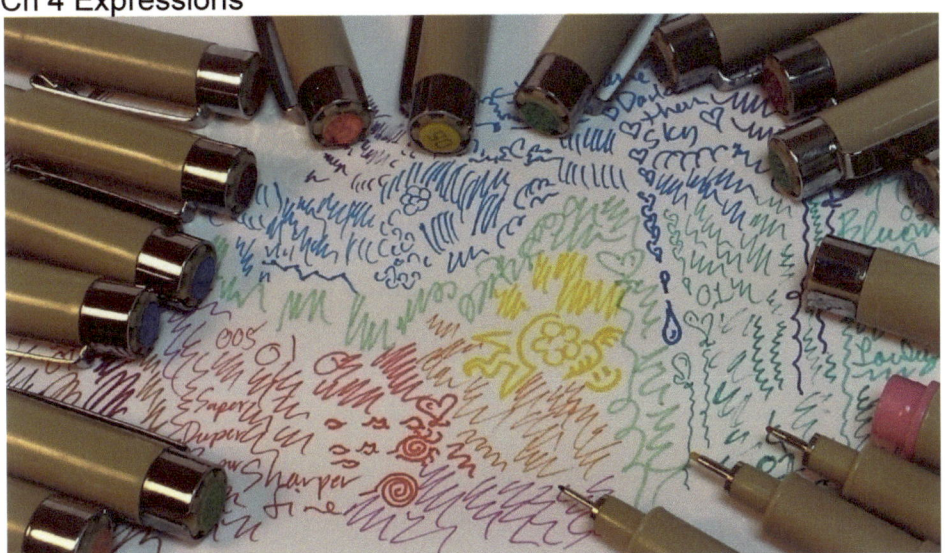

Suggested tools;
Quality artists pigment pens in various sizes and shades including white
Cotton swabs
Clear acrylic spray
Clean, well-lit work surface
Paper to test out pigment pens and to keep the ink fresh
A place masked with newspapers, preferably outside in which to seal features
with acrylic spray

I have experimented with brushes and different kinds of paints but I have settled
on using pigment pens to apply the expression to the faces of the tiny dolls I
design. Smallest size commercially made art brushes were not fine enough or
that the paints and inks dried too quickly under the bright lights I use to illuminte
this stage of the work.

As with the previous steps of work, washing your hands often will prevent
accidental pigment transfer and remove the build up of oils that make up the
finger print left behind.

Since I use super glue in the many stages of application it is wise to limit the
areas you handle the figure and how often it it touched.

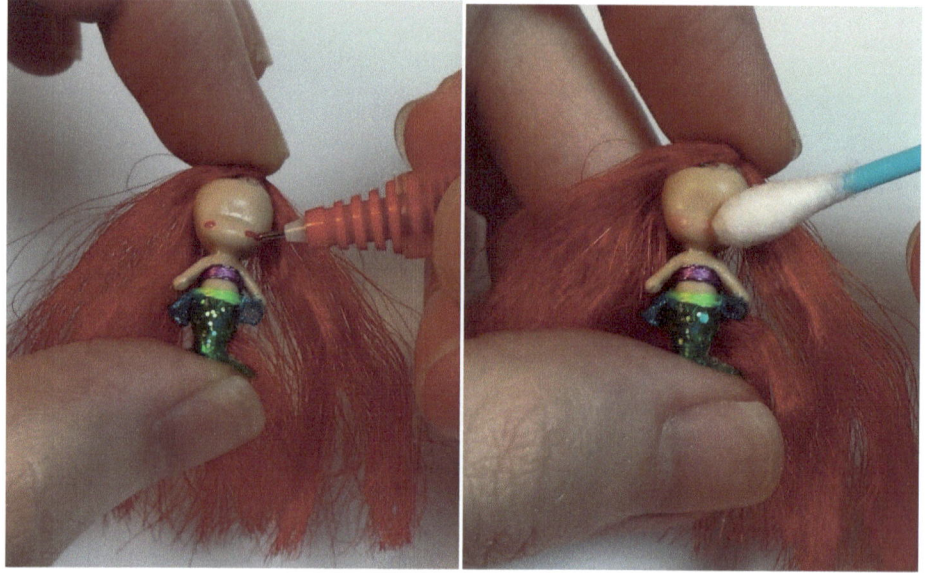

Use the red pigment pen to draw a blush line.

A clean, dry cotton swab works best to blend the blush into a faint glow that compliments the semi translucent pigment used in urethane.

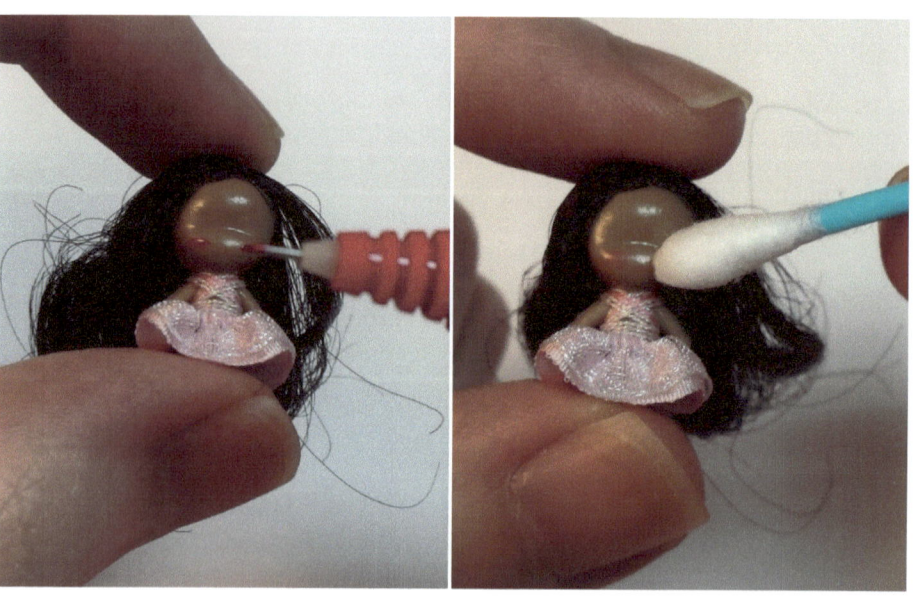

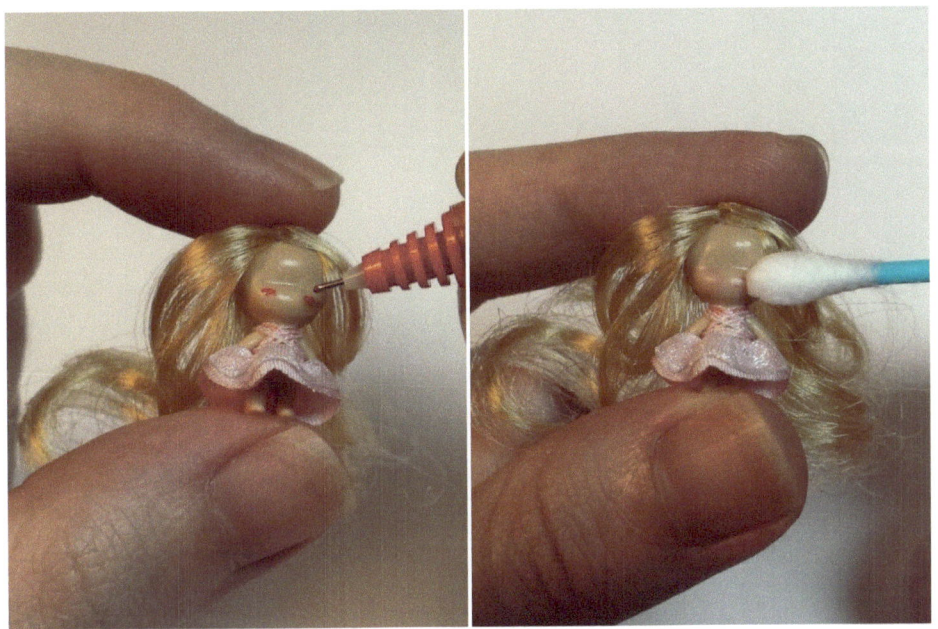

Be sure to blend the liquid pigment as soon as it is applied.

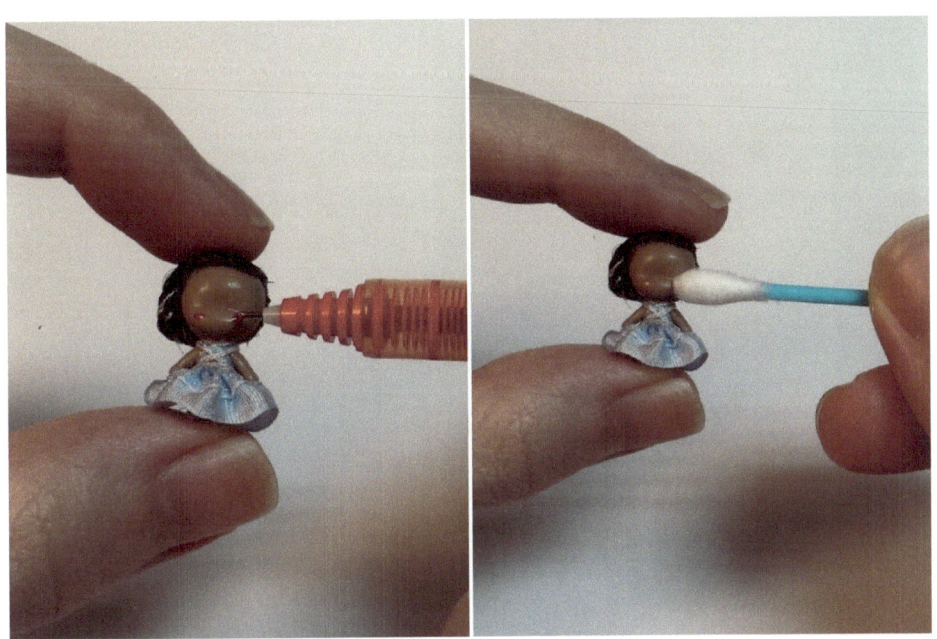

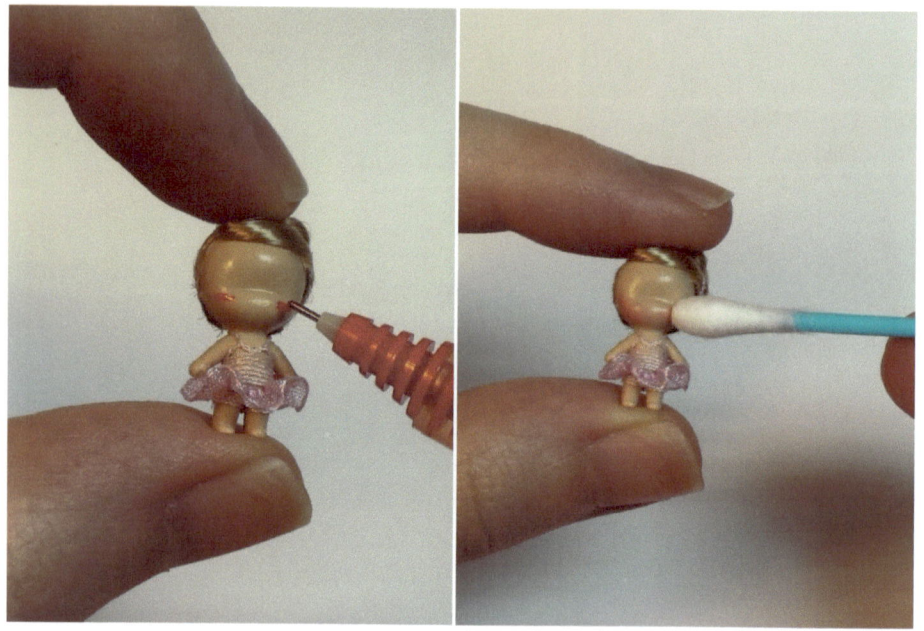

The longer the time gap between application and blending can lead to uneven coverage.

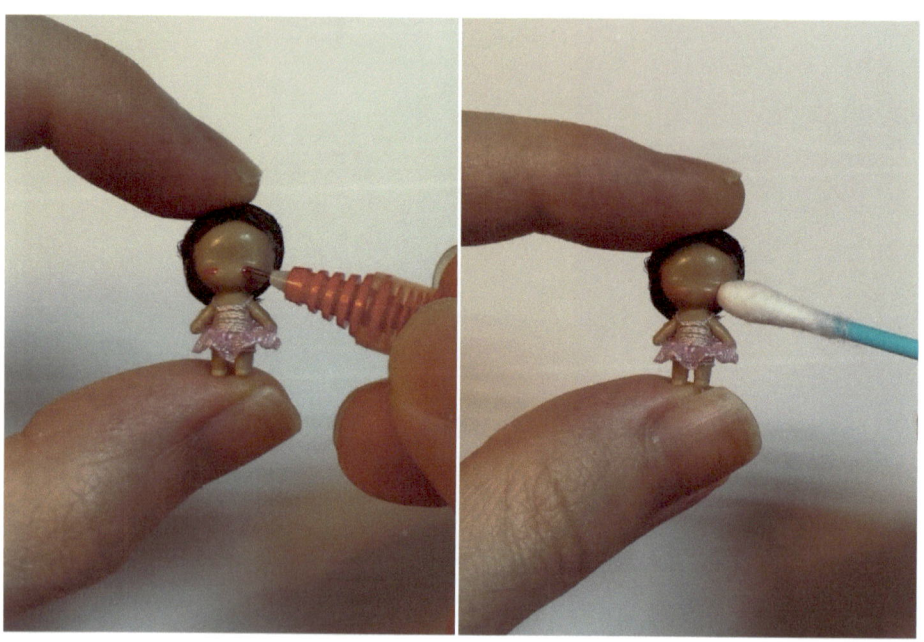

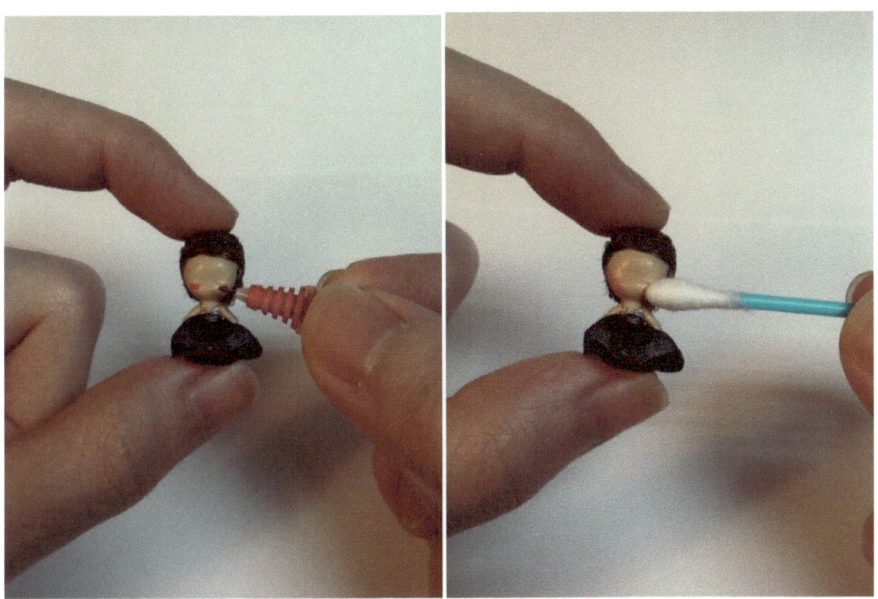

After the red pigment has cured for about a minute, add the white of the eyes to figure by drawing them on with the white pigment pen.

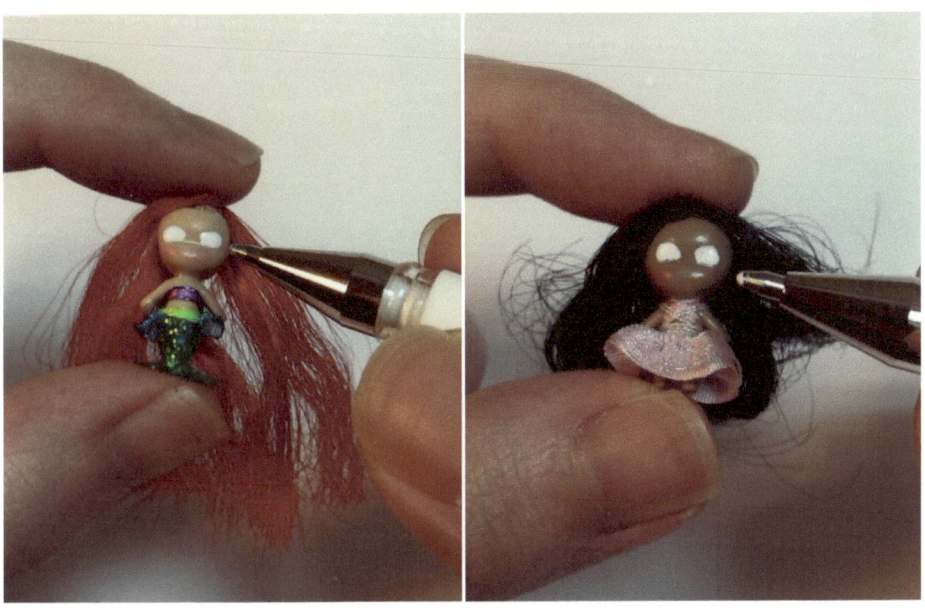

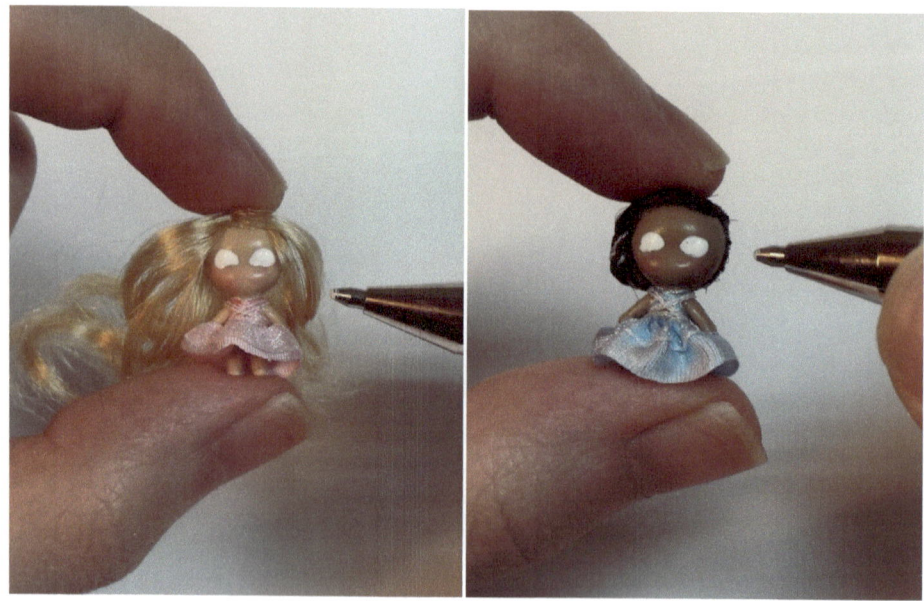

You many experiment with using white acrylic based paints, but I had difficulties applying small quantities of paint with out it drying quickly on the brush under hot lights.

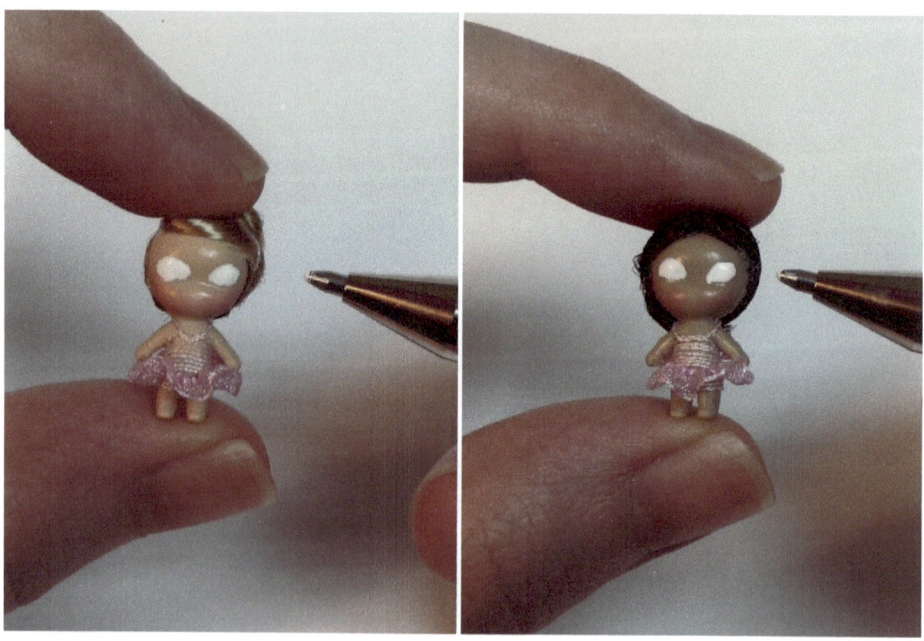

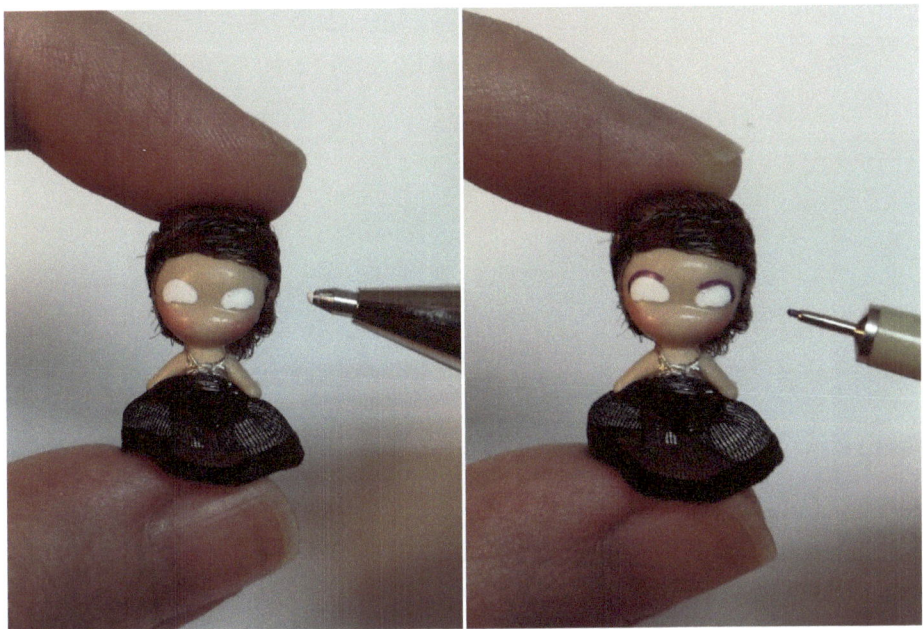

After the white pigment has sufficient time to cure, you may advance to the next step of adding color to the eye.

I use a lamp to provide enough heat to aid in the curing process between adding pigments next to each other to prevent the colors running together.

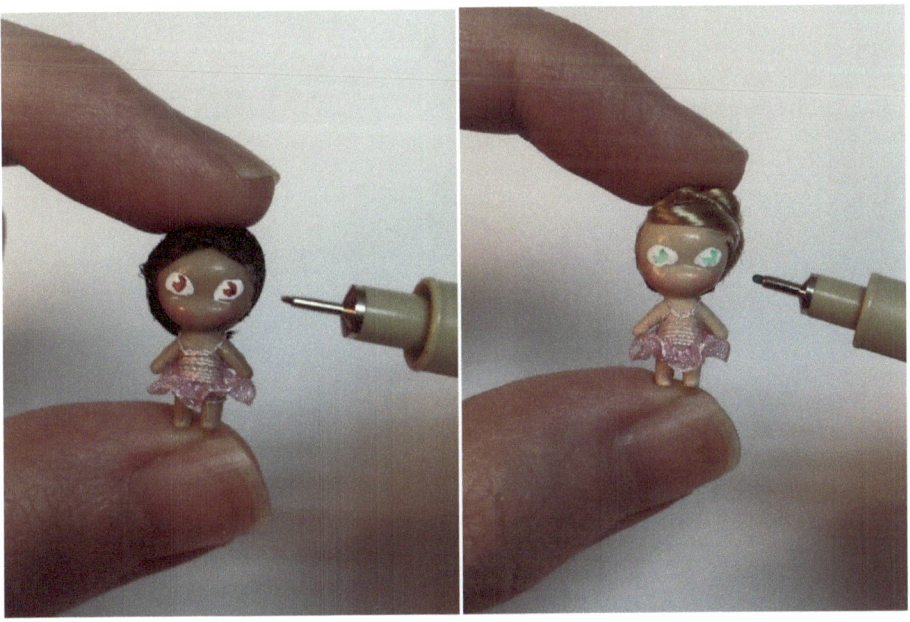

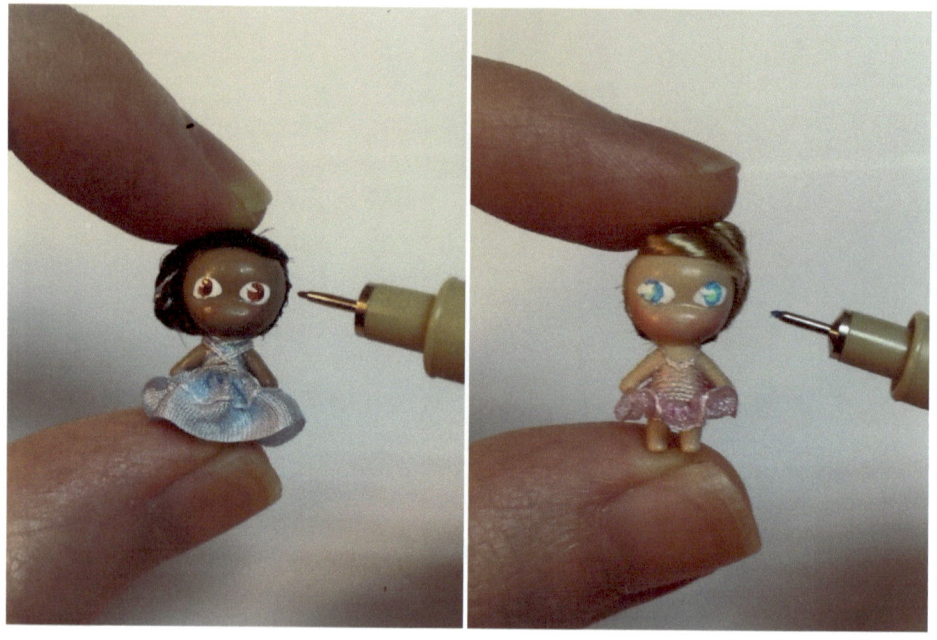

As the eye pigments are added, you may layer the colors to add depth to the finished product. Be certain to allow for cure time.

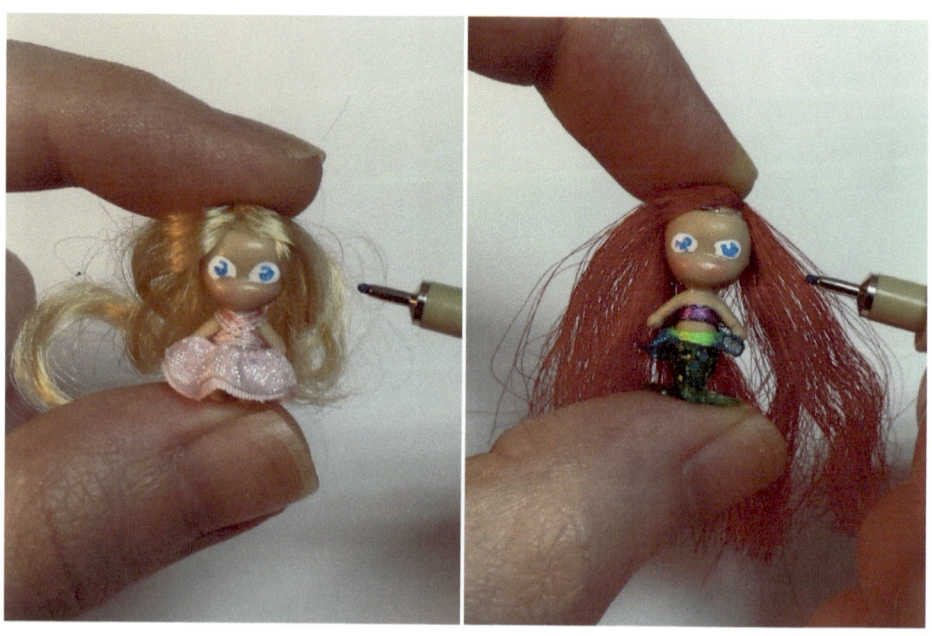

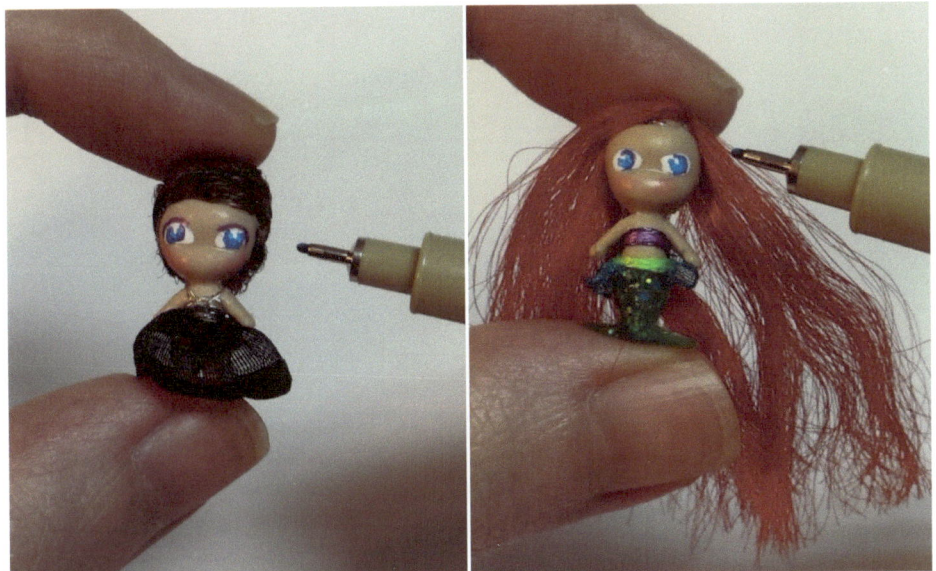

When deciding on the eye hues, you can use a color wheel to assist in creating contrasting or complimentary shades as apposed to the rest of the composition.

The hair shade you choose can help in making this determination.

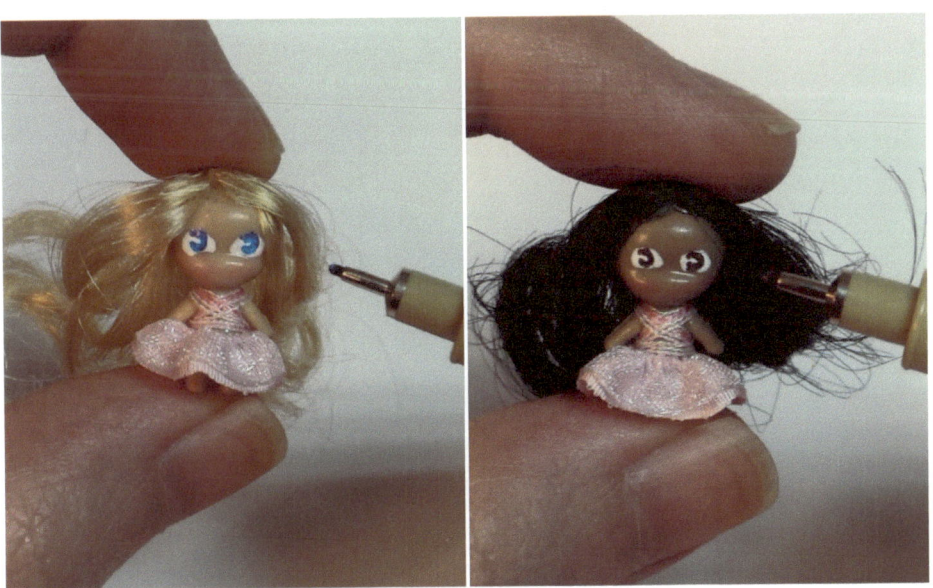

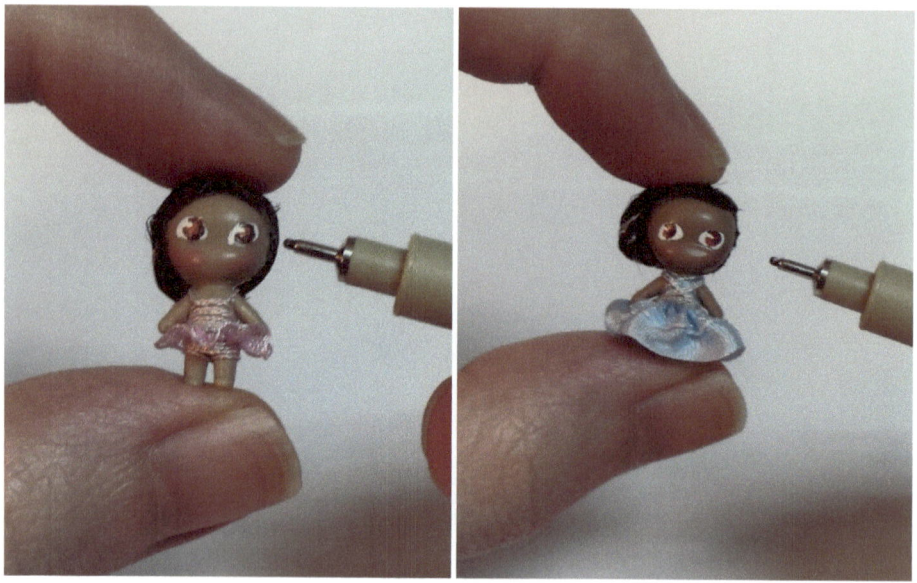

Use different shades of the same hue to create depth of the eyes. Keep in mind the position of the catch light in the eye of the figure.

While adding layers of pigment, avoid accidentally drawing over the white space that implies light.

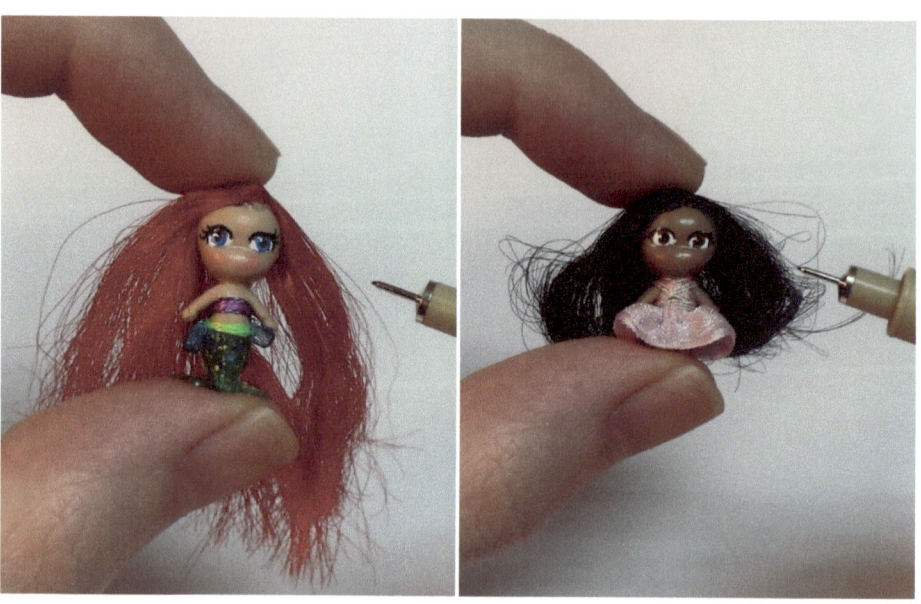

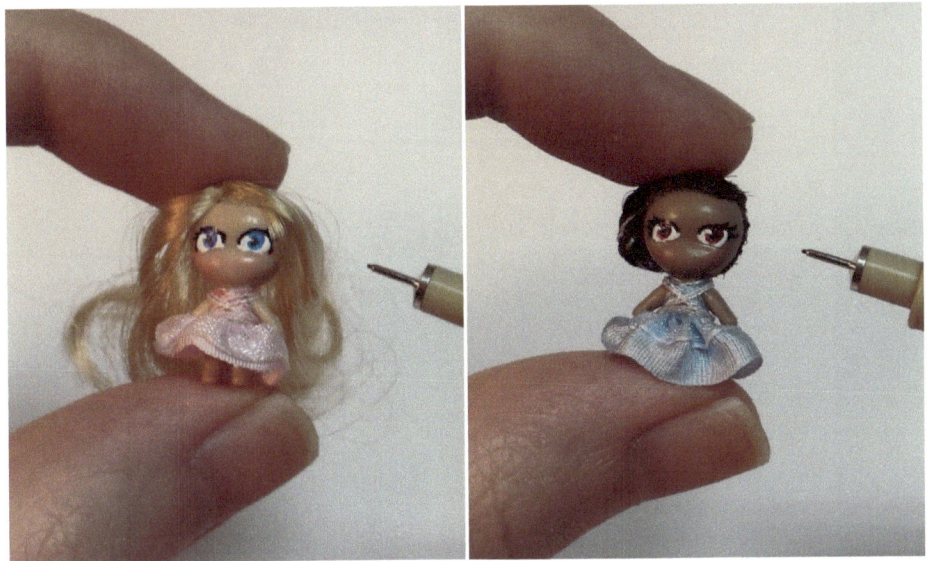

Add the upper lashes and pupil to the figure.

Be certain the other pigments have completely cured to prevent colors running together.

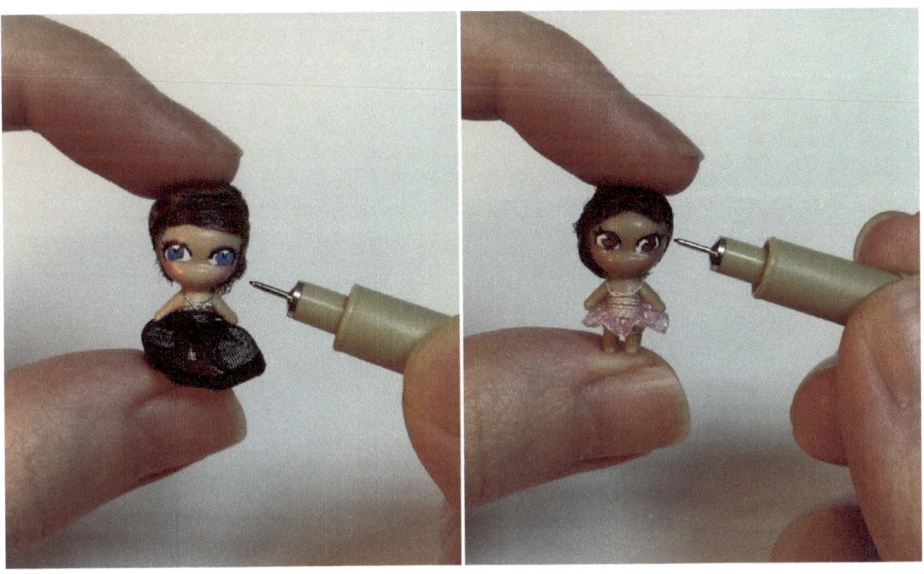

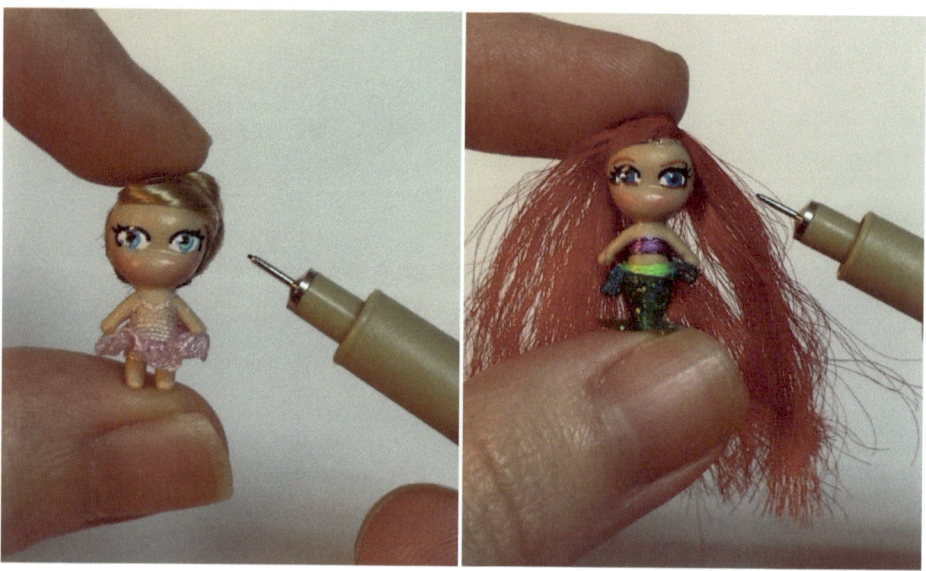

As you create the upper lashes, keep in mind the next step of adding lower lashes and how it will affect the composition.

The brown shade used ends up blending purposefully into the black lash line. Betwen strokes, clean the pen of any pigments accidentally lifted in the process.

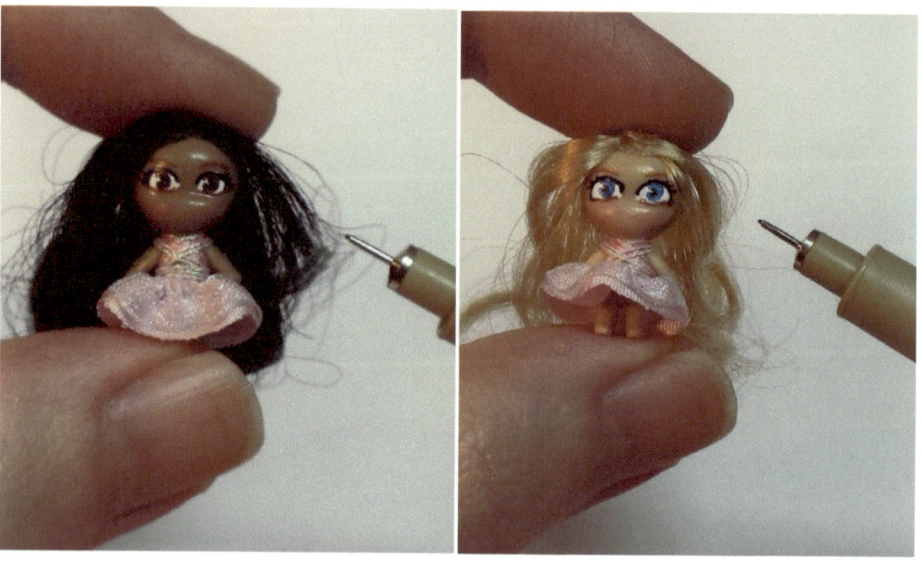

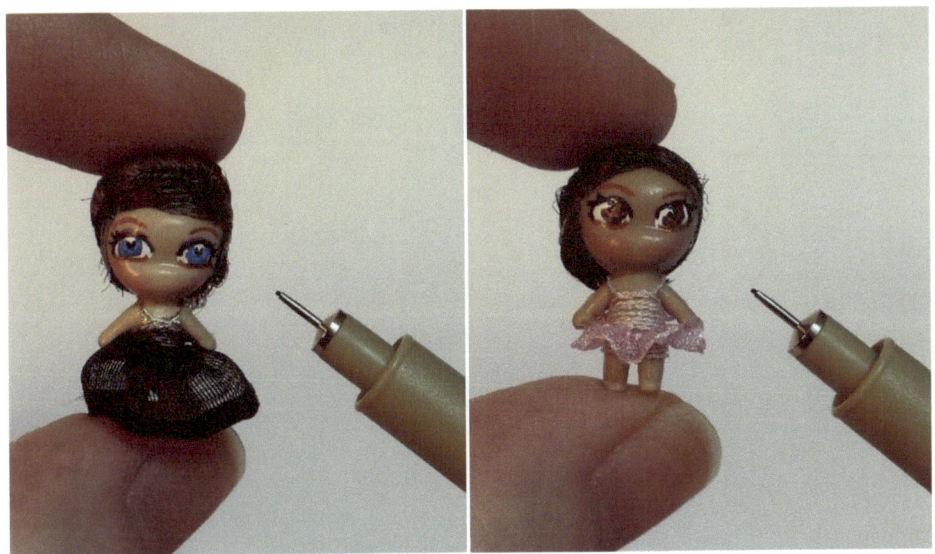

Add brows by starting above the colored iris of the eye and end just past the lash line.

Drawing on a test sheet is most important at this state to prevent transfering the pupil and white of the eye to the eye brow.

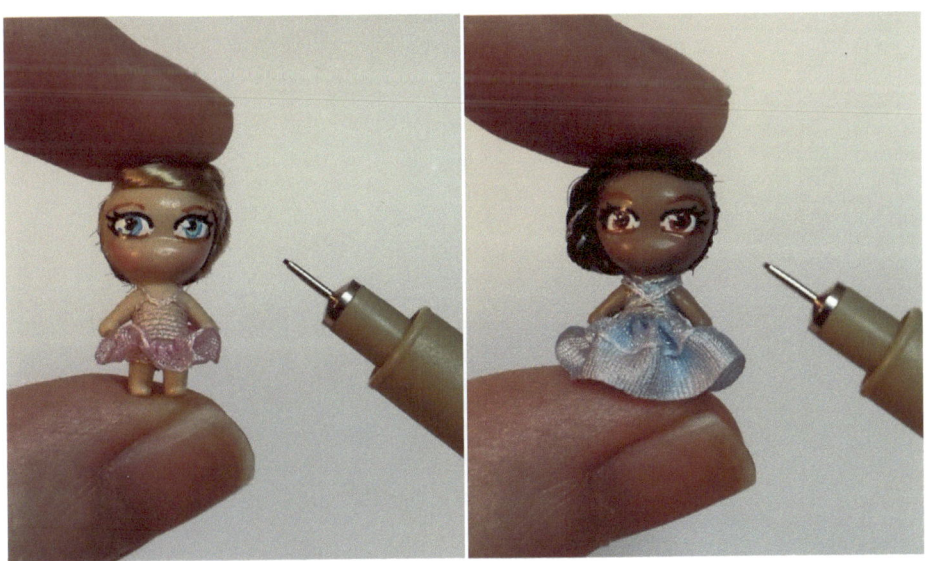

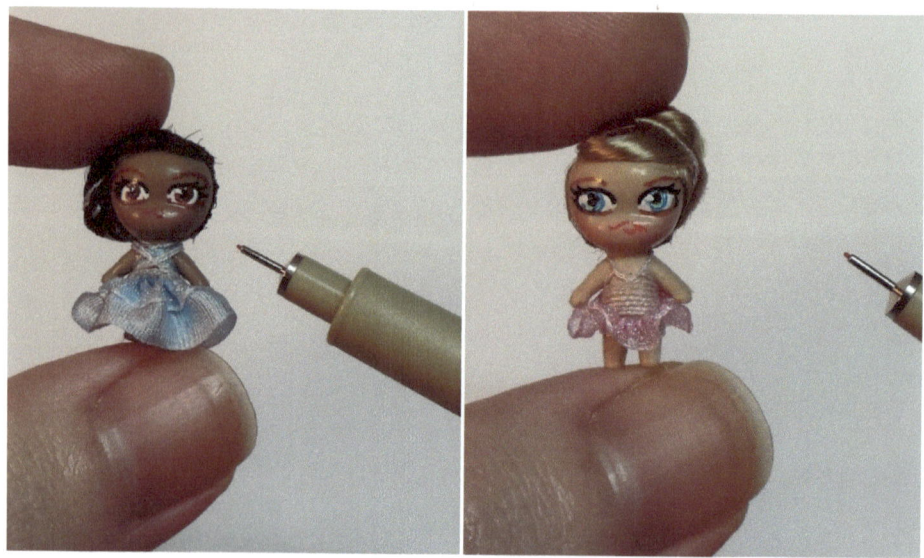

I use pink shades and red for the mouth depending the hair color, eye shade and costume chosen for the character.

There are many ways of implying expression with the smile you choose to draw.

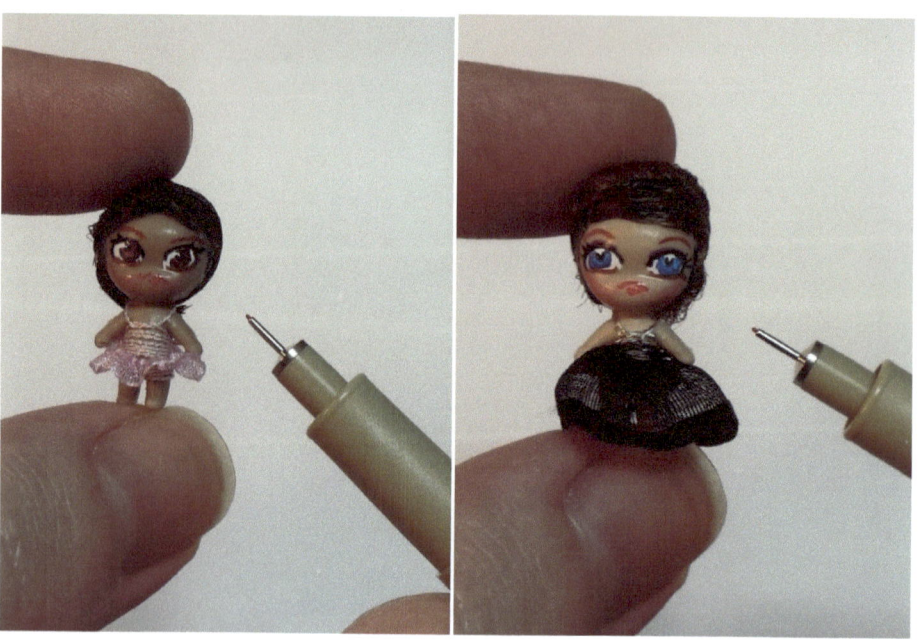

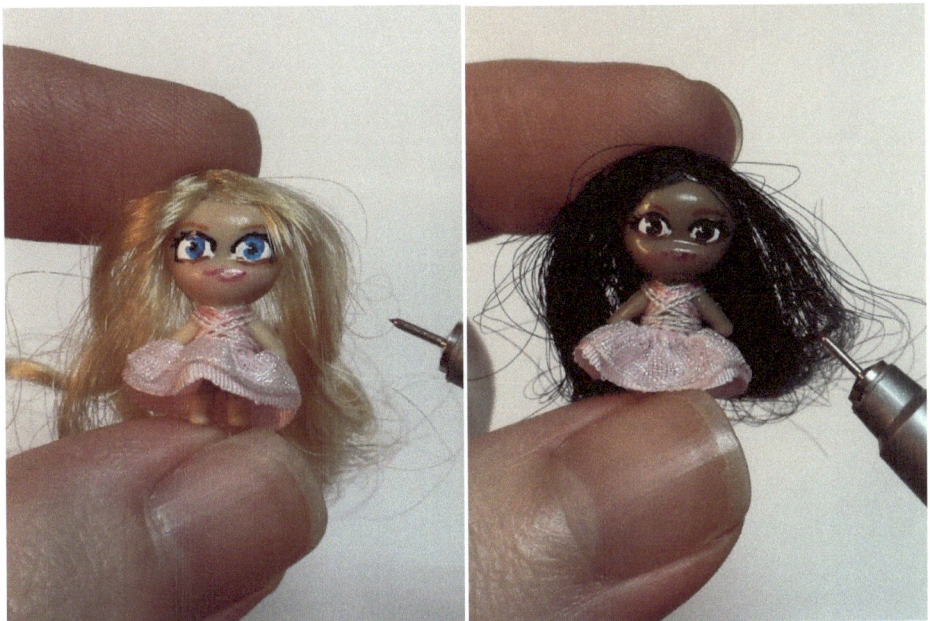

These figures illustrate more mouth and smile designs. While drawing on the expression in every stage, take extreem care not to touch it because it is not permenant at this stage. Although it is permenant ink, it reacts differently on urethane as it does to paper products the pigments are designed for which leads to the next step; sealing the expression. Prepare paper board by cutting a hole.

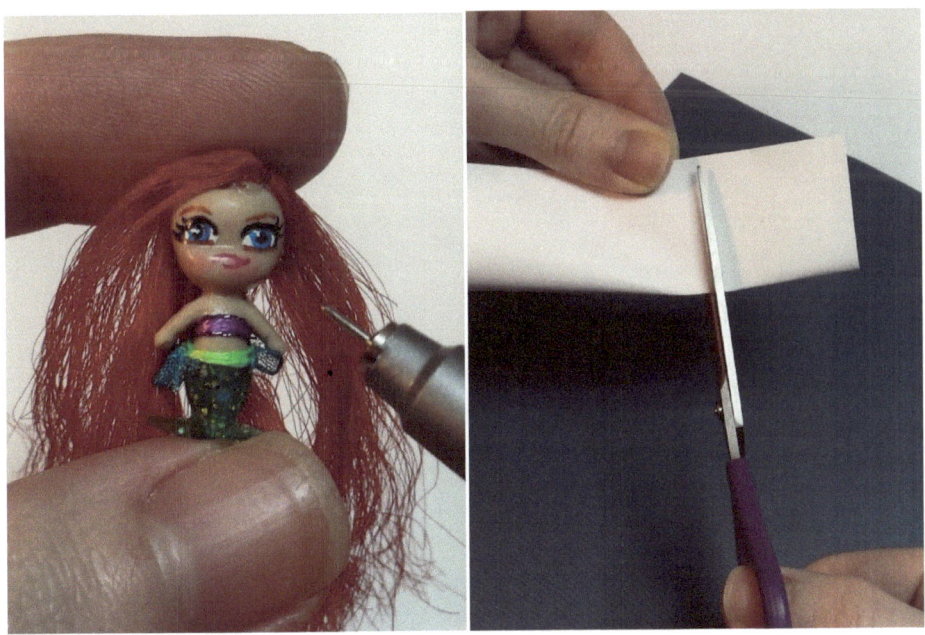

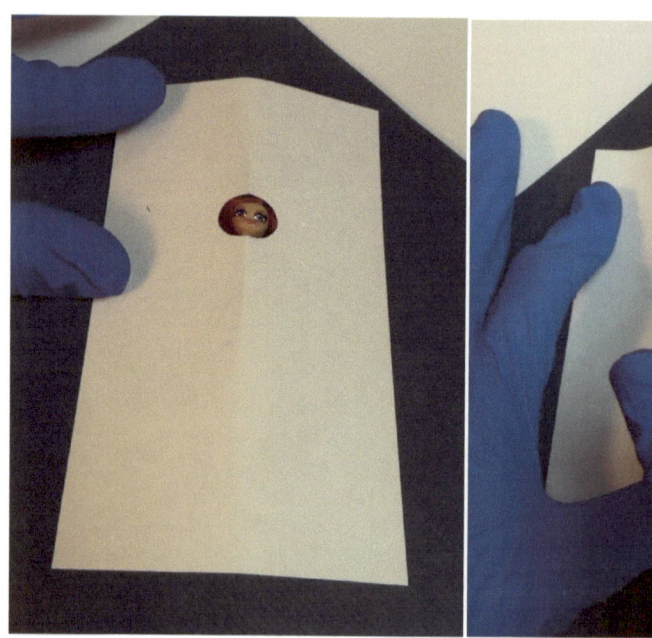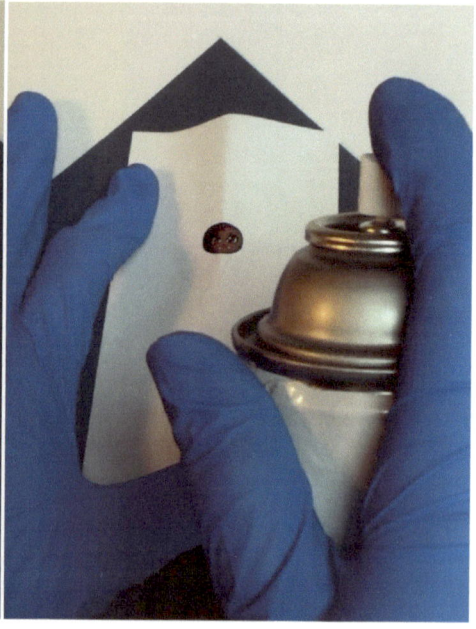

Mask the figure with the paperboard leaving the face area exposed.

Protect your hands while you apply clear urethane according to manufacturer's instructions.

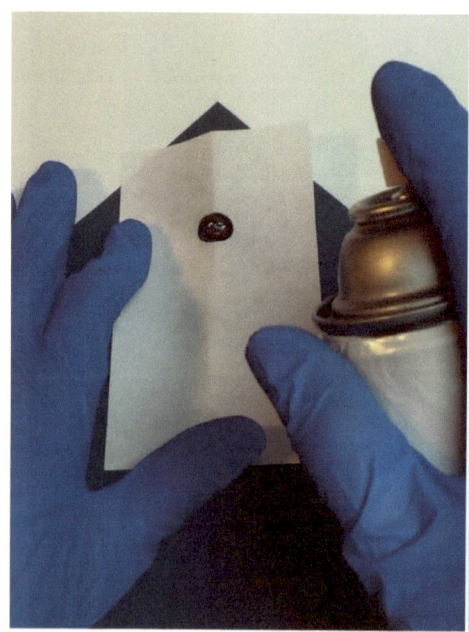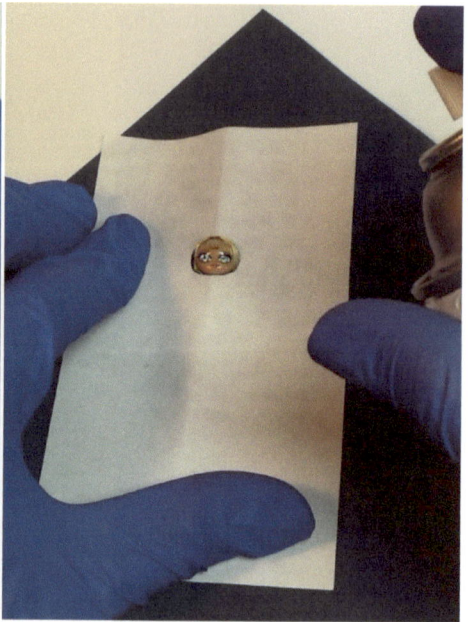

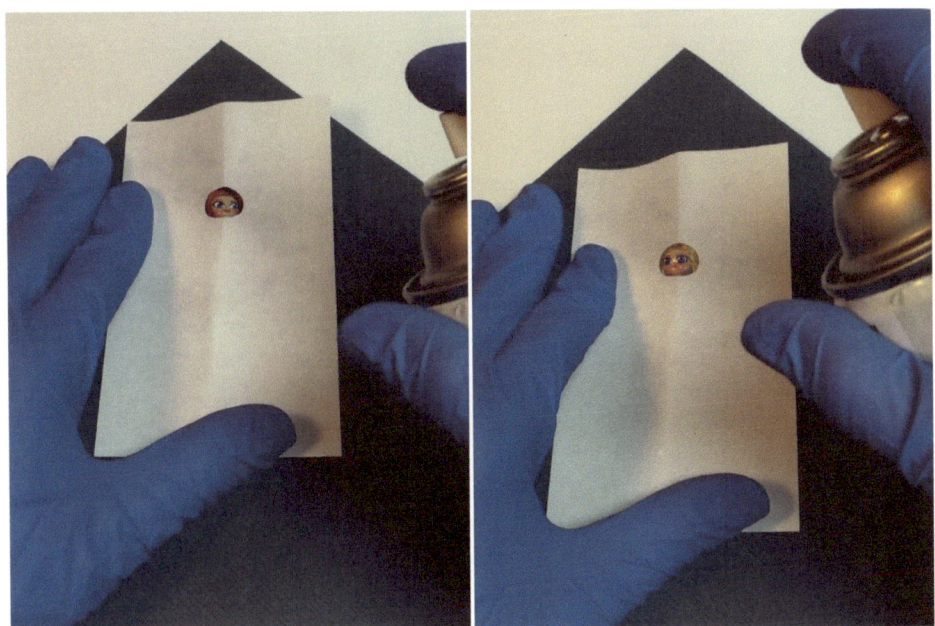

As you spray the figure, use short bursts of spray using a distance of about 16" from the figure.

Use sweeping motions. Inspect the face to ensure all the area is properly covered but not thick.

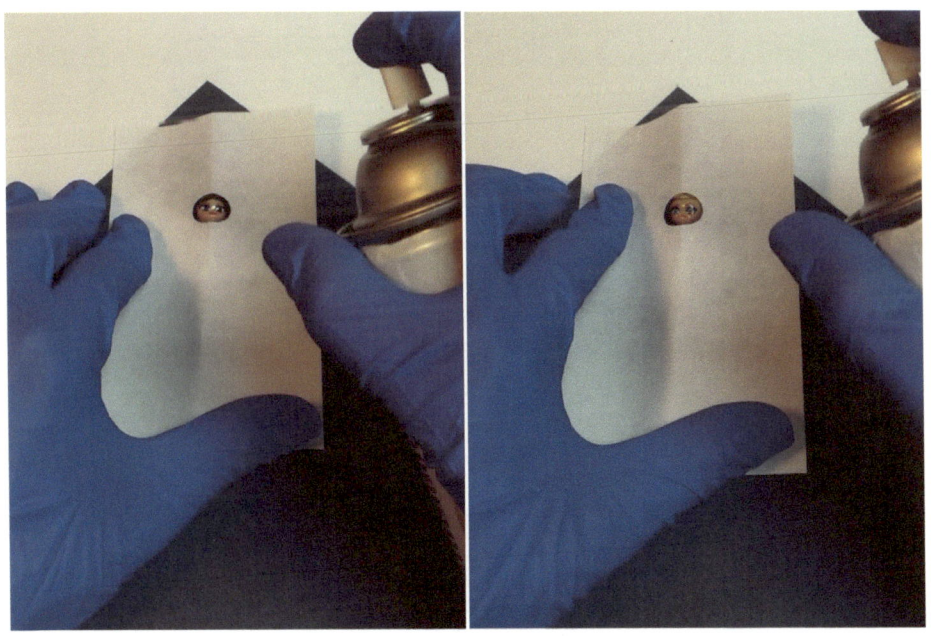

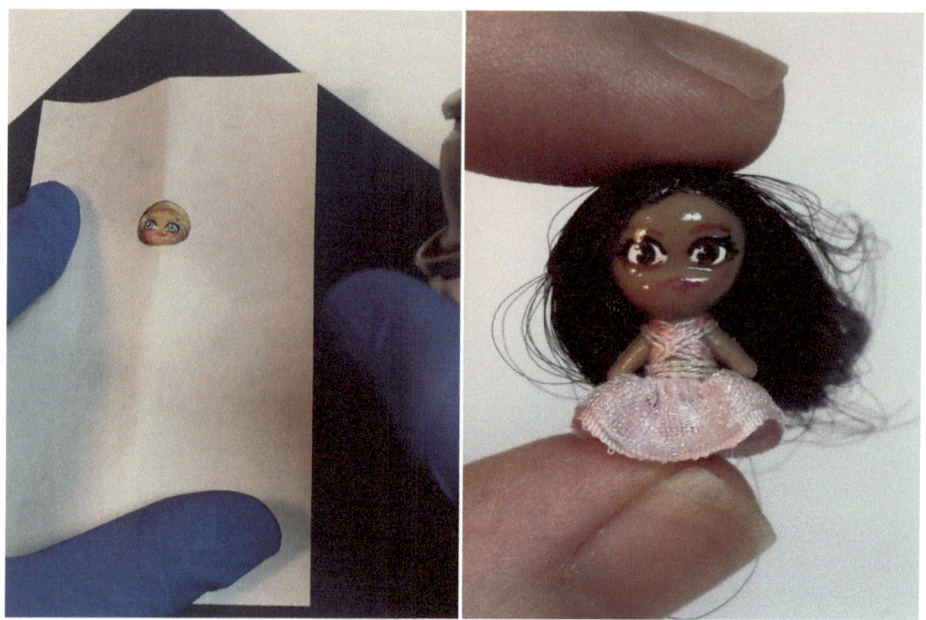

The expression can run if the spray is not applied in light layers.

After the face is properly sealed, place on waxed paper to cure for about 3 hours, which is longer than the cure time on regular surfaces. Urethane coated with acrylic needs to cure longer to insure no transfer of the facial expression.

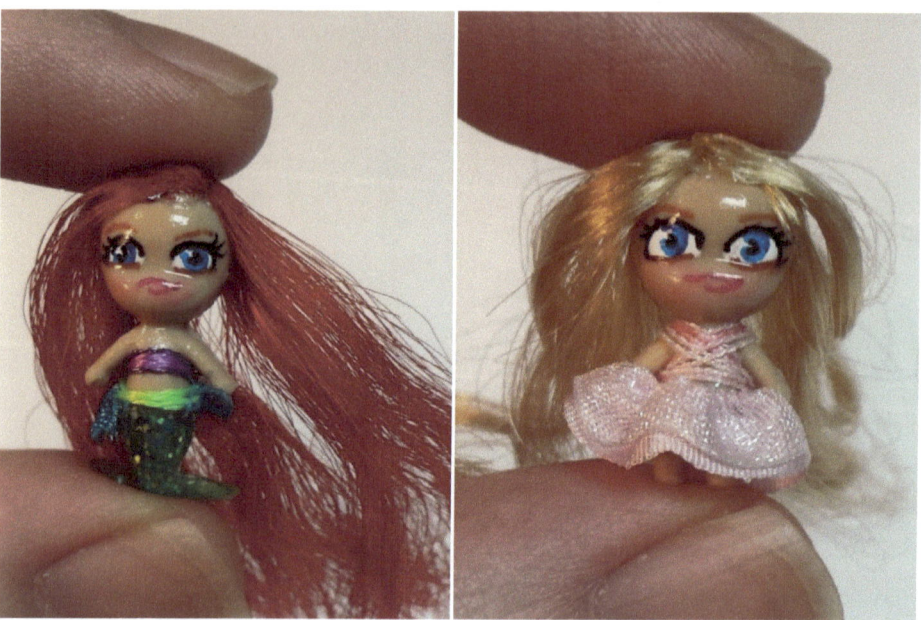

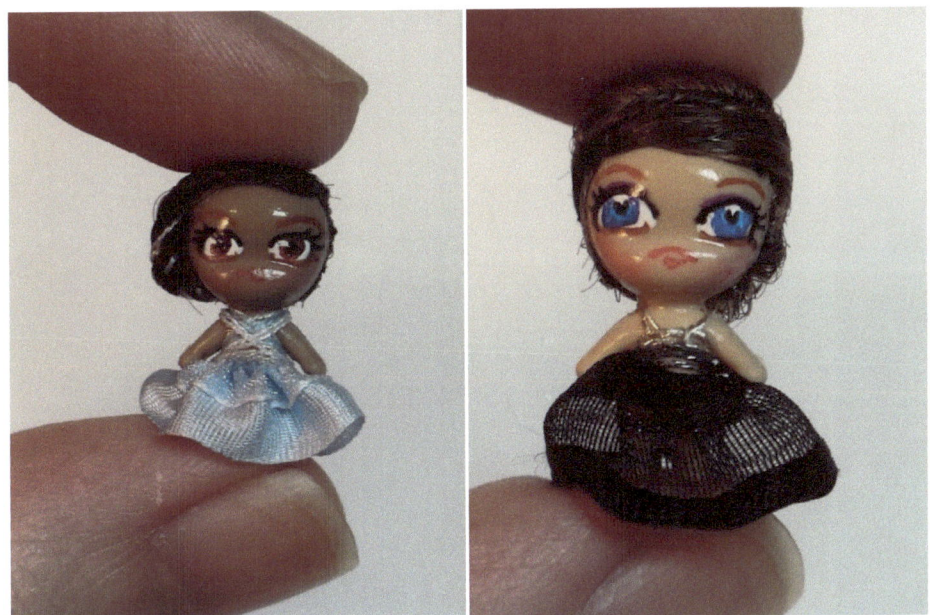

After the features are cured, you may add accessories to the figure.

The dolls can be stored long term after this cure time inside individual plastic bags. I like to store them in plastic after the face is sealed and before adding accessories to prevent dust from sticking to the expressions.

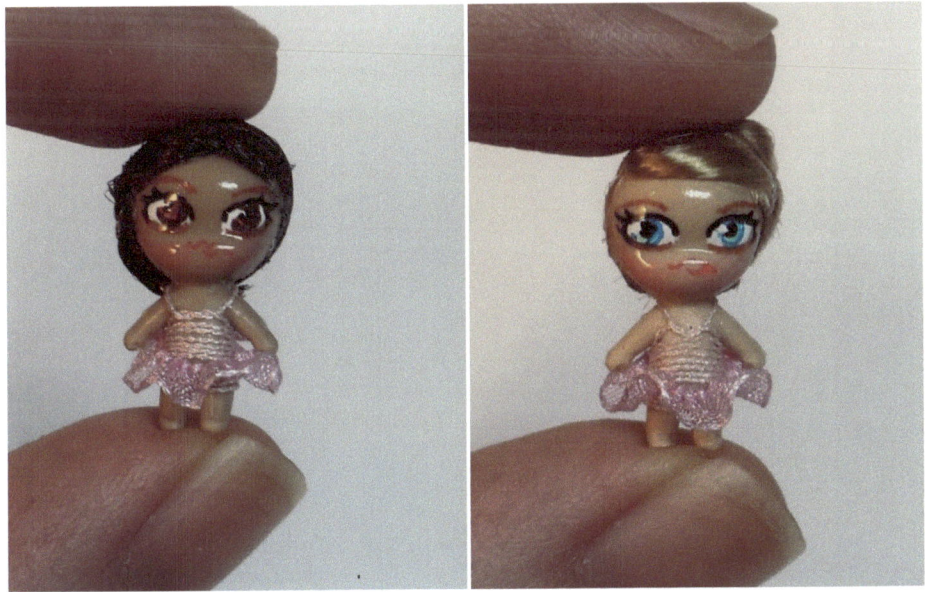

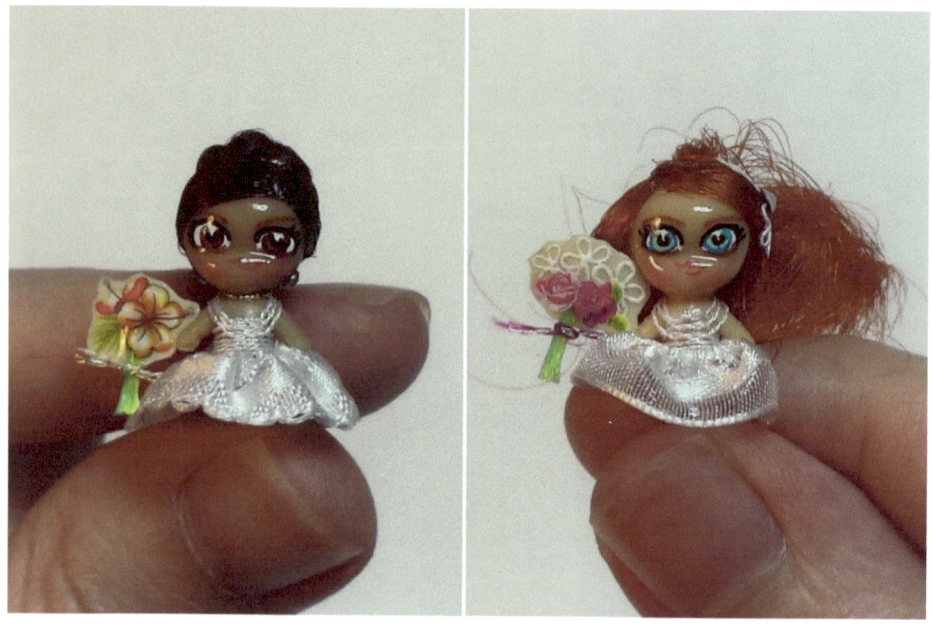

These are a few more examples of hair styles with plaits, floss accents and decals.

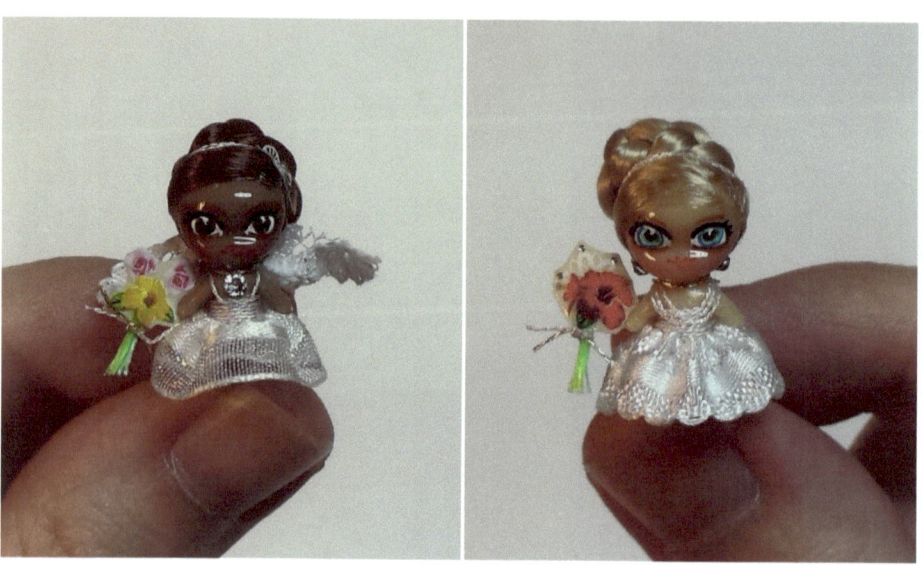

Ch 5 Accessories

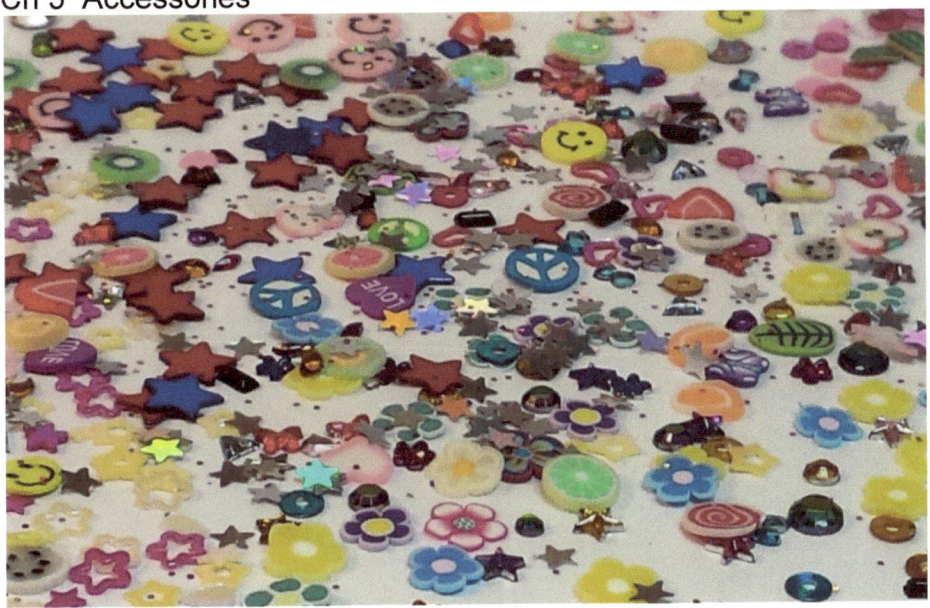

You will need a lot of super glue and tooth picks as well as wax paper and foil.

There is no end to the accessories suggestion list, only that it must be small.

Acrylic paint works best for shoes but, unlike the painted on bodysuit, the heels and toes receive the most wear with regard to painted surfacs. Allow for at least 45 minutes cure time before attempting to make the figure "stand."
As long as the accessories and glitters are compatable with with the adheasives used, the sky's the limit.

I often create thin sheets of glitter or effects embedded urethane to cut out to depict many objects that I can't find commercially such as space ray blasters and musical instruments. I use nair art decals and millefiori in place of many kinds of accessories but don't let that limit you. There is more to accessories than purses and shoes

As with any stage of creation, it is very import to have a clean, well lit work surface and that you wash your hands often. Avoid touching the doll as much as possible while it is being produced. It is easy to transfer oils and dirt by accident. Another important thing to recogize is when you are finished, to prounounce your creation complete and leave it alone in a clean, temperature controled, ventilated space to finish curing up to 24 hours.

Store in plastic bags to prevent dust from collecting on your finished piece.

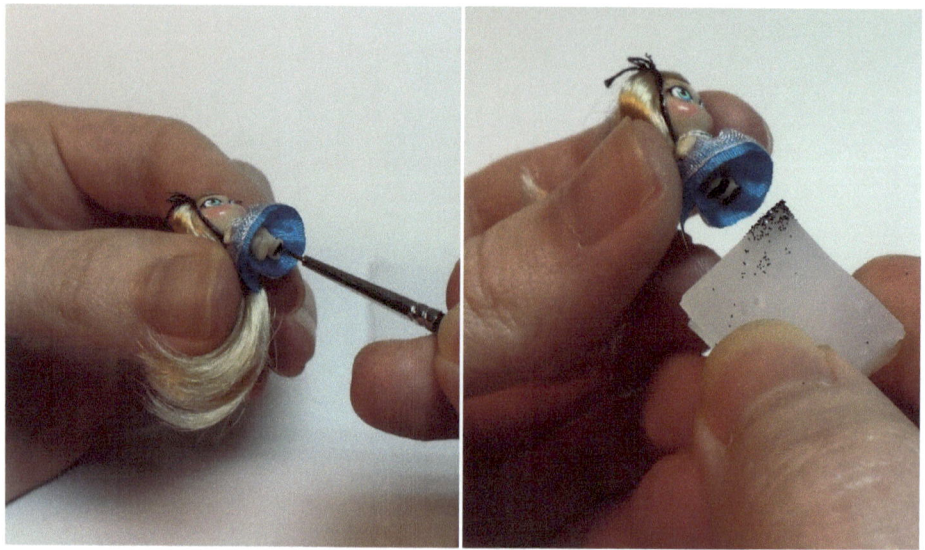

Acrylic paint works well to create shoes.

I add black glitter with a silicone tool to give them a little extra shine.

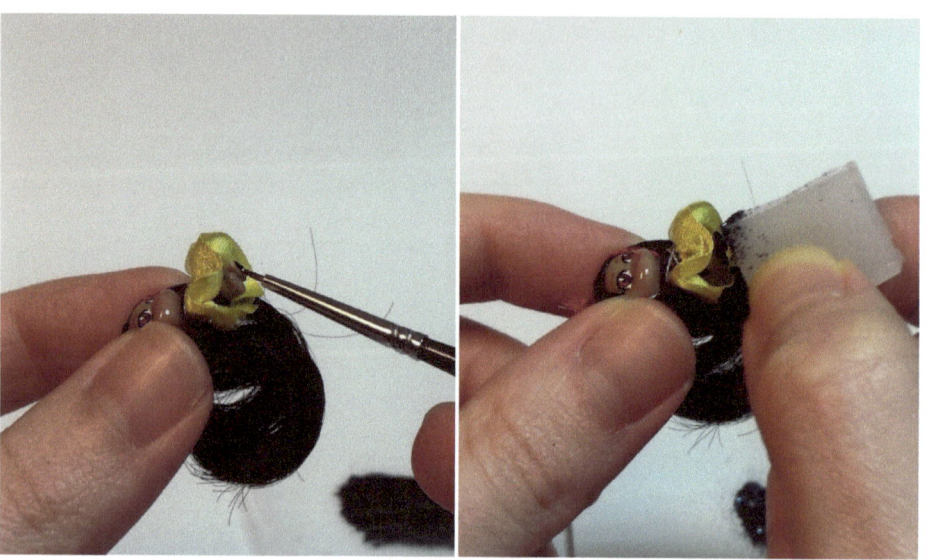

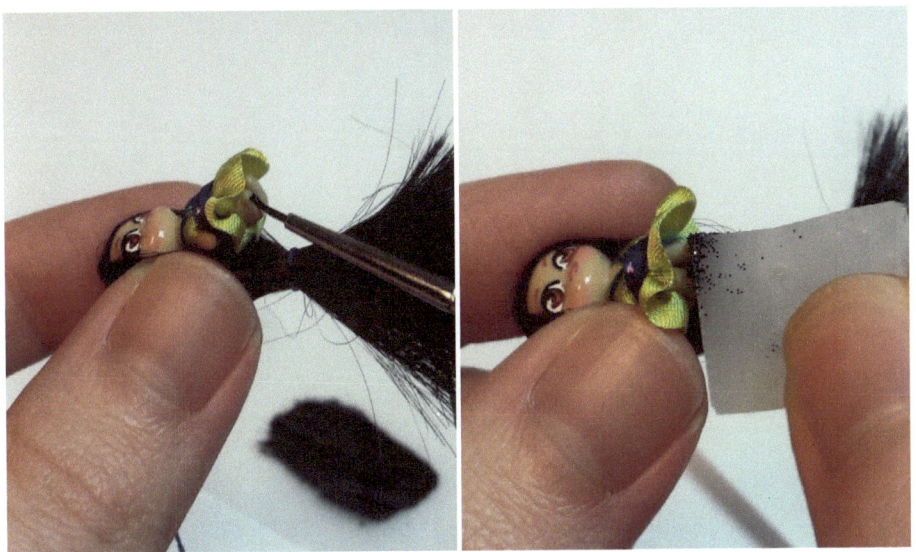

The acrylic paint only likes to hold onto the glitter within about 10-30 seconds after it is applied, depending on the temperature and humidity of your work space.

The acrylic paint acts as a glue adhering the glitter into place.

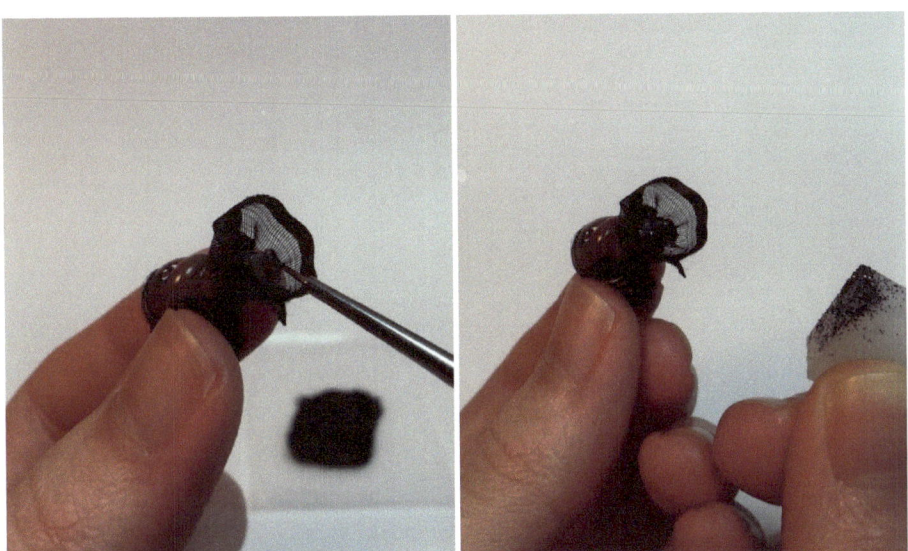

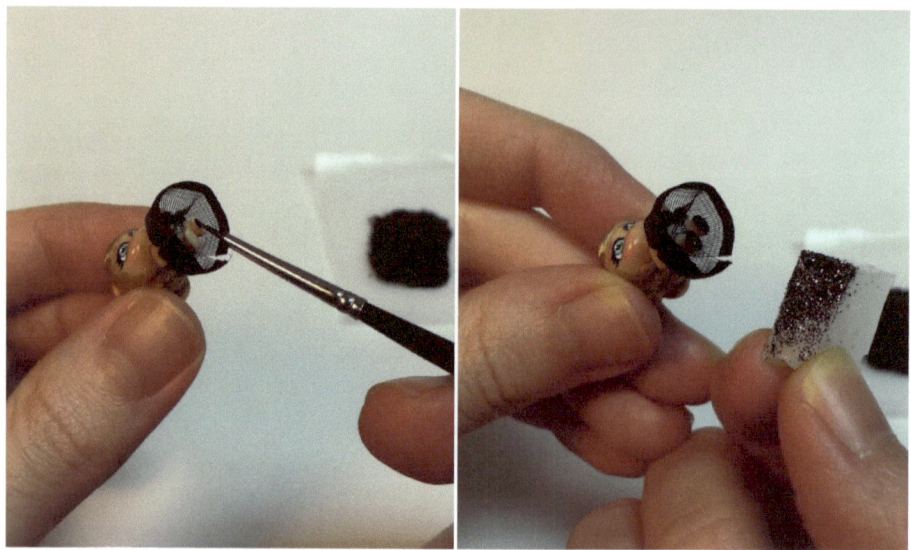

If the glitter is applied too soon, it tends to puddle on the silicone tool and covers the glitter, preventing it from shining. Watch for the acrylic to form a "skin" where the paint begins to dry on the surface, changing from shiny to satin. This is the optimal time to apply glitters.

Other designs require more elements and preperation. This floral design includes a sparkly crystal to catch the light.

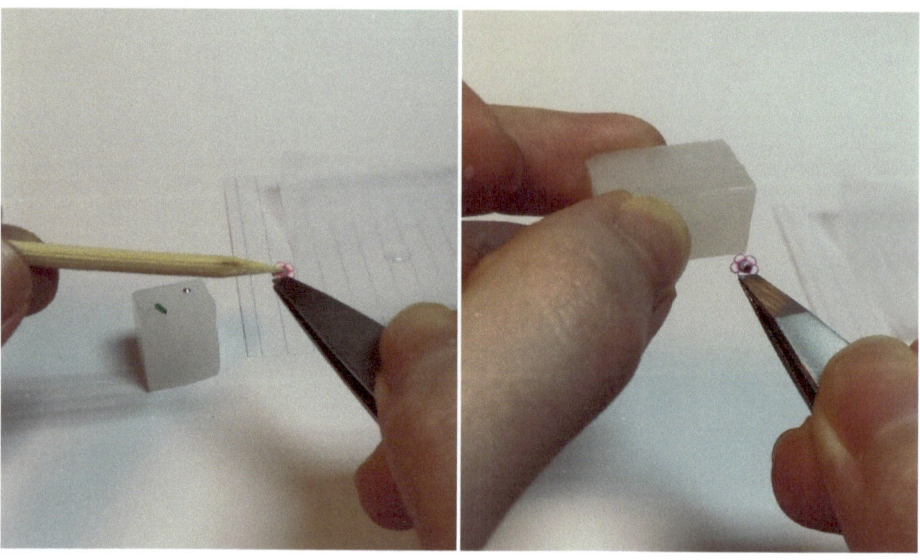

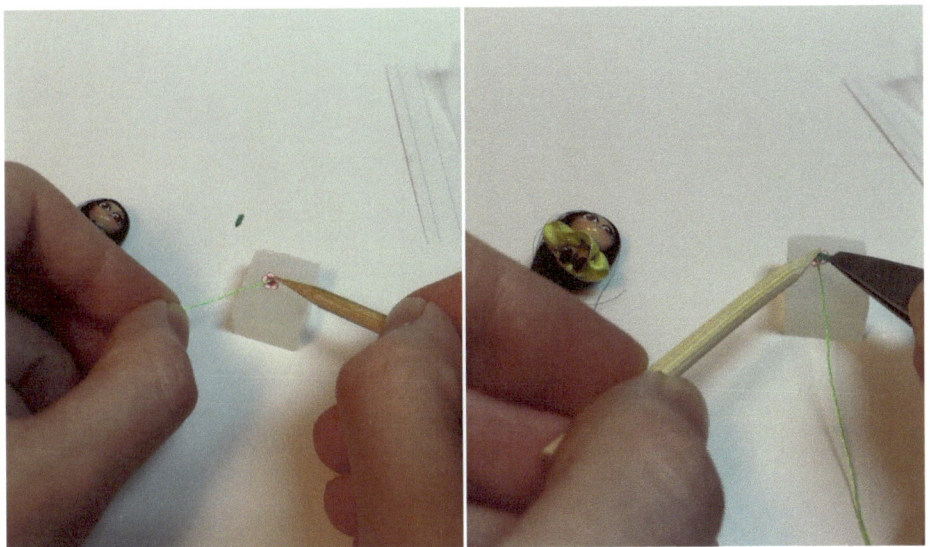

Floss is added to represent a stem. A mili leaf is glued at the base of the flower.

The stem is trimed to size and glued onto the figure.

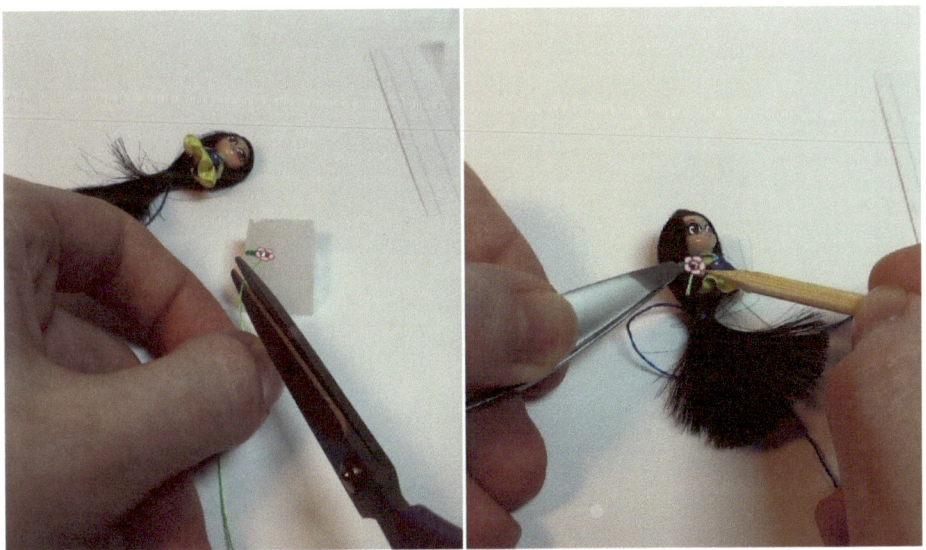

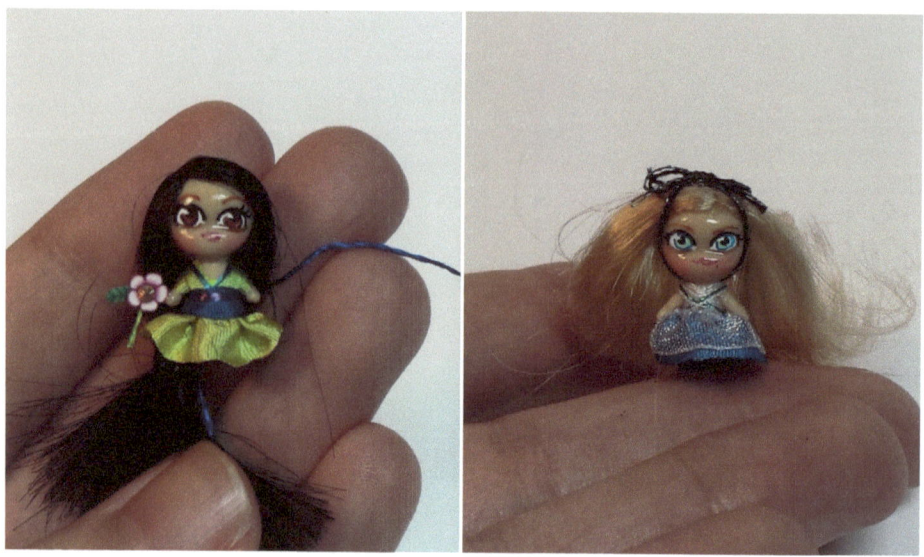

The small addition of the accessory completes a figure. Often we are temped to add more but sometimes simplicity is the best choice.

The chosen elements together create a composition of artistic expression.

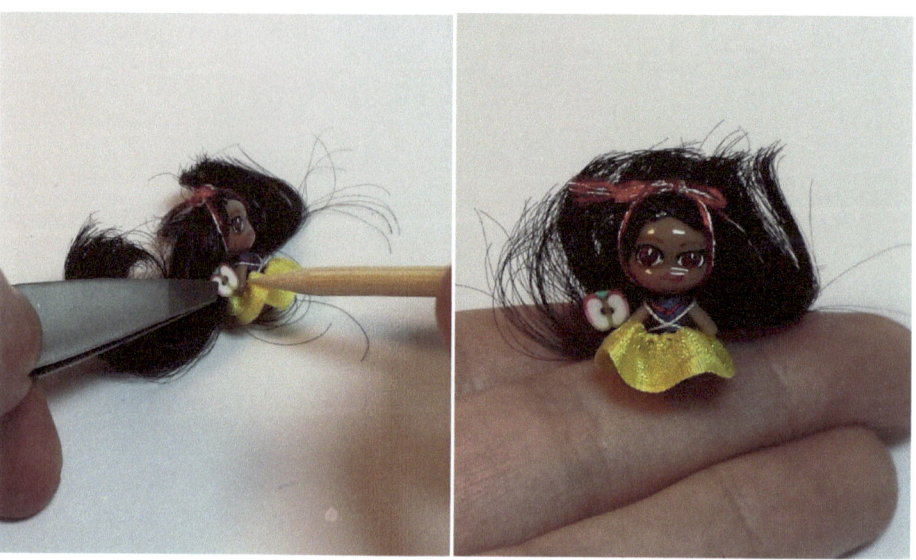

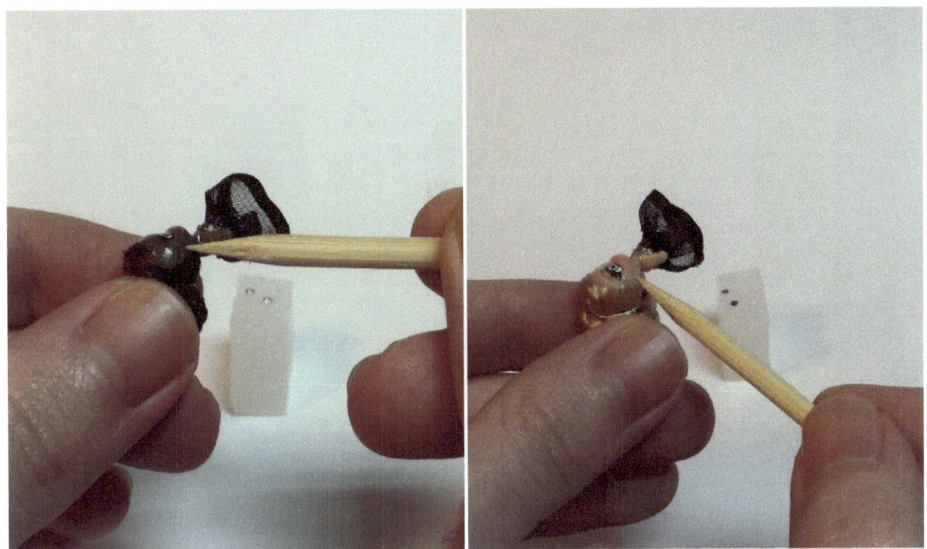

Crystals are added to imply earrings.

They give the finished figure an element of polish and shine.

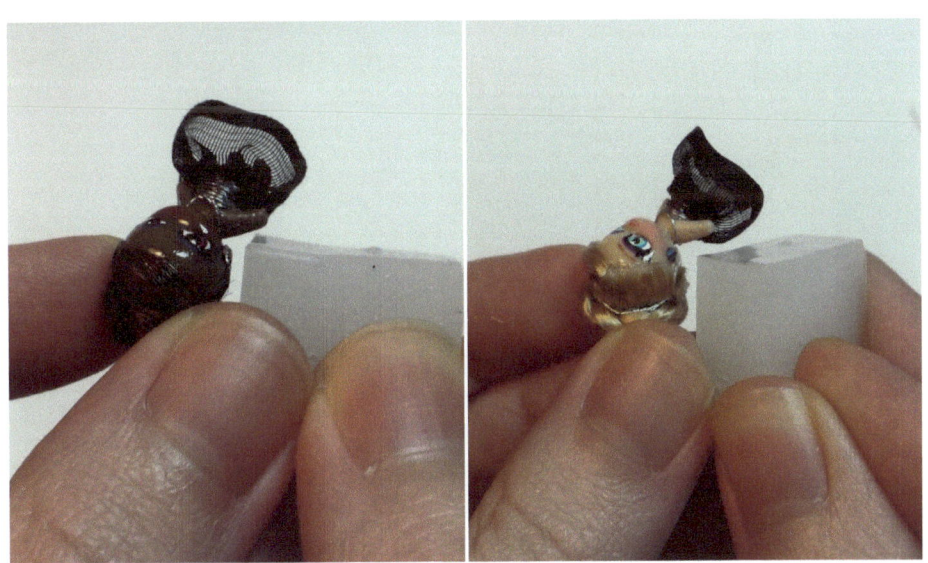

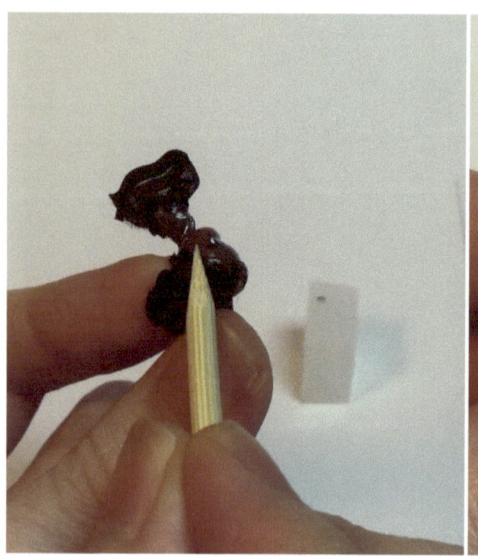 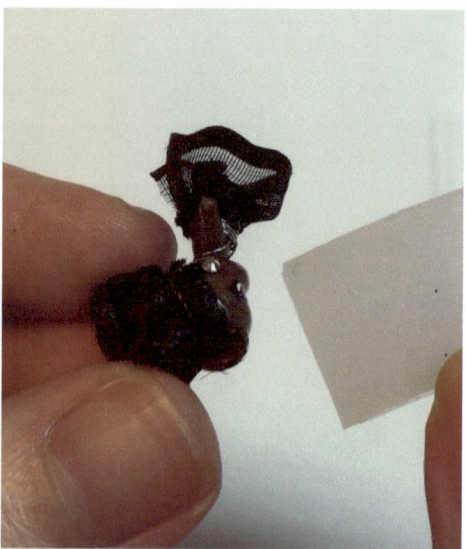

When choosing the finishing details, look to all the other elements to create a complimentary or contrasting effect.

Some accessories can tell stories.

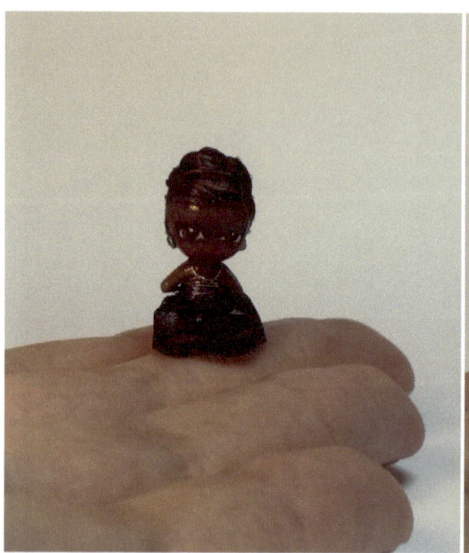 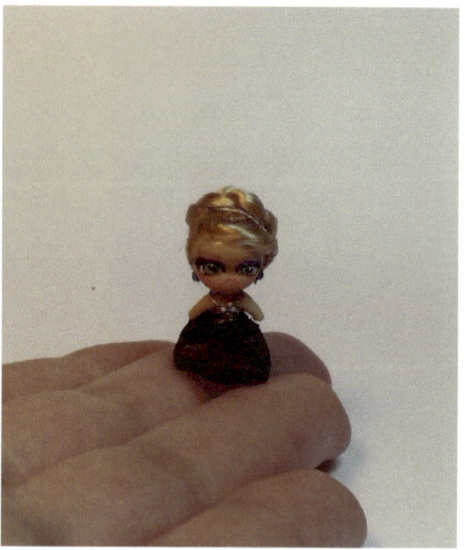

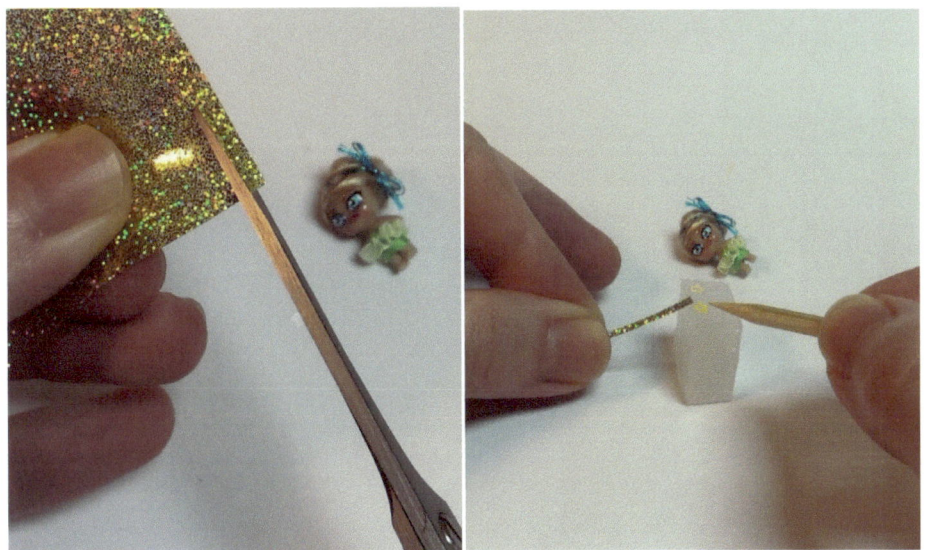

Fairy wands are created with gold glittery sheet urethane, cut to size.

Shimmery stars and flowers are glued onto the ends of the tiny wands.

Wing pattern is drawn on a post it note pad to prevent it from slipping as the wing is cut out.

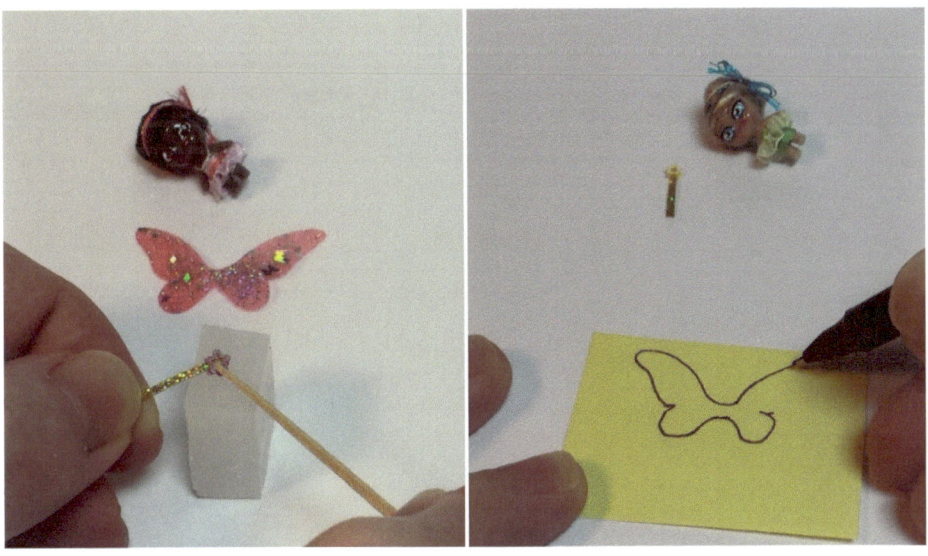

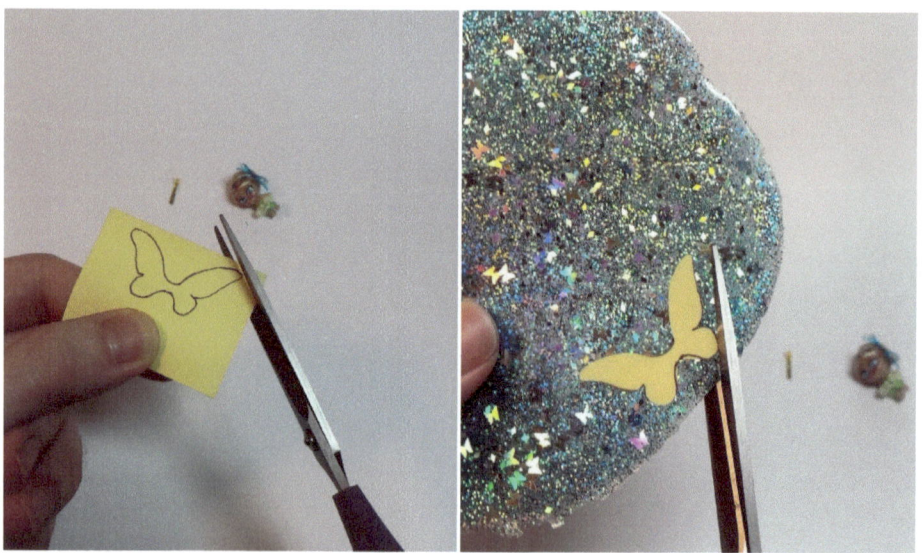

The wing pattern is trimmed and placed on a sheet of glittery, aqua sheet urethane and cut out with sharp shears.

The wing is prepped with super glue and nail decals are placed with a bamboo skewer end.

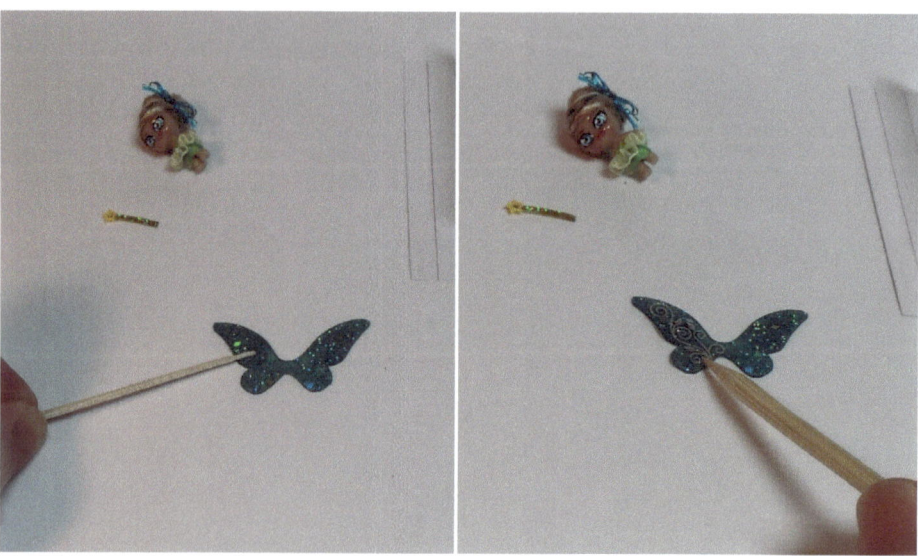

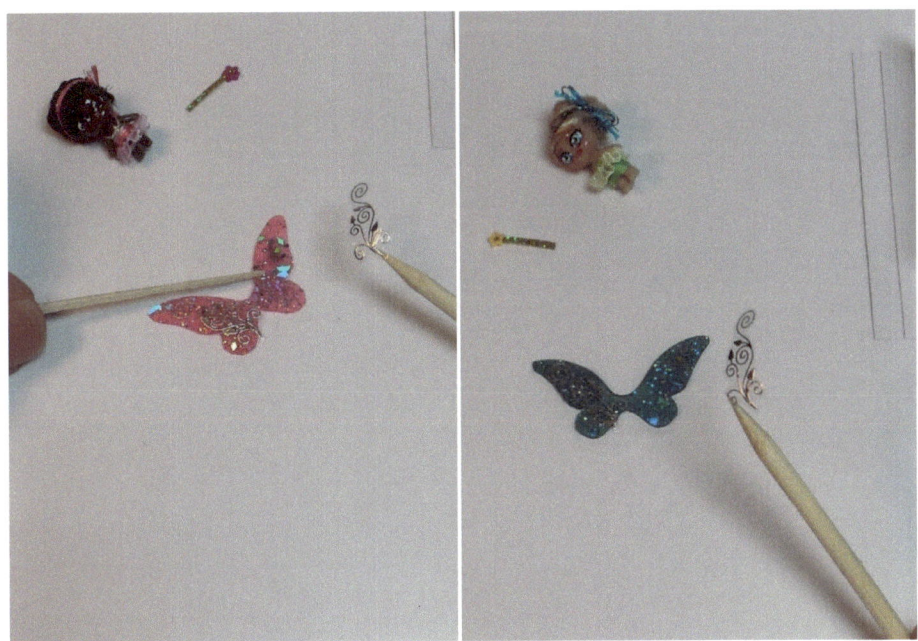

Sometimes, I like the design to mirror each other and sometimes an asymetrical design is visually appealing.

Trim any excess flush to the wing edge.

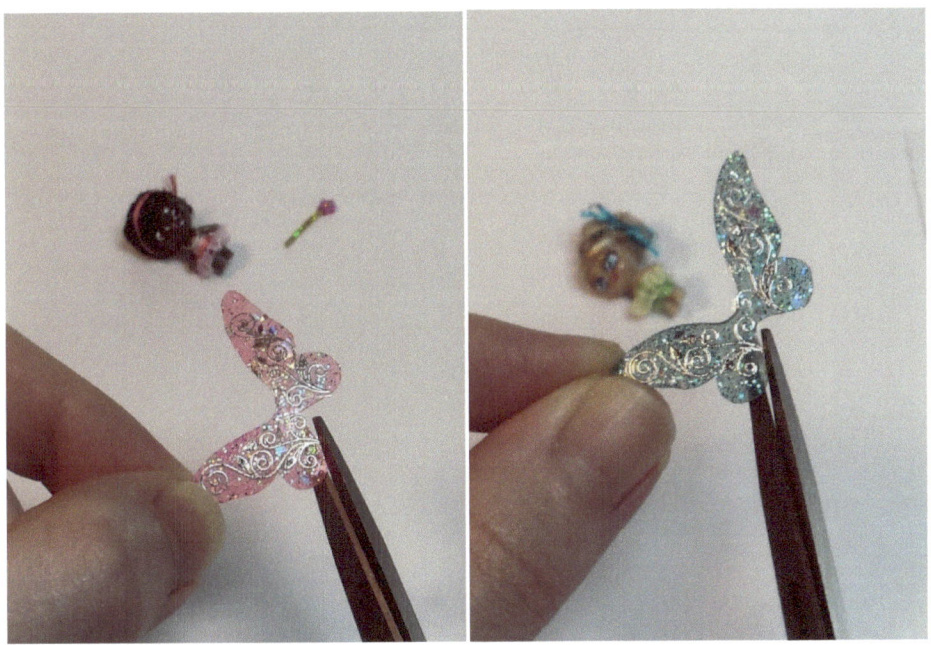

115

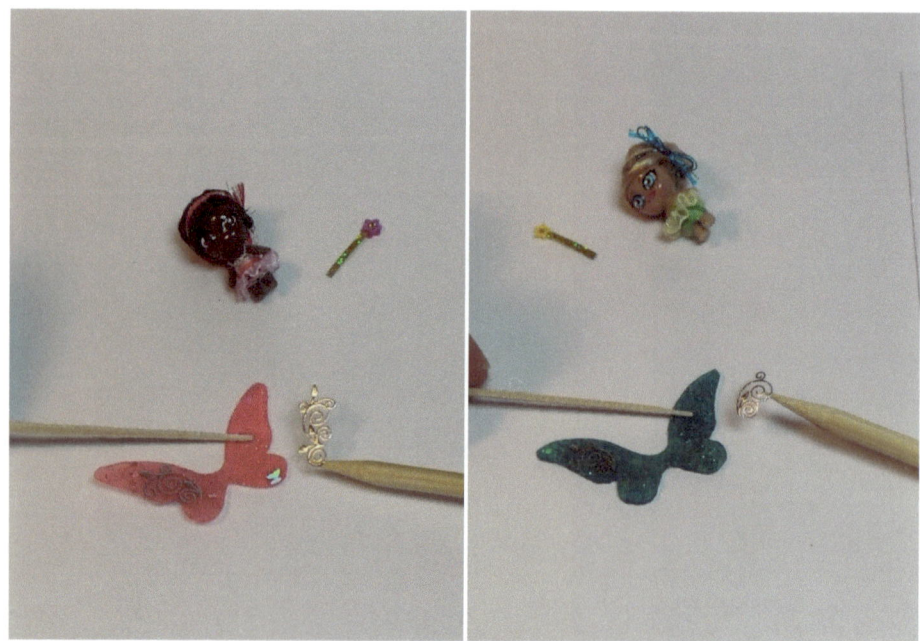

After the wing has cured for about 2-5 minutes, turn it over and glue more nail decals to decorate the fairy wings. When the wings have totally cured, prepare the back of the figure with super glue.

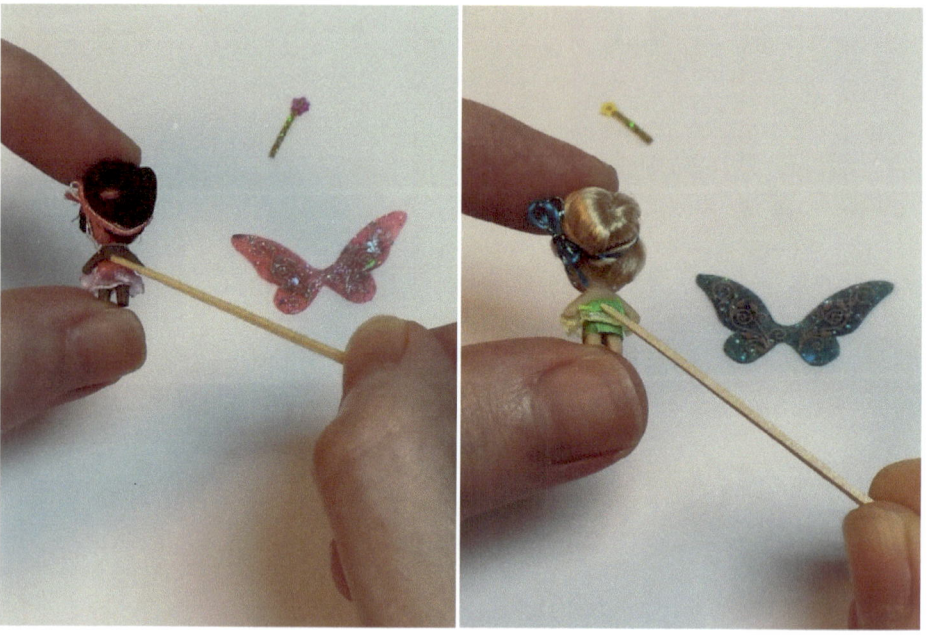

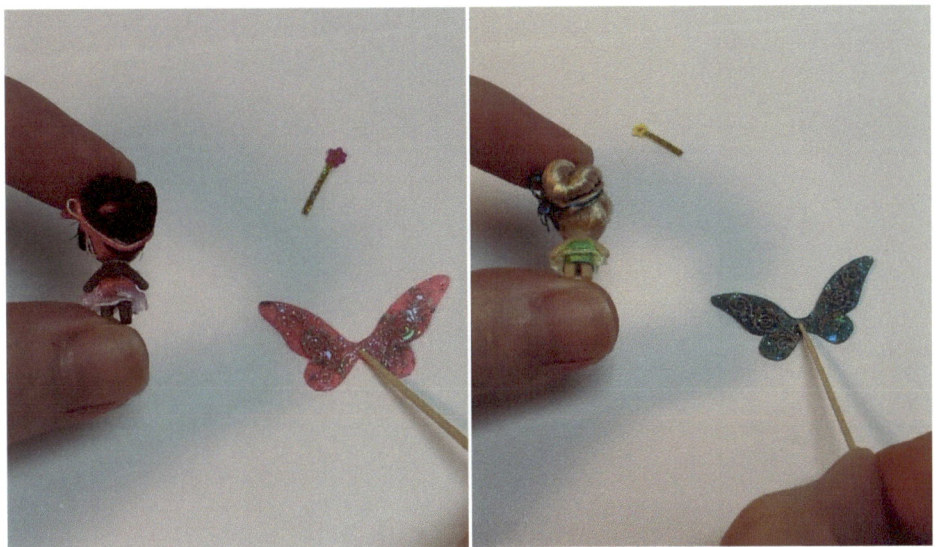

Place a droplet onto the wings and set it onto the back of the figure.

Use a silicone tool to apply pressure for about 30 seconds. Allow the wings to set for between 2-5 minutes before handling.

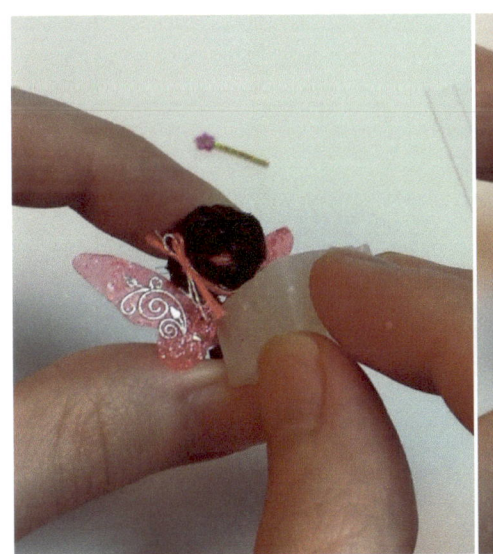
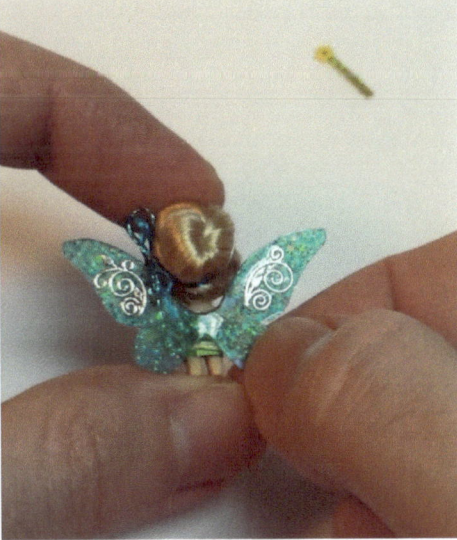

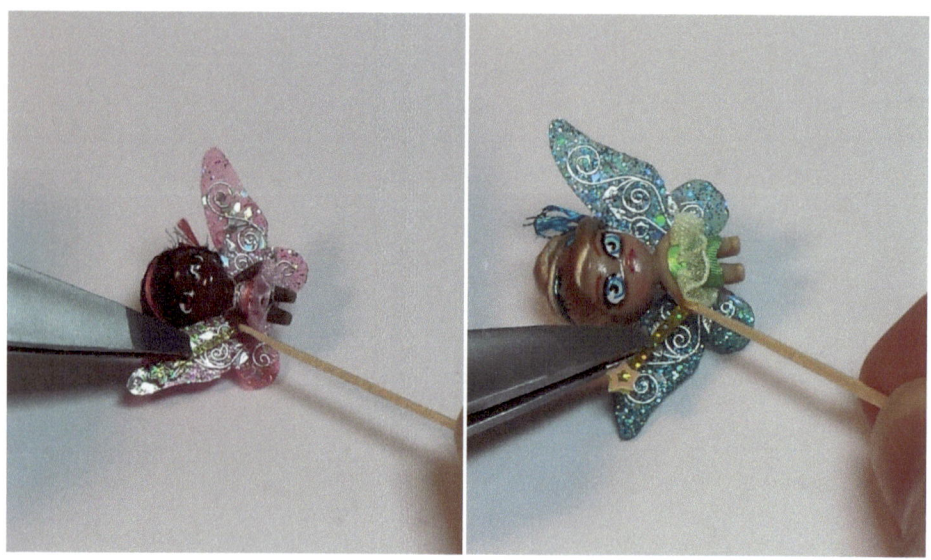

Use tweezers to hold the wand as you glue it into place.

Paint the shoes with acrylics. Mix colors on waxed paper with a toothpick before using a brush to apply pigment.

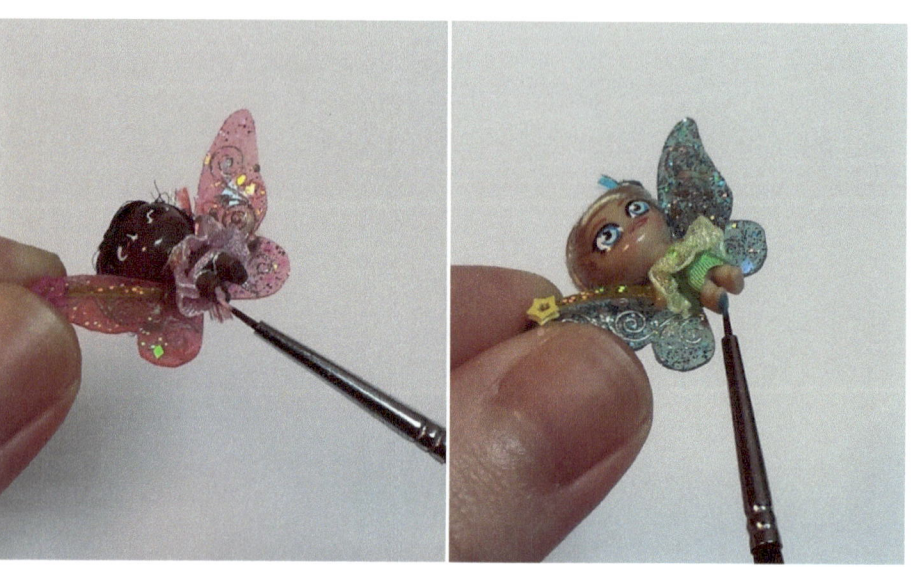

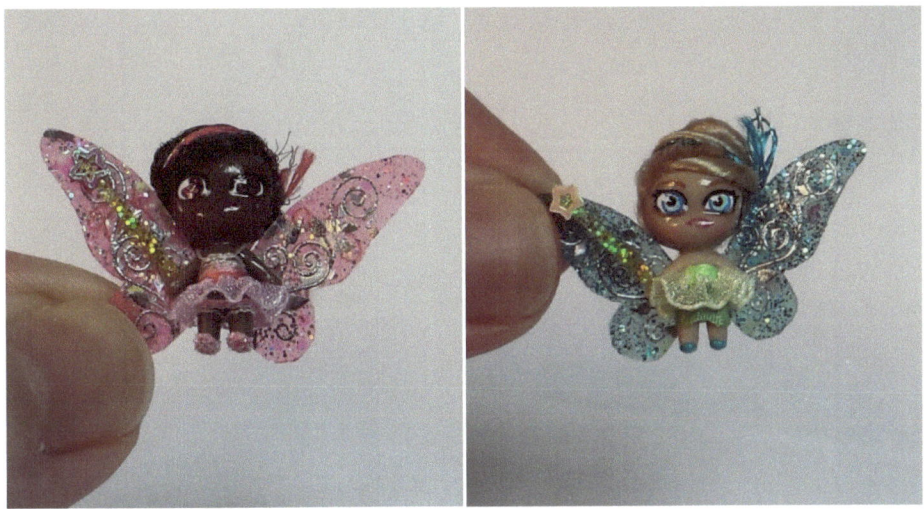

This is the finished product. Every element was chosen before assembling the final figure.

This bride doll has shimmery crystal sugar glitter applied to her white shoes by using the silicone tool.

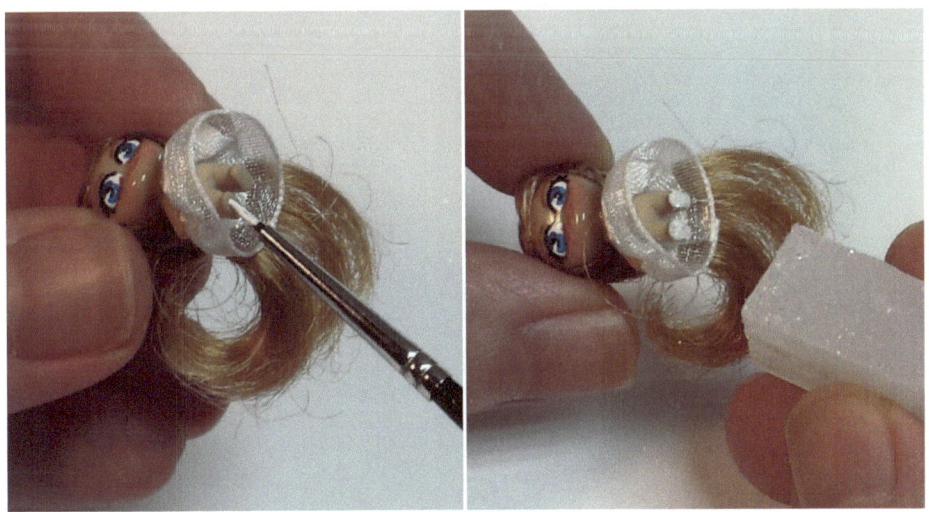

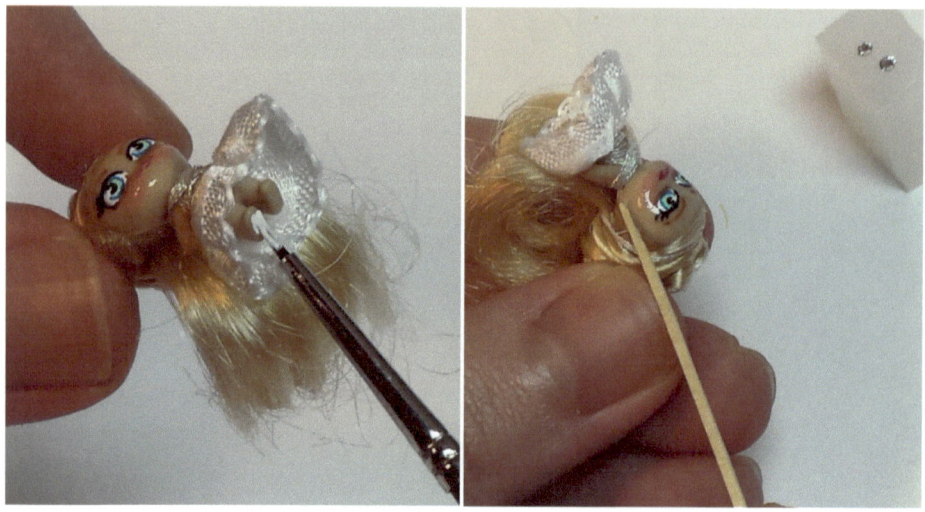

While applying the crystal type glitter as apposed to the holograpic type glitter, use the same method of watching for the acrylic paint to cure only to the point that the surfce is no longer shiny but still tacky.

These dolls are given crystal earrings to add sparkle to the figure.

The silicone tool is important in ths step to prevent fogging from the vapor of the super glue reacting with residue from your finger print.

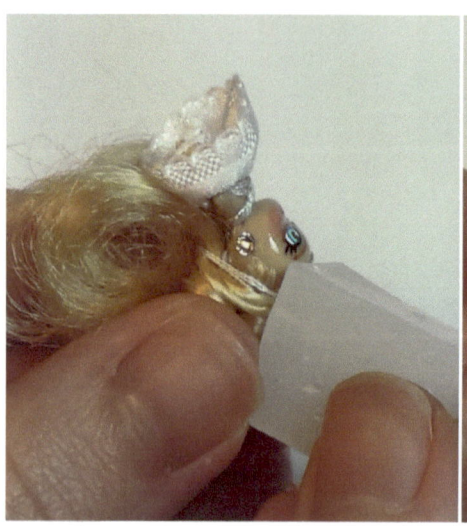
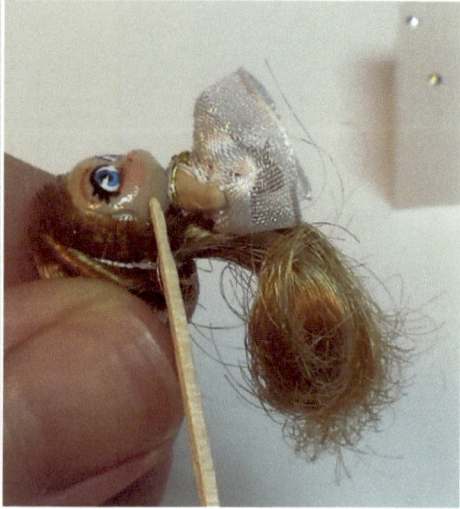

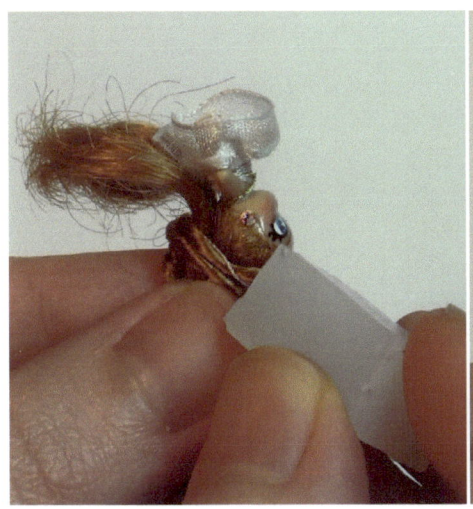 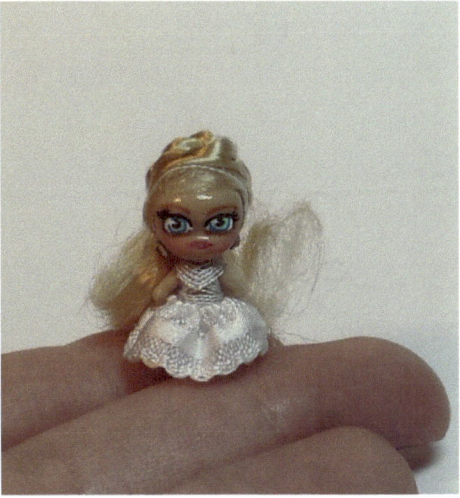

Choose a complimentary or contrasting hue of crytals to set off the features of your doll or to compliment the overall design.

Use the silcone tool to apply pressure to ensure the crystals are firmly attached.

This doll has red acrylic shoes painted over her white acrylic socks.

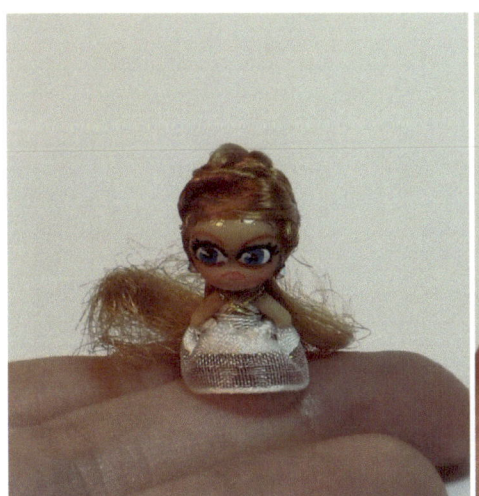 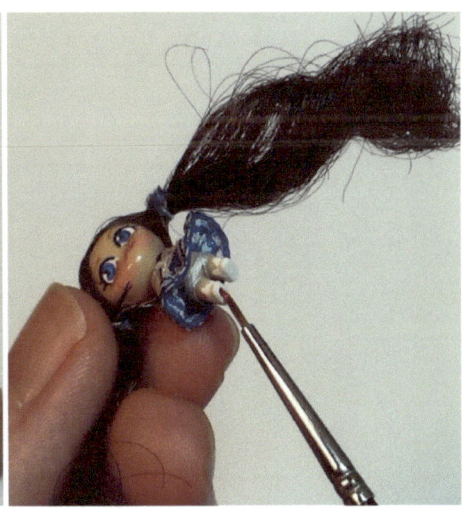

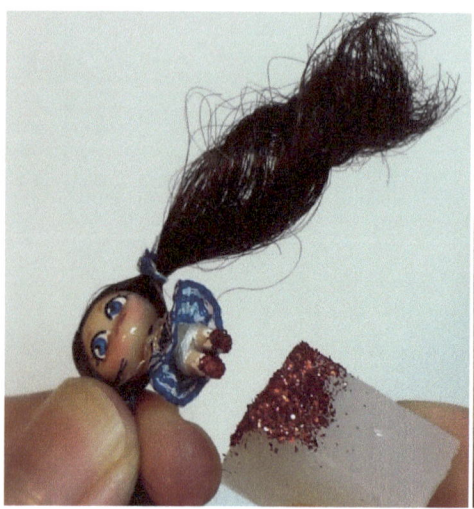 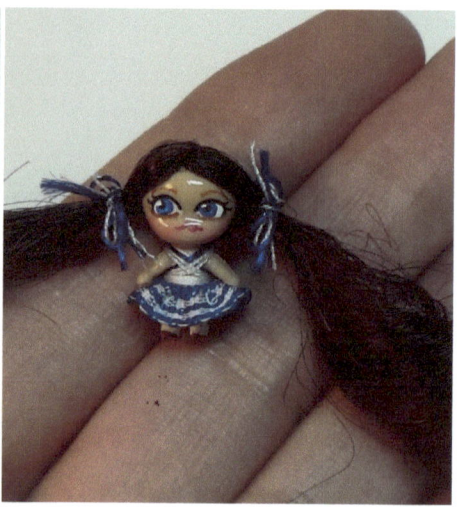

Mixed shades of red holographic glitter is applied to the shoes using the silicone tool. After the shoes cure for about 10 minutes, use a medium paint brush to brush away any stray glitter.

This doll's brown and iridescent twist floss necklace is given a "pearl" pendant.

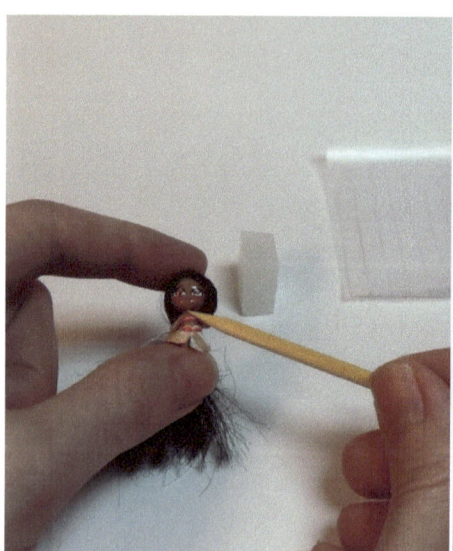 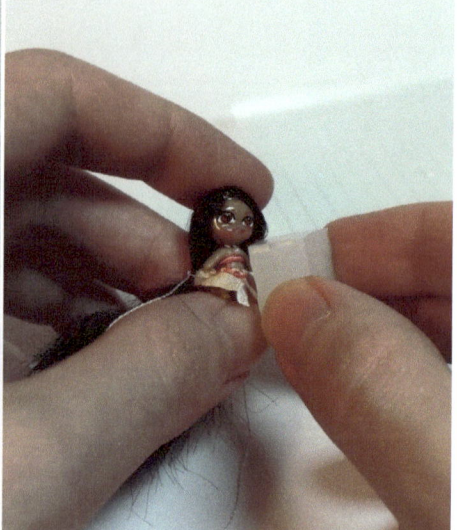

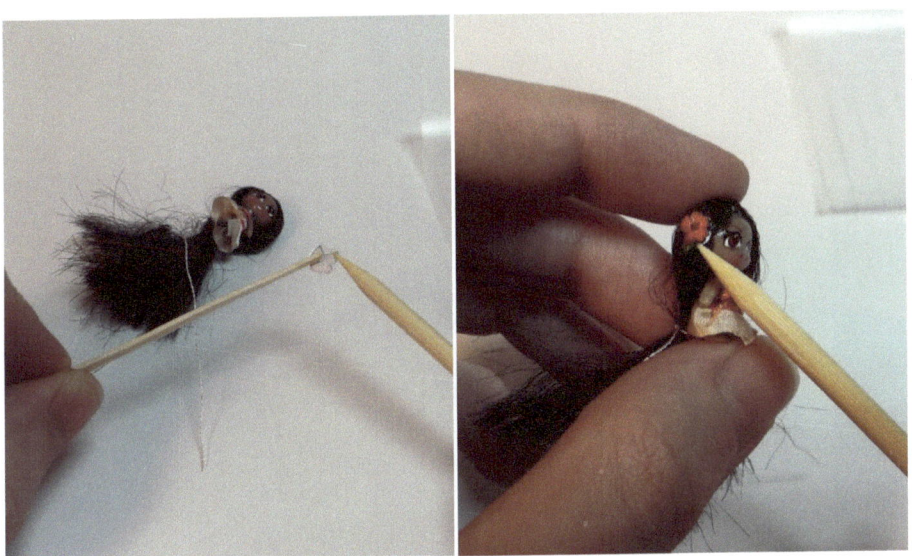

While holding a floral decal with the pointed end of a cut bamboo skewer, place a small quantity of super glue onto the decal using a tooth pick.

Transfer the decal to the figure. You may use the silicone tool to press the decal gently onto the surface. Allow the super glue to cure between 2-5 minutes before storing.

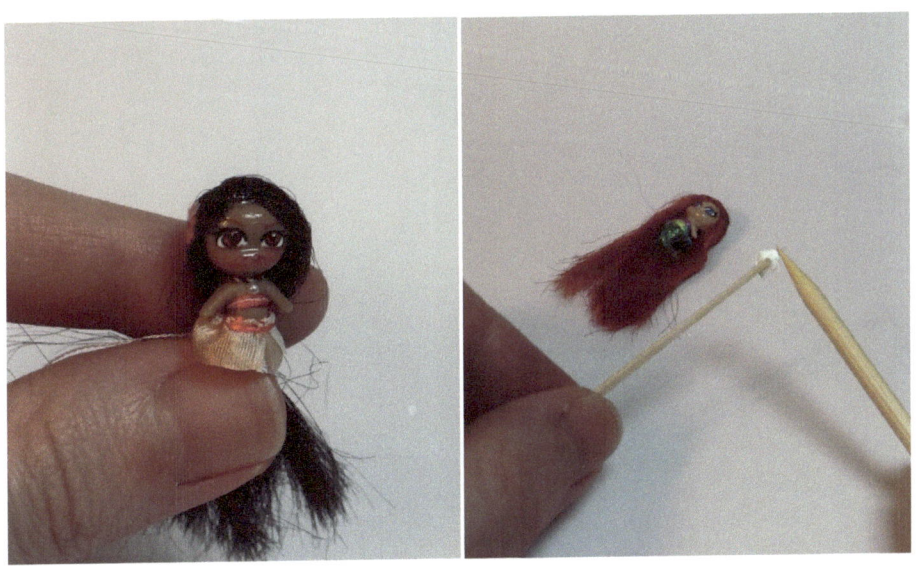

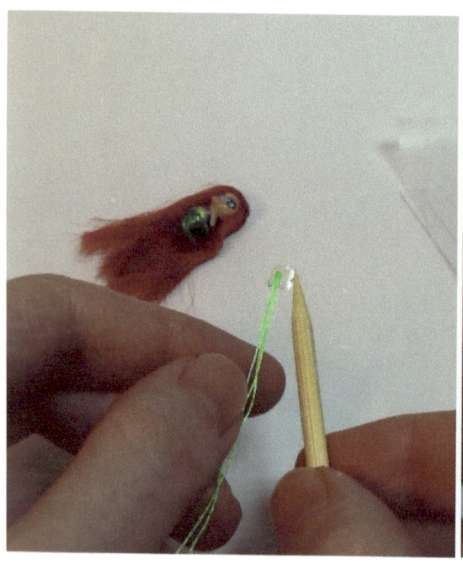 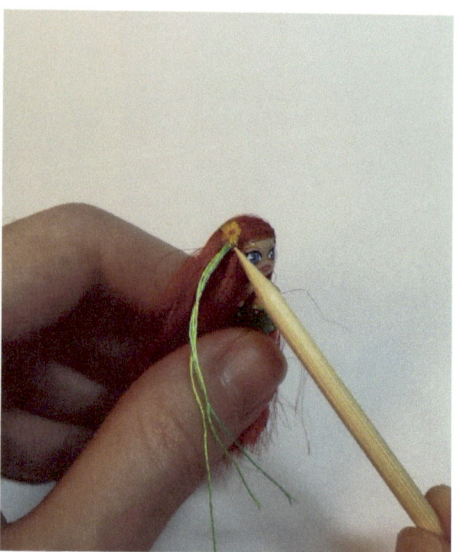

This floral decal has "seaweed" implied with green shades of floss glued onto the back side.

Allow the decal to cure for at least 30 seconds before adding more super glue to the back of the decal to secure to the side of the head of your figure, in this case a mermaid. Trim the ends to size.

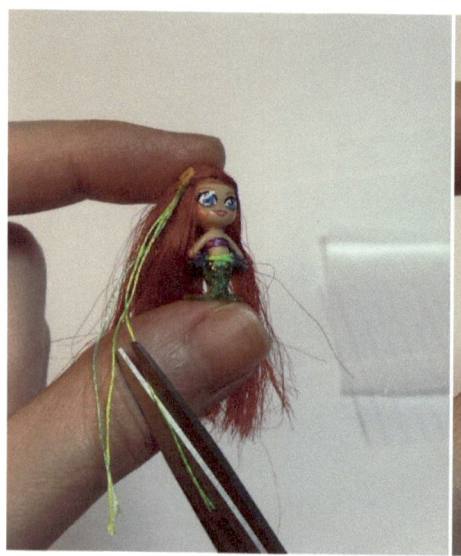 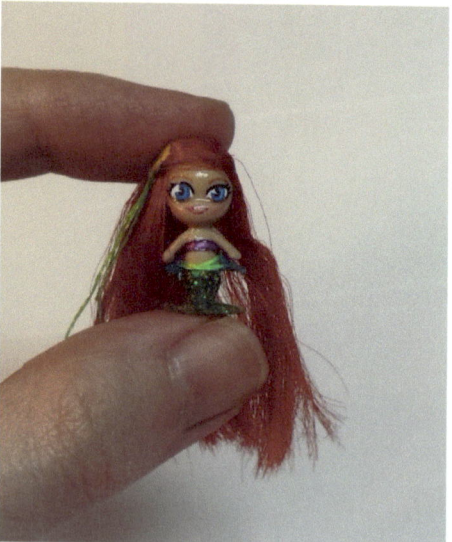

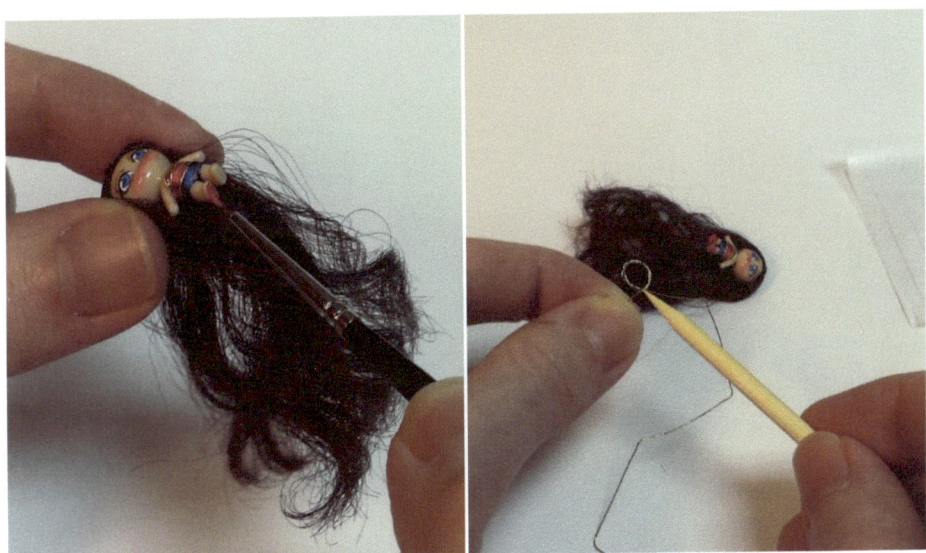

Paint the shoes onto this figure with red acrylic. Allow to cure about 10 minutes before handling. Create accessories with golden floss looped and glued into place.

Prepare golden braid with glue to prevent the ends from fraying.

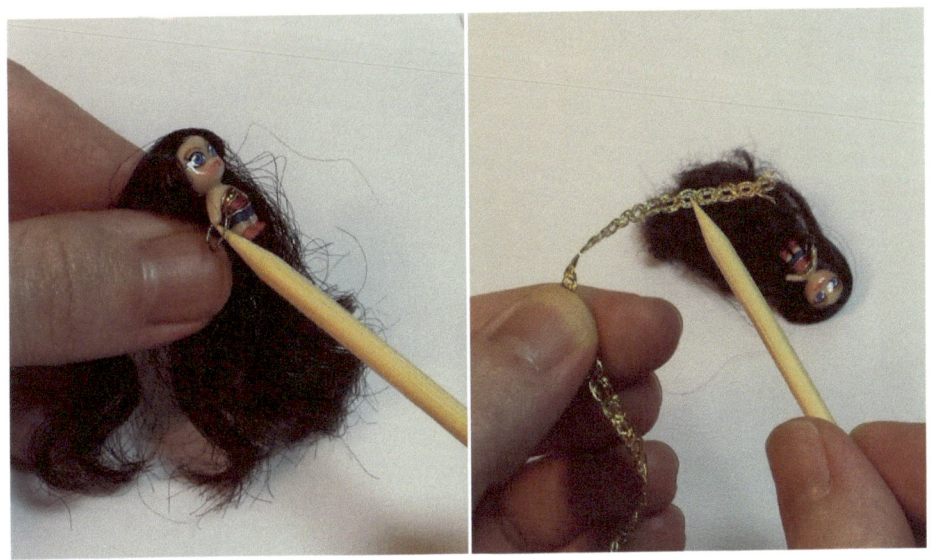

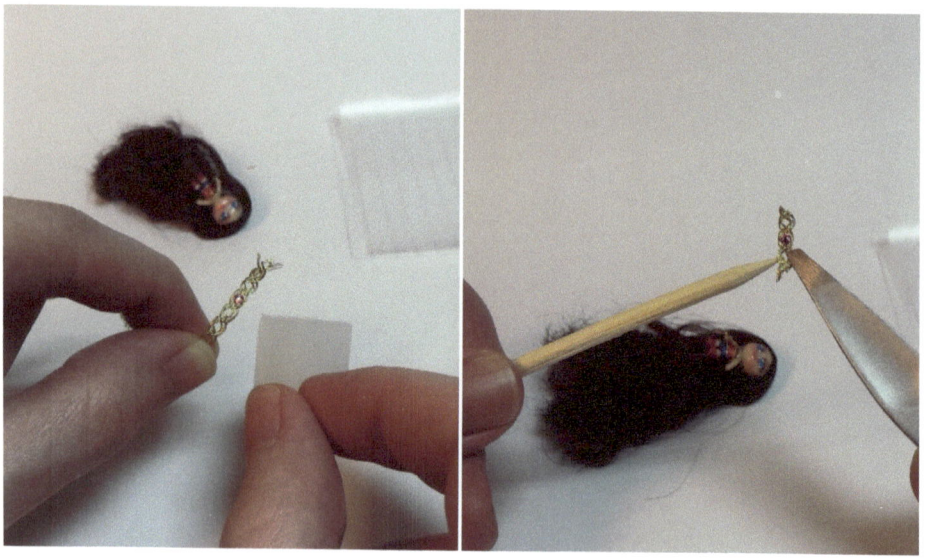

Use silicone tool to glue crystal gem onto the braid. Allow the glue to cure about 5 minutes before trimming the ends.

Use super glue and tweezers to secure the tiara onto the figure.

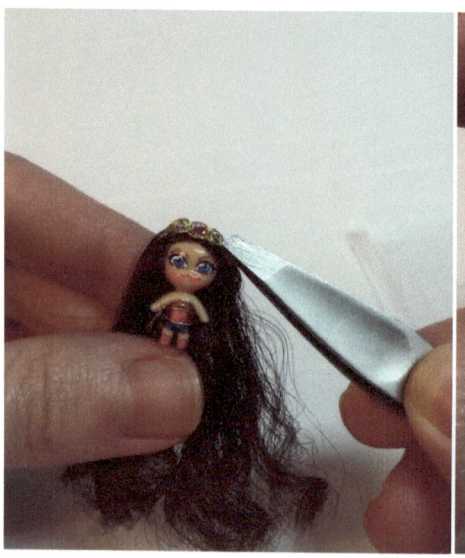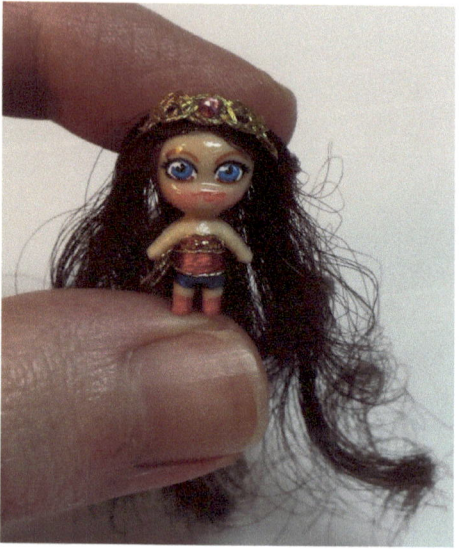

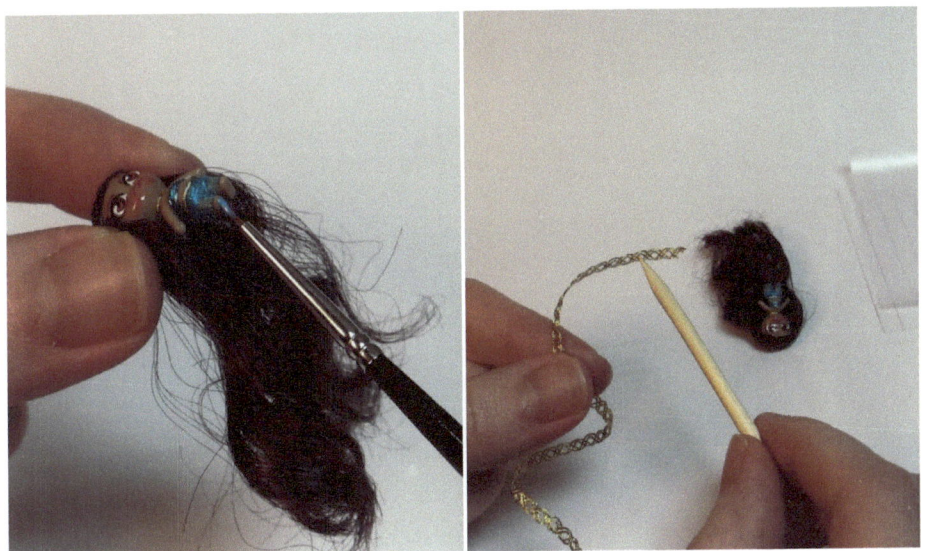

Mix acrylic paints to the desired shade with a toothpick before using a small brush to apply it.

Prepare golden braid with super glue. Use silicone tool to transfer crystal gem onto the braid. Trim the braid to size.

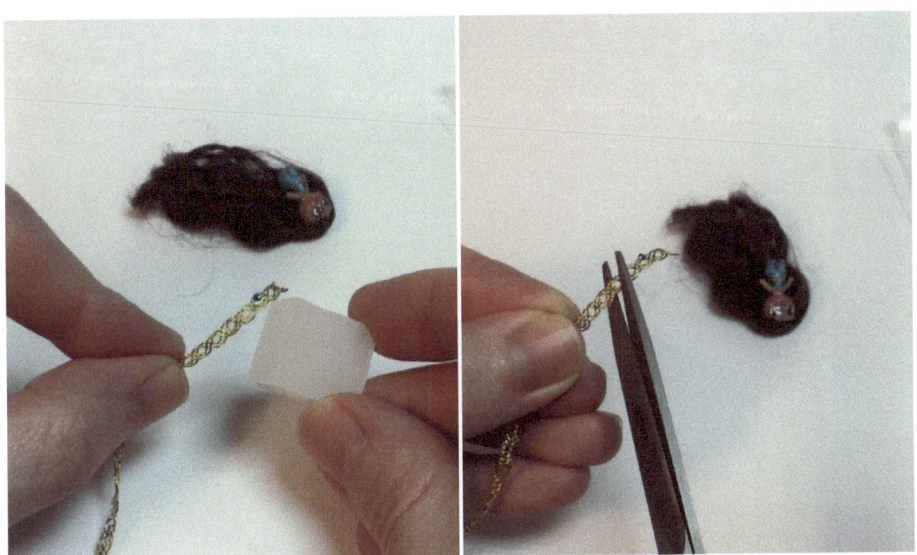

127

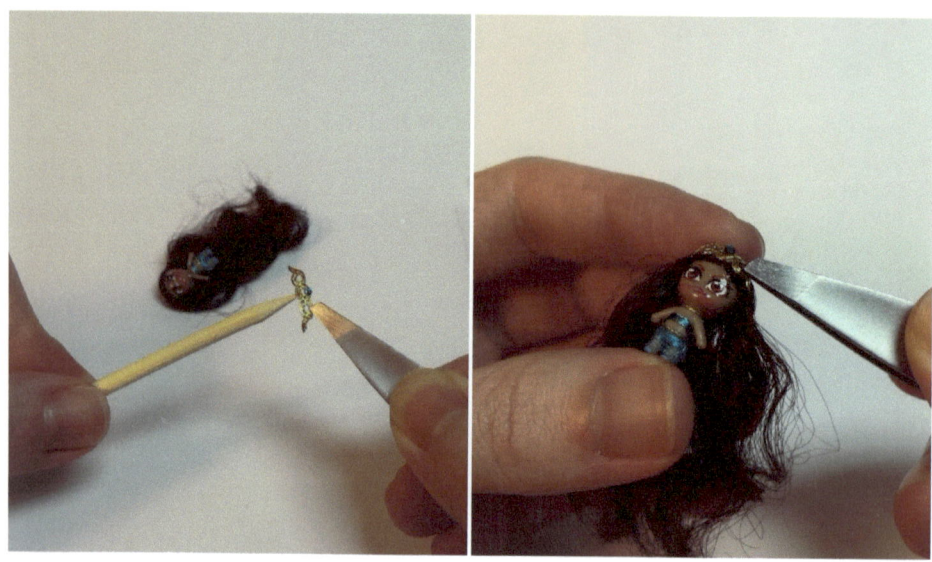

Use super glue and tweezers to secure tiara onto the head of the figure.

Use a toothpick to transfer a small quantity of super glue to target area. Use silicone tool to afix crystal gems onto the head of the figure to imply earrings.

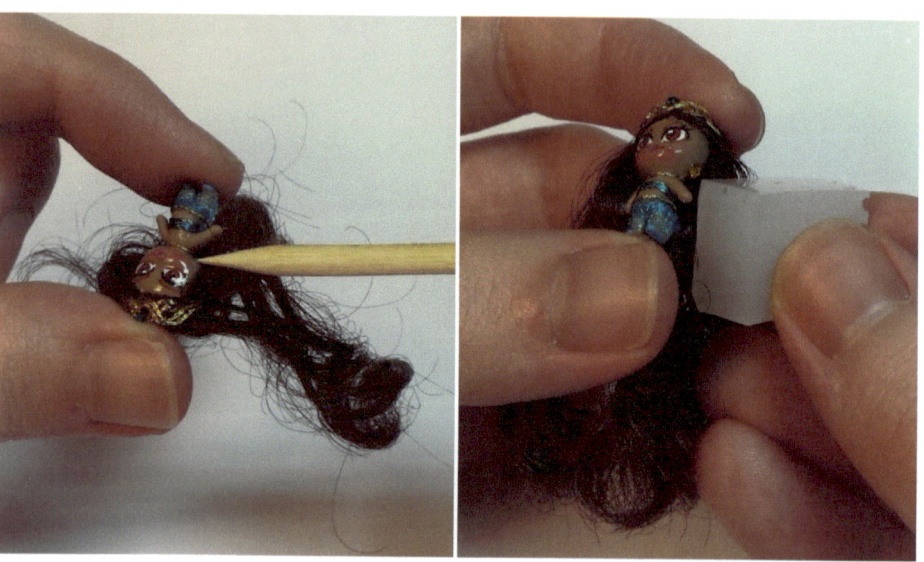

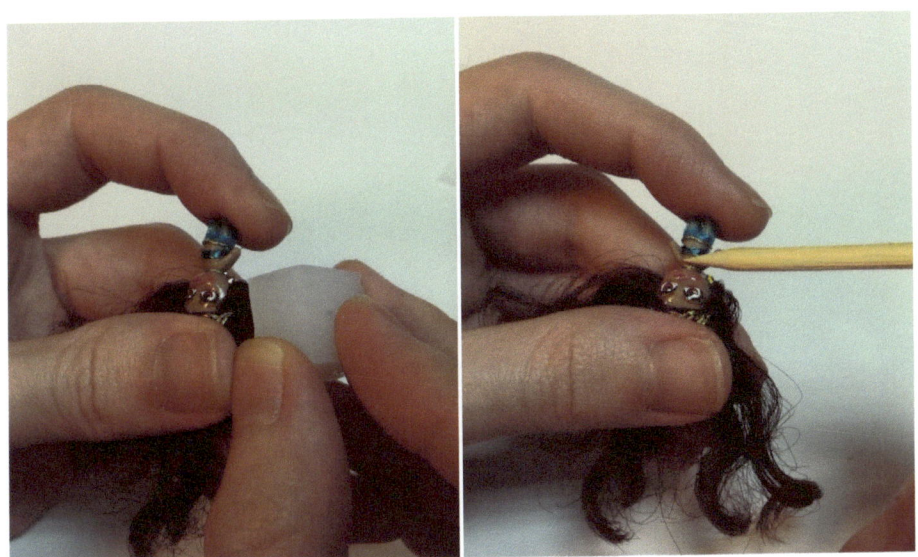

Use care not to accidentally transfer super glue onto other parts of your figure or your fingers.

Super glue does not readily stick to the silicone tool, so it is ideal to use to apply pressure to glued medium.

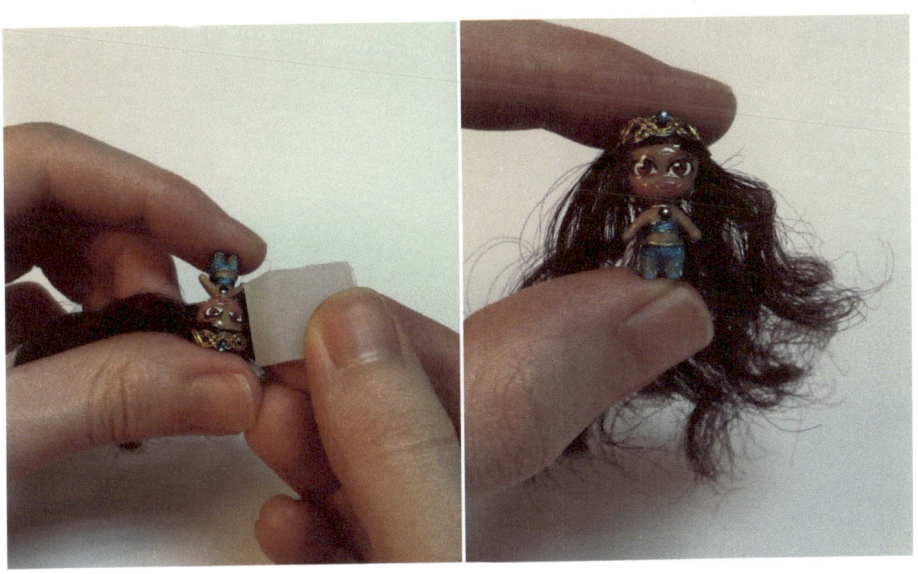

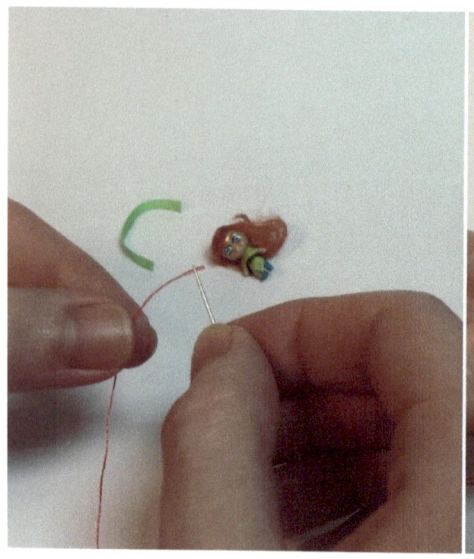 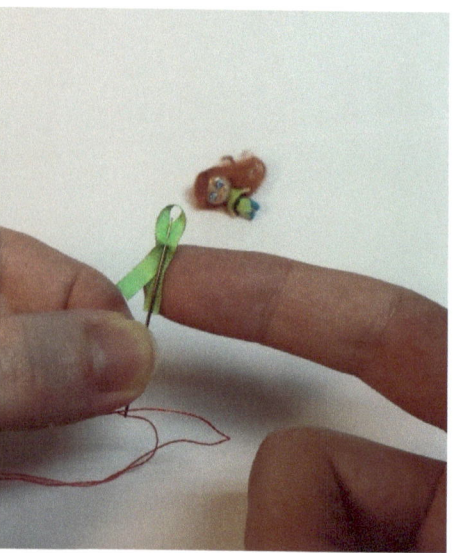

Thread a bright piece of floss to imply a feather. Stitch silk ribbon together and add a small quantity of super glue with a tooth pick to imply a hat.

Trim the ends to size. Allow the "feather" ends enough length to represent the intended design.

.

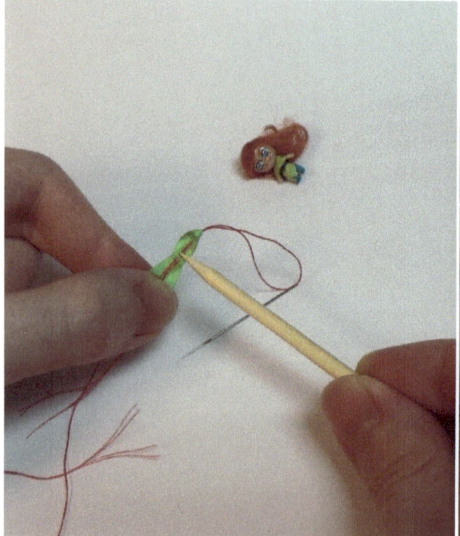 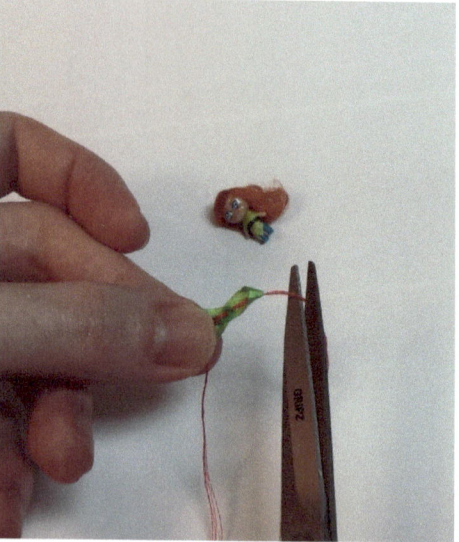

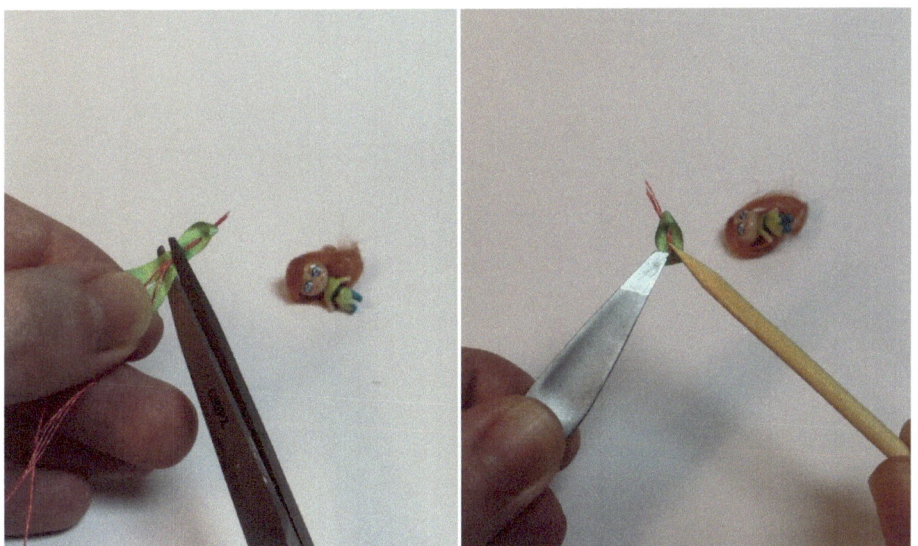

After the super glue has cured on the silk cap for about 2 minutes, trim it to size and use tweezers and a tooth pick to affix the cap onto the head of the figure.

Use a contrasting shade of acrylic paint to imply shoes and complete this costume design. Allow the acrylic to cure about 30 minutes before long term storage in plastic.

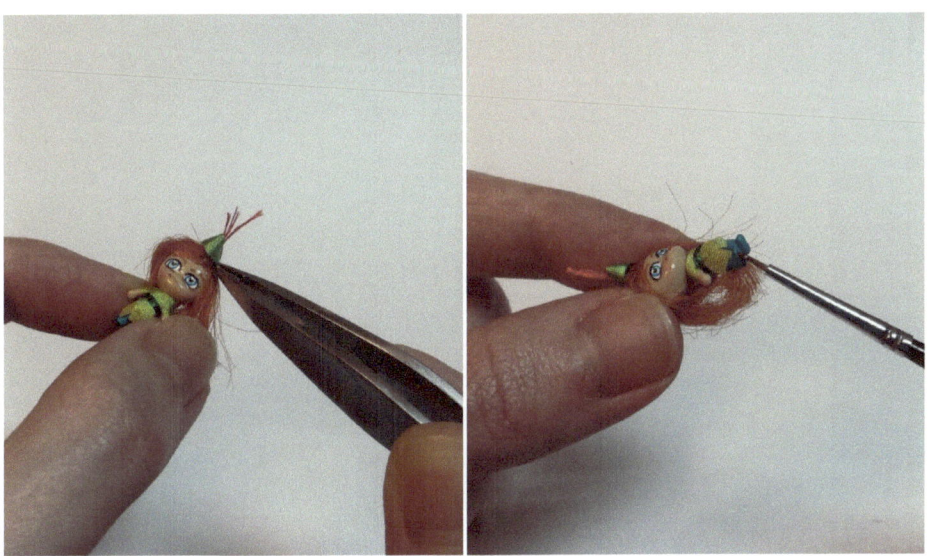

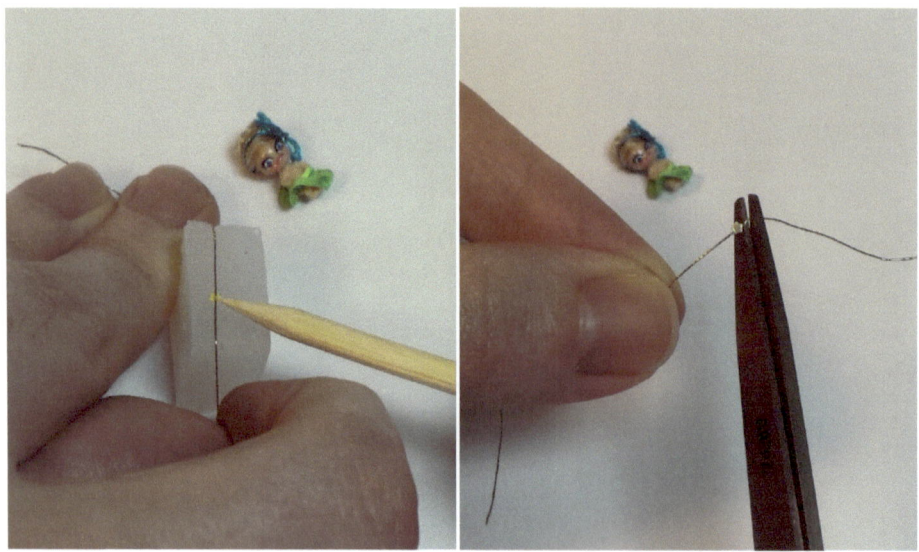

Use golden floss to create a wand. Use super glue to afix the tiny star shaped nail decal.

Cut wings to size from sheet urethane decorated with glitters.

Prepare the wings with super glue to afix them to the fairy doll.

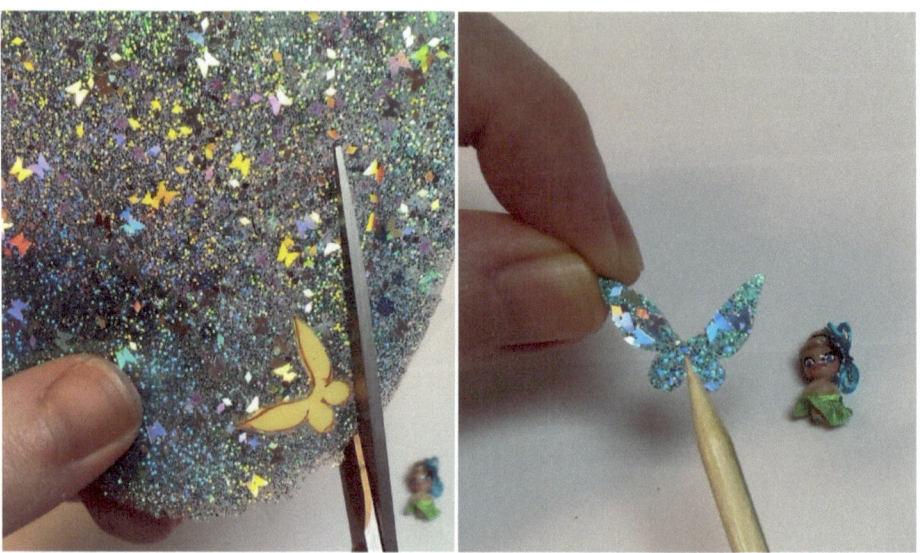

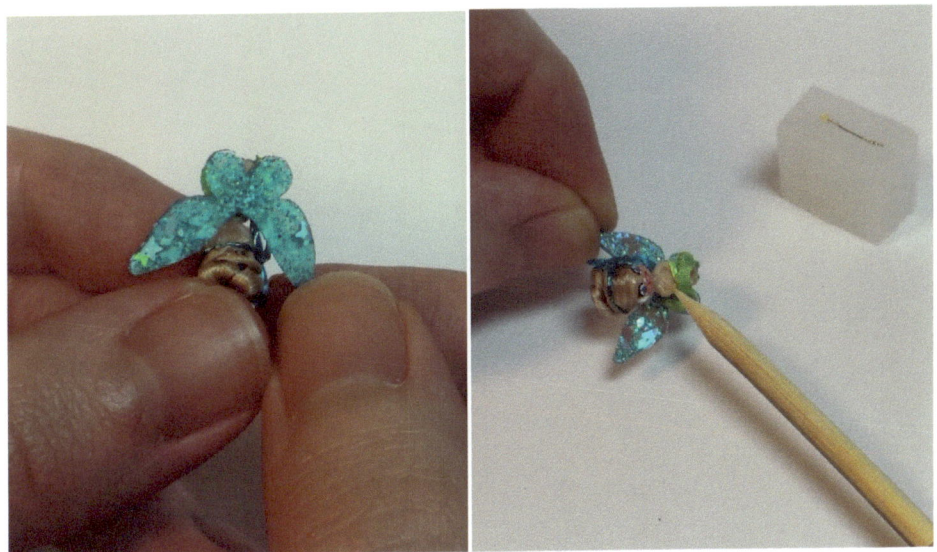

Use the silicone tool to apply pressure to the wings.

Apply a small quantity of super glue to the figure with a tooth pick. Use tweezers to hold the wand into place until the glue has started to cure, about 30 seconds. Allow the glue to finish curing for between 2-5 minutes until you handle it or store

.

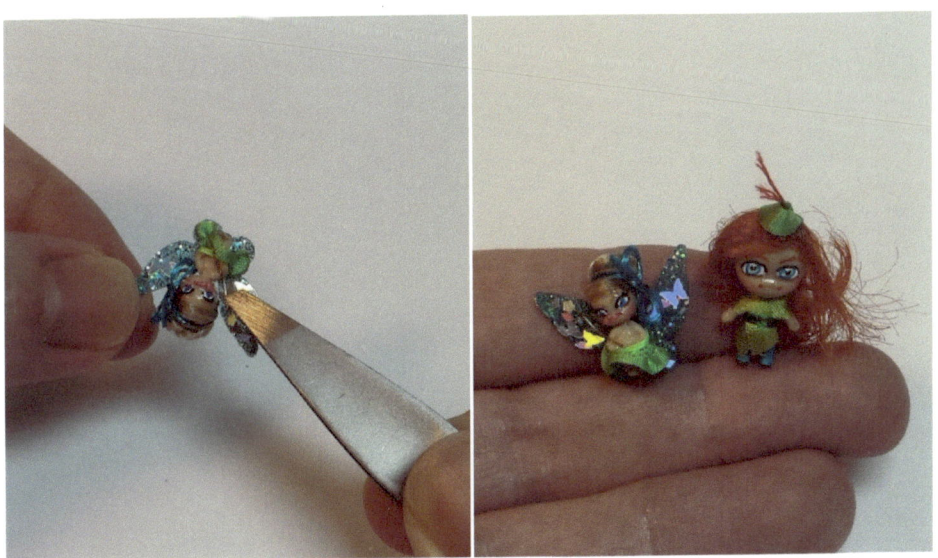

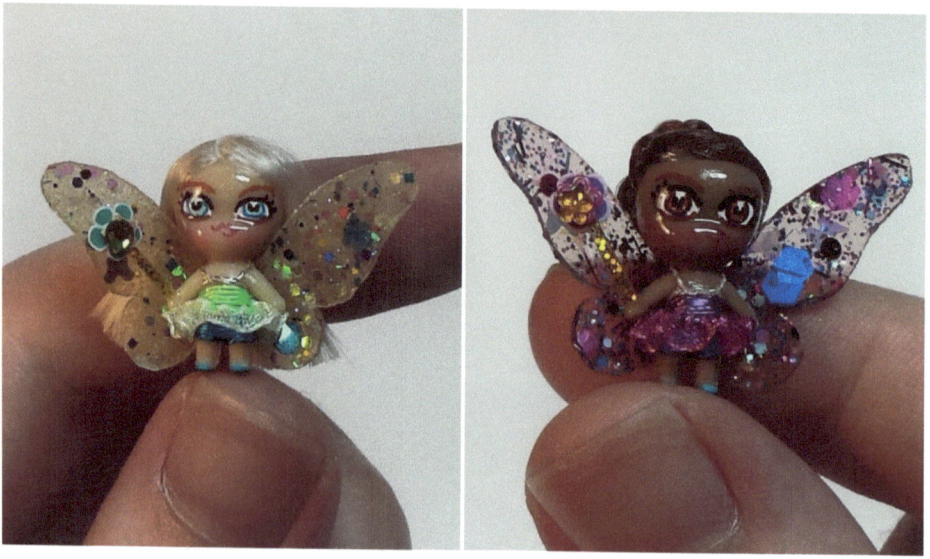

Here is a few more examples of different accessories I have used to create fairies. Note the different shades of wing glitter and alternative wand decorations.

You can use your imagination to create a new variation of a theme.

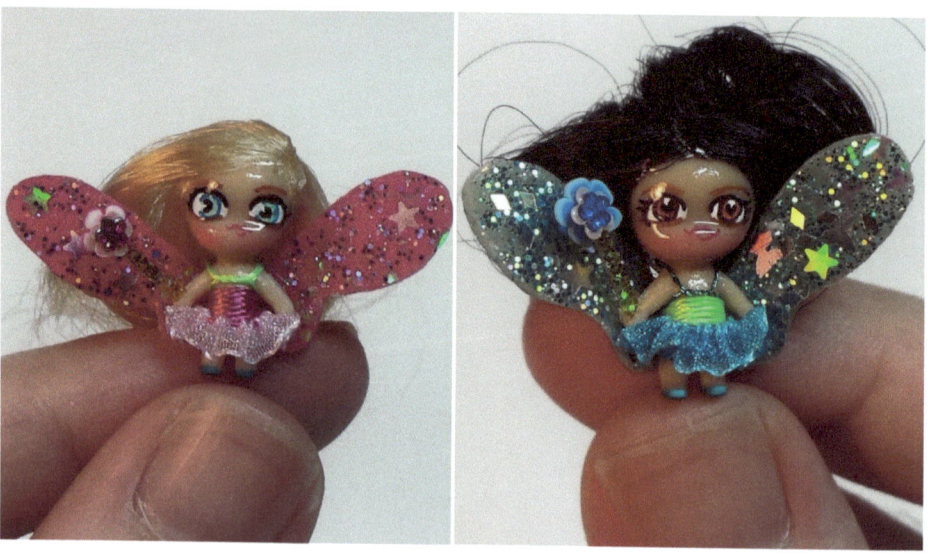

Ch 6 Finesse

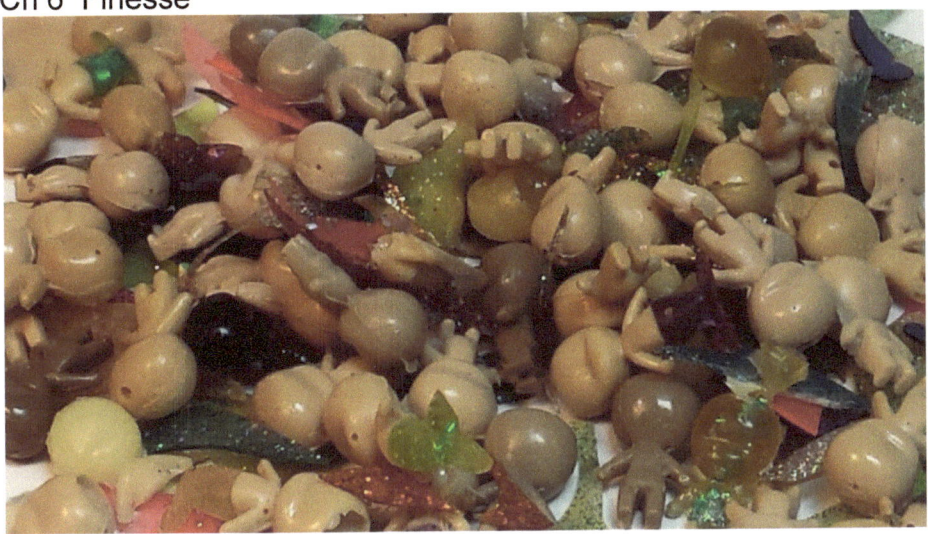

Although there are many online classes and videos on the subject, there is a difference experiencing learning the casting process in person, hands-on. If you can find local classes on the subject, it is always a good idea to learn from an expert, with proper protection and ventillation in a well-lit, clean space.

While experimenting, we found many ways that did not work and that is part of the process. The need to experience and experiment with many methods until settling on one which we refer to as a free-mold where the object is suspended and freed by xacto knife method and not using a release agent like 2 piece molds require because of the chemicals I choose to use.

There are many kinds of indrustrial rubber compounds and resin to create sculpture with. This artistic guide is not meant to only show the reader how to create new artistic expression from a vintage discontinued doll but that there are many kinds of figures in which to re-create using endless combination of colors and effects such as ponies and horses, animals, trolls, monsters, robots, aliens, fairies, princesses, mermaids, the list is endless. When re-creating an already existing object, be certain to state that is is a re-creation and not the original object. Artists often use different labels for their creations so as not to confuse the two to the undiscerning eye.

When learning the process, and making mistakes, many things happen that is beyond your control and that will lower your ratio of successful pour and assembly. We have destroyed a vacuum chamber while in the middle of creaton. Whole containers of open chemicals have been dumped and luckily we placed enough newspapers masking off the work area AND immediate floor space that prevented chemicals from reaching the table and floor surfaces.

Dried out pigments would crack and send small micro-chips of intense, consentrated paint into carpeting beyond where the floor space was masked off.. Care should be taken to vacuum up dry pigments. Liquid pigments can leak if not stored upright. Stains are not easy to remove because of the dense colors. Use water dampened rags to wipe up surfaces and throw them away. Don't use anything except for water or a commercial dye remover sparingly to remove wet pigments.

Don't allow failure to stop you from proceeding to learn. There are many ways to get it wrong. Perfect molds have been cast and after a few days of a heat wave, we fould the chemicals had spoiled, smelling badly with a cloudy appearance. Chemicals do not last and become more oxidized with each use. The two parts that make up the composition of the urethane compound becomes darkened when exposed similar to copper when exposed over time becomes a pale aqua with patina. As the chemicals darken, they become less and less usable. Always combine chemicals thoroughly to insure correct reaction to cure properly.

The silicone used in the process reacts to the atmosphere, eventually becoming unusable so be certain to observe the condition of your chemicals when your first open the factory seal and as you use it over time to note how it is aging and reacting to atmosphere. For this reason you need to use a gas blanket to remove the moisture from the air space within the container every time it is re-sealed after each use. This slows down the oxidization process considerably so be sure not to forget this important step.

Some urethane chemical compositions can darken when exposed to direct sunlight as well as how silicone will discolor and darken after long term exposure to air. It doesn't necessarily change the way a silicone mold functions but after it discolors, you might not want to recycle it into new molds. Silicone molds break or tear on occasion when the mold slips while your gloves are coated with sticky materials or while teasing material into the smallest crevaces. It might not look bad at first but often silicone will continue to tear along the path of least resistance.

Figures with small appendages or highly detailed surfaces often trap small air pockets creating bubbles. They can be drawn out by placing figures into the vacuum chamber a second time if necessary. Be sure to allow these remaining bubbles to escape without pulling too much material out of the mold in the process. Even after pouring molds thousands of times, our success rate is still not 100%. Keep track of your success rate over time.

It is easy to become disorganized with the many tools and materials that is required, so it is a good idea to add a clean up regiment for this art form. It is not difficult to have threads, fabric scraps and glitter clutter up the work space.

Store materials properly to prevent dust and dirt from coming into contact rendering them unusable. Wash your hands often to prevent any unseen accidental contamination by chemicals or transfering dirt onto your art.

While dressing the figures, ribbon can tear and threads break as fabrics are gathered to create full skirts. While applying final touches such as acrylic paint, it is easy to slip and paint part of the costume and a decision whether to start over needs to be made. In each step of the process, some mistakes can't be fixed. This is why patience is required and understanding that you will not learn it all overnight. Every time you make a mistake, you are learning how it doesn't work so don't discount the learning curve while accounting for the failure rate. It never completely disappears, it decreases over time with each casting experience.

Hair is the hardest part of making these dolls right after creating the usable figure. I look to characters and professional hair design for inspiration. Some are more difficult than others to replicate and not all nylon dolls hair is created equal. Some hair is soft and fine and has a low melting point so keep in mind how much time you expose it to the heat required to apply it to the head of the figure.

Practice is always a good when applying facial features. Sketch out ideas first and note iris color for character design. Use light and even pen strokes to get the colored pigments to stick to the white part of the eye and not hard enough to lift the layers of pigments. Handle the figures as little as possible and especially while the facial features are curing after clear acrylic finish is applied. .

It is easy to launch materials and tiny accessories through the air losing them because of their size or ruining them beyond repair. While trimming excess floss take are not to cut the costume or hair, ruining the compostion. Don't allow these kinds of failures to stop you from continuing to learn about this art form.

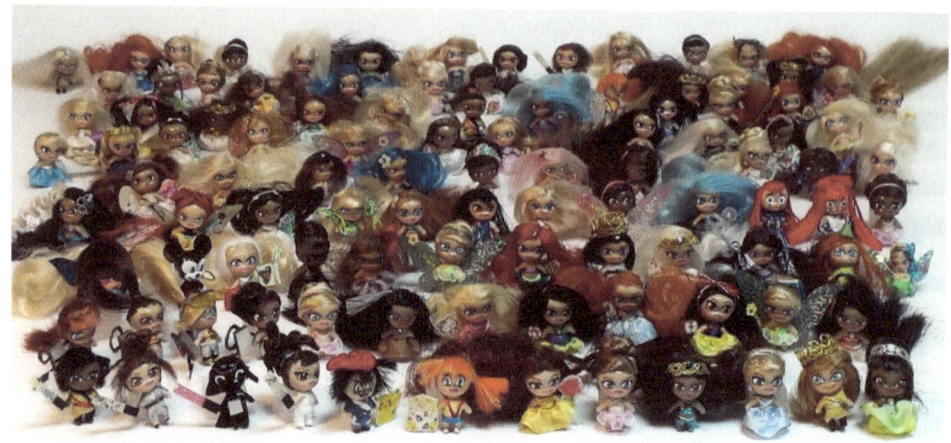

The real question is, what are you going to create?

The possibilities are endless.